Writing Southeast Asian Security

This book is a critical analysis of how the discursive and material practices of the "War on Terror" influenced security politics in Southeast Asia after 9/11. It explores how the US-led War on Terror, operating both as a set of material practices and as a larger discursive framework for security, influenced the security of both state and non-state actors in Southeast Asia after 9/11. Building on the author's own critical security studies approach, which demands a historically and geographically contingent method of empirically grounded critique, *Writing Southeast Asian Security* examines some of the unexpected effects that the discourses and practices of the War on Terror have had on the production of insecurity in the region. The cases presented here demonstrate that forms of insecurity were constructed and/or abetted by the War on Terror itself, and often occurred in concert with the practices of traditional state-centric security. This work thus contributes to a larger critical project of revealing the violence intrinsic to the pursuit of security by states, but also demonstrates pragmatic opportunities for a functioning politics of theorizing security.

This book will be of much interest to students of critical terrorism studies, critical security studies, East Asian, and Southeast Asian politics, US foreign policy, and IR in general.

Jennifer Mustapha is an Assistant Professor in Political Science at Huron University College, Canada. She researches and teaches critical international relations, security studies, and Southeast Asian regional relations.

Routledge Critical Terrorism Studies

Series Editor: Richard Jackson
University of Otago, New Zealand

This book series will publish rigorous and innovative studies on all aspects of terrorism, counter-terrorism, and state terror. It seeks to advance a new generation of thinking on traditional subjects and investigate topics frequently overlooked in orthodox accounts of terrorism. Books in this series will typically adopt approaches informed by critical-normative theory, post-positivist methodologies, and non-Western perspectives, as well as rigorous and reflective orthodox terrorism studies.

Terrorism, Talking and Transformation
A Critical Approach
Harmonie Toros

Russia's Securitization of Chechnya
How War Became Acceptable
Julie Wilhelmsen

A Critical Theory of Counterterrorism
Ontology, Epistemology and Normativity
Sondre Lindahl

Narratives of Political Violence
Life Stories of Former Militants
Raquel da Silva

Islam and Sectarian Violence in Pakistan
The Terror Within
Eamon Murphy

Writing Southeast Asian Security
Regional Security and the War on Terror after 9/11
Jennifer Mustapha

For more information about this series, please visit: www.routledge.com/Routledge-Critical-Terrorism-Studies/book-series/RCTS

Writing Southeast Asian Security

Regional Security and the War on Terror after 9/11

Jennifer Mustapha

LONDON AND NEW YORK

First published 2019
by Routledge
4 Park Square, Milton Park, Abingdon, Oxon OX14 4RN
605 Third Avenue, New York, NY 10017

First issued in paperback 2023

Routledge is an imprint of the Taylor & Francis Group, an informa business

© 2019 Jennifer Mustapha

The right of Jennifer Mustapha to be identified as author of this work has been asserted by her in accordance with sections 77 and 78 of the Copyright, Designs and Patents Act 1988.

All rights reserved. No part of this book may be reprinted or reproduced or utilized in any form or by any electronic, mechanical, or other means, now known or hereafter invented, including photocopying and recording, or in any information storage or retrieval system, without permission in writing from the publishers.

Trademark notice: Product or corporate names may be trademarks or registered trademarks, and are used only for identification and explanation without intent to infringe.

British Library Cataloguing-in-Publication Data
A catalogue record for this book is available from the British Library

Library of Congress Cataloging-in-Publication Data
A catalog record has been requested for this book

ISBN: 978-1-03-256979-6 (pbk)
ISBN: 978-1-138-95778-7 (hbk)
ISBN: 978-1-315-66153-7 (ebk)

DOI: 10.4324/9781315661537

Typeset in Times New Roman
by Wearset Ltd, Boldon, Tyne and Wear

Publisher's Note
The publisher has gone to great lengths to ensure the quality of this reprint but points out that some imperfections in the original copies may be apparent.

Contents

	Preface	vi
	Acknowledgements	vii
1	An introduction to writing Southeast Asian security	1
2	The politics and ethics of critical approaches to security	13
3	In search of monsters: US foreign policy in East and Southeast Asia	41
4	Here be monsters! "Experts" and the mapping of terror	63
5	Irruptions of the War on Terror in Southeast Asia: gender, sovereignty, and constructions of insecurity	89
6	Bicycle wheels and noodle bowls: making sense of (South) East Asian regional relations after 9/11	119
7	Beyond the Bush Doctrine: new narratives and new questions	136
	Conclusion: future questions in writing Southeast Asian security	152
	Index	160

Preface

This book is based on my doctoral thesis, and for a variety of reasons – both personal and professional – some time has passed since its first iteration. It has been substantially updated to reflect new research, new information, and the ongoing work that I have been doing to refine my own theoretical and practical understanding of the puzzles that motivate me. Getting this book to publication has reminded me of all the new questions I have been asking in the years since I obtained my PhD – not just about my research area, but about the whole world of academia and my own purpose in it. It has reminded me of the degree to which an effective scholar is always learning, always revising, and always being thoughtful about *why* they do the work that they do. I hope that this book reflects that, and that readers will find it useful and engaging.

Acknowledgements

I am forever grateful for the support of Richard Stubbs and Marshall Beier, who greatly influenced my ideas and research on this project. Thanks also to Lana Wylie, Richard Jackson, Netina Tan, and the anonymous reviewers for their encouragement and helpful suggestions. I also need to acknowledge my academic peer group and our ongoing chats about our work and our lives. You know who you are, and how much you all mean to me. And, finally, writing projects demand the support, love, and patience of partners, children, parents, family, and friends who are like family. Unbounded thanks are always due to all of you. To S and Z most of all, I love you.

1 An introduction to writing Southeast Asian security

I started my post-graduate research in the fall of 2006, a mere five years after the events of September 11, 2001 and relatively early into the era of contemporary security politics that followed. The terrorist attacks of 9/11 were still relatively fresh and the ensuing American-led "War on Terror" was in full swing. As with the fall of the Berlin Wall, 9/11 became a pivotal event that prompted a firestorm of (re)theorizing in the field of International Relations (IR) and in the social sciences more generally. Scholars, students, policy makers, and popular pundits asked questions like: How has 9/11 changed the world? What did September 11, 2001 *mean*? Why has "9/11" itself come to be used to refer to the events of that day?[1] What values and ideas are now held to be true in the after-space of a post-9/11 world? These questions, and more, animated the landscape of post-9/11 theorizing. Academic responses to the terrorist attacks were varied.

Old-guard realists initiated a chorus of academic *Schadenfreude*, almost cheerfully refuting Fukuyama's (1992) *End of history* and its attendant liberal visions of a Kantian post-Cold War peace spreading across the globe (see Krauthammer 2002; Walt 2002; Kaplan, Kristol, and Whitfield 2003). And for those skeptics who had been doubtful of the "globalization thesis," so in vogue throughout most of the 1990s, the events of 9/11 and the divisive fractures in world politics that followed seemed to support their rejection of a more optimistic view of globalization (see Friedman 2002; Falk 2003). For them, 9/11 meant that the very idea of globalization had been delegitimized by the terrorist attacks since perhaps globalization itself had acted as a catalyst for the rise and reach of *Al-Qaeda*. Relatedly, devotees of Huntington's (1993) *Clash of civilizations* thesis believed that 9/11 had vindicated him as an underappreciated Cassandra figure. His theories of fractious "civilizational" relationships gained renewed interest in policy circles. Despite the obvious conceptual and analytical shortcomings of Huntington's *Clash* thesis, the message of 9/11 has continued to be framed as part of an ongoing era of clashing civilizations.

Through such a lens, although the United States continues to exist as the world's lone super power and although "Western civilization" continues to be understood as the superior incarnation of a linear progression of human history, 9/11 nevertheless revealed that the US – and, by proxy, Western civilization – had come under attack by evil, counter-civilizational forces. The obvious corollary to

2 *Introduction*

this was that Western civilization itself must be defended. This way of seeing the world after 9/11 ushered in a (re)appearance of ethno-nationalist and militaristic thinking in security politics. It also led to an ongoing preoccupation with bordering practices that focus on difference and "otherness" vis-à-vis the resurgent import-ance of "security" itself, which is readily evoked in all of its interconnected discur-sive and material forms: *national* security, *border* security, *Homeland* security, *aviation* security, *societal* security, and so on. In other words, the terrorist attacks of September 11, 2001 have come to be seen as a defining rupture in contemporary security politics, and we now reside in the temporal space of the "post-9/11" era. This tendency we have, as a human species attempting to make sense of our exist-ence, and to chart a linear history punctuated by distinctive ruptures in time, comes to inform our understanding of the world. There is a "before" and there is an "after," and while we are in the "after" space we tend to selectively forget the significance and relevance of things that came "before."[2] And when we do look back, our view of the past comes to be informed by whatever "apparent truths" (Jackson 2005) now define the "common sense" of the present.

As a student of politics in this post-9/11 "after" space, I became intrigued by the meta-narratives that were emerging from the discourses surrounding 9/11 and the ensuing War on Terror. These narratives appeared to possess a set of unwritten rules that necessarily foreclosed certain ways of responding to 9/11. This was observable at all levels of discourse: popular, academic, and policy. It was a discourse framed as *Good* against *Evil* and *Us* versus *Them*. These senti-ments were deployed in the post-9/11 narratives in a doctrinaire and ahistorical way because, as mentioned, when we are in the "after" space, we tend to selec-tively forget the significance and relevance of the things that came before. To ask questions about the historical context or motivations of terrorist groups like *Al-Qaeda* was perceived, at worst, as apologia for terrorism; and, at best, as inappropriate and disrespectful. This was the intellectual climate within which the Bush Doctrine was conceived and the so-called "coalition of the willing" began their bombing of Afghanistan and invasion of Iraq as part of a global military response to 9/11.

This was also the setting in which I was introduced to Campbell's *Writing security: United States policy and the politics of identity* (1998). In the context of the Cold War, Campbell (1998) theorizes that US national identity was highly dependent upon characterizations of the external threat of an adversarial *Other*. This was achieved through a scripting of US identity contingent upon its opposi-tion to the identity ascribed to that threat, which must be depicted as both patho-logical and alien (Campbell 1998, 30–33). Ultimately, the emphasis on fear and danger within US national security discourses during the Cold War became crucial to the scripting of US national identity itself as a defender of freedom and upholder of Western civilization. Hence, the repetitive articulation of danger in US foreign policy discourses was not just a reference to "… threats to [American] identity or existence: it [was] its condition of possibility" (Campbell 1998, 13).

In late 2005, and in a nod to Campbell, Jackson published *Writing the war on terrorism: Language politics and counter-terrorism*, which critiques the

Introduction 3

discourses of "otherness" deployed by the Bush administration in response to 9/11. In his analysis, Jackson argues that these discourses were consciously and carefully deployed in order to justify mobilization for Bush's declaration of war against global terrorism. The degree to which Jackson contends that the political elite consciously and strategically chose the language that they did is debatable,[3] but the main arguments made in *Writing the War on Terrorism* are persuasive: first, that it was not inevitable that the 9/11 terrorist attacks would be construed as an act of war that required a national-level military response, but rather, this interpretation and subsequent actions represented a political choice made by the Bush administration; second, that the dominant narrative of the War on Terror was reproduced and reinforced via its institutionalization in powerful discursive sites such as the news media, popular culture, government organizations, and other social and political structures; and third, that these War on Terror discourses were more than just words and propaganda, and produced tangible irruptions into the "real" world of domestic and foreign policies (Jackson 2005).

Jackson convincingly argues these points. He makes a compelling contribution to the broader argument that, while the most obvious component of Bush's War on Terror was its material military dimension, an equally significant (if not more significant) aspect of the War on Terror as it relates to security is that its discourses also operated – and continue to operate – as a powerful social and political narrative of security. In other words, the discourses of the War on Terror have operated as a kind of hegemonic security narrative and "discourse" in this sense "involves not just speeches by politicians ... but also the symbols they appropriate, the myths and histories they refer to, the laws they pass, the organizational structures they create, the decision-making procedures they follow and the actions they undertake" (Jackson 2005, 19). The War on Terror as a narrative is specifically a *security* narrative. That is, it is a discursive framework within which the definitions and practice of security take shape. It can be seen as a *hegemonic* security narrative because it has successfully achieved domination in the sense that it is a narrative where its "regimes of truth" (Foucault 1980) have come to be taken for granted as the foundation for policy and public debate. These "regimes of truth" contain powerful political, cultural, and institutional meaning (Geertz 1973; Gusterson 1999) and come to be through "multiple political practices, related as much to the constitution of various subjectivities, as to the intentional action of ... subjects" (Campbell 1998, 17). This does not mean that there is no disagreement among scholars and policy makers around and within these topics, but there is widespread acceptance that 9/11 was a significant event and that the War on Terror continues to be a significant historical context in which we still find ourselves.

Within this context, an academic cottage industry on related topics has emerged since 9/11. This has included work on the broad subjects of terrorism and counter-terrorism; radicalization and extremism; the shape and significance of political Islam; counter-terror policies; the efforts of state authority to legislate and enact "domestic security," and many other related issues. Much of this work has occurred in the so-called "mainstream"[4] of political science and IR,

4 *Introduction*

and under the rubric of traditional security studies – where the state is the referent object of security and the analytical focus is on the threat of terrorism as an existential and somatic threat to the state (Jarvis and Holland 2014). The War on Terror then, in both its material practices and as a broader hegemonic security narrative, operates within a framework of understanding that is closely tied to the mainstream of security studies in both the academic and policy worlds.

There is, however, a growing body of inquiry and policy work that utilizes distinctly *critical* approaches to the study of security and more specifically, to the study of security in the context of terrorism and counter-terrorism as it relates to 9/11 and the War on Terror. This critical work is diverse, inter-disciplinary, and it varies in content and purpose. Within it though, there is a general shift in emphasis away from focusing solely on the existential threat of terrorism to the sole referent object of the state. Instead, critical security approaches – broadly defined – delve into deeper ontological questions about the nature of security itself and are interested in referents of security other than the state. They also examine the myriad effects that terrorism *and* counter-terrorism, as well as terrorists *and* state authority, can have on the production of insecurity. Related to this, critical security approaches seek to bring nuance to strictly modernist and positivist epistemologies and methodologies by using approaches that highlight inter-subjectivity; that question relationships between knowledge and power; and that acknowledge the significance of academically marginalized but crucial aspects of global politics, such as discourse and gender.

Flowing from this, Jackson's (2005) observation that the War on Terror "imposes its interpretation of political reality on … society and rationalizes, legitimizes and normalizes the practices of counter-terrorism" (20) supports a critical security approach that inquires after the security politics and practices of the ongoing War on Terror. Political violence, broadly defined, is perpetrated by both state and non-state actors and experienced by both state and non-state actors alike, but mainstream IR approaches to terrorism tend to focus entirely upon the state as the referent and non-state actors as the threat. This only tells part of the story, and as Said (1993, 2012) might argue, a *contrapuntal* analysis of the War on Terror is required to delve into its many layers (Chowdhry 2007). The point of this project, it bears noting, is not to discount the threat of terrorism as far as it does exist. Rather, the point is to *also* ask different questions than the ones that are asked by the security establishment, in order to reveal some of the less obvious security implications of both terrorism and our reactions to it.

Along this register, there are a host of interesting lines of inquiry that can be charted to examine the implications of the prevailing security narratives that continue to serve key descriptive, constitutive, and performative functions in the contemporary security landscape. A critical security exploration of War on Terror discourses can contribute by inquiring into specific empirical examples and cases that demonstrate the importance of these security narratives in shaping identities, framing political "problems," and influencing the lives of groups and individuals. In other words, it asks the question: what can a critical security analysis "see," that a conventional security analysis does not?

Importantly, the pervasive influence of War on Terror *meta*-narratives is observable in a variety of different contexts – conceptually, historically, and geographically. We increasingly see that the political discourses in different geographic regions have come to be framed within the context of War on Terror security narratives (Holland 2012). We have seen this in political discourses and policies in Europe around refugees and mass migration (Hellwig and Sinno 2017); in the electoral politics of recent elections in both North America and Europe (Schmidt 2017; Bogain 2018); and in a variety of regional issues in the Middle East, South Asia, and Africa among others. East Asia – and Southeast Asia in particular[5] – is another geographic area that is influenced and affected by War on Terror security narratives but has been largely neglected in terms of critical security scholarship. For a variety of reasons, this makes it a particularly interesting region in which to direct our attention.

First, Southeast Asia has been identified as another "front" in the War on Terror both by academics and by policy practitioners (Higgott 2004). Second, there is the fact of "strong state" authority, which is understood to be characteristic of many East and Southeast Asian governments. This has long been of interest to researchers who examine the implications of strong states on factors such as economic development and practices of democracy (Ba 2014). In the context of the War on Terror, a host of novel questions arise related to the role that the strong state plays: for example, when Southeast Asian governments co-opt the War on Terror discourse as a means to silence political dissent, or conversely when fear of terrorism undermines the legitimacy of the elites in these "strong" states (Noor 2006; George 2015). A third reason for turning our attention to the region is that there has been a proliferation of work pertaining to Southeast Asian security as it relates to the War on Terror, but much of this work resides in the so-called mainstream of IR, and under the rubric of traditional security studies.

Hence, the analysis in this book is undertaken with the view to help remedy the relative paucity of *critical* security analyses focused on East Asia and Southeast Asia.[6] As mentioned, while much has been written about security, terrorism, and US foreign policy in the region, most of it is grounded in decidedly conventional IR analytical approaches that regard the state as the primary object of security. These types of analyses essentialize the threat of terrorism in ways that fail to problematize a wholly state-centric understanding of security or that various forms of *in*security arise from state-responses to terrorism itself. Such approaches also tend to ignore the role that discourses and ideas play in the larger security narratives that regional actors both construct and operate within.[7] Further, the vast majority of the literature on security in Asia is not focused on terrorism or counter-terrorism, but around realist balance-of-power issues and constructivist analyses of institutional norms and the state-centred security architecture of the region.[8] Hence, when one considers that the existing critical security literature on Southeast Asia, which is only just beginning to emerge, is a small sub-set of an even smaller sub-set of the existing literature on regional security, there is a gap that is waiting to be filled by approaches that find their pedigree in critical post-structuralist epistemologies and methods.

6 *Introduction*

The questions that drive this book

This book seeks primarily to explore how the US-led War on Terror, operating both as a set of material practices and as a larger discursive framework for security, influenced the security of both state and non-state actors in Southeast Asia after 9/11. Building on my own previously formulated critical security studies approach (Mustapha 2013), which is rooted in Stephen K. White's notion of "weak ontology"[9] and demands a historically and geographically contingent method of empirically grounded critique, *Writing Southeast Asian security* examines some of the unexpected effects that the discourses and practices of the War on Terror have had on the production of insecurity in the region.

The larger research question driving the book is as follows: *What can a critical security analysis tell us about the production of insecurity that a more conventional security analysis cannot?* And more specifically, *what can a critical security analysis tell us about the impact that the War on Terror, operating as a hegemonic security narrative, has had on Southeast Asia after 9/11?* In exploring these questions, the cases examined in this book demonstrate that forms of insecurity in Southeast Asia after 9/11 were constructed and/or abetted by the War on Terror itself, and that these forms of insecurity occurred in concert with the practices of traditional state-centric security. This book thus contributes to a larger critical security project of revealing the many ways that the pursuit of security by states in the context of the War on Terror can contribute to insecurity. Further, the specific cases and examples examined in this book point to important critical security questions about the War on Terror in Southeast Asia that remain unexamined, pointing us to important new lines of research and inquiry.

The following chapter conceptually and theoretically contextualizes the empirical cases explored in the book by analytically situating and explaining a "weak ontology" based critical approach to theorizing security. It makes the case for this approach, and for the benefits of employing (modified) post-structuralist methods of analysis that stress the interwoven relationships between knowledge, power, and subjectivity in constructing security knowledges and practices. In emphasizing these points, Chapter 2 also argues for the strengths of utilizing White's (2000, 2003, 2005, 2009) idea of "weak ontology" in *re*constructing foundations, in order to move beyond *de*construction and to make space for engagements with the (contingent) empirical realities of actually occurring security logics (Mustapha 2013). By focusing on the role of knowledge-production; the importance of ontological theorizations of critical security; and by deploying a context-specific, reflexive, and empirically grounded method similar to what Wyn-Jones (1999) might call "immanent critique," it is possible to engage critically with the politics and ethics of security practices in Southeast Asia in the specific context of the War on Terror.

Chapter 2 then turns to existing IR scholarship that endeavours to explain and understand security (and insecurity) in East and Southeast Asia. It surveys the dominant literature on Southeast Asian security and highlights the debates between realist and conventional constructivist scholarship, identifying the conceptual gaps in the existing literature, and introducing the critical ideas that are emerging. Notably, this chapter regards academic "bodies of literature" as discourses and narratives themselves: frameworks within which the theory and practice of IR and security operate. Approaching academic bodies of literature discursively allows us to recognize that these are not homogenous or monolithic areas of inquiry, because each contain unique and sometimes competing representations of the subjects that they pertain to. Understanding this, it is important to critically engage with these literatures in ways that recognize which points of view are privileged and which are marginalized.

Chapter 3 delves into the powerful constitutive effects of US foreign policy in East Asia after 9/11 and argues that the Bush Doctrine set the stage for how the War on Terror itself continues to operate as a dominant security narrative in the region. This chapter first explores the various ways to define and approach "foreign policy," ultimately arguing for a critical constructivist analysis of foreign policy as informed by David Campbell's (1998) persuasive call to reorient our understanding of it. Campbell (1998) sees "foreign policy" as performative and constitutive, and as a boundary-producing practice "central to the production and reproduction of the identity in whose name it operates" (68). As such, it is an integral aspect of the narratives of *Self* and *Other* that both construct and define threats and the security practices of states in response to those threats. Chapter 3 also engages in a critical reading of the Bush Doctrine and the *2002 National Security Strategy* as the foundational (con)text of the security narratives of the ongoing War on Terror. Along these lines, the argument is made that the US-led War on Terror, as a foreign policy narrative, operates through discursively constructed "regimes of truth." Finally, the chapter sketches out significant aspects of US foreign policy towards East Asia in particular, revealing both the continuities and discontinuities in US policy from "before 9/11" and into the "post-9/11" era. This is the context in which the empirical cases of the following chapters are examined.

Chapters 4 through 6 are conceptually linked through the use of a critical security lens to explore regional examples of specific security issues. Here we see a persistent theme emerge: that the "common sense" of the War on Terror has introduced the idea of risk-mitigation and the management of emergent threat as central organizing logics of security practices and policies. Chapter 4 scrutinizes common assumptions present in the "expert" understandings of terrorism in the region within the context of War on Terror discourses and challenges three commonly made claims that have emerged out of the post-9/11 security narrative and related "expert" discourses on Southeast Asian terrorism. These claims are inter-related and flow into one another: first, *that all forms of political Islam necessarily represent an imminent threat of terrorism*; second, *that there exists a regionally cohesive radical Islamist identity with robust organizational and ideological links to Al-Qaeda and the Islamic State (IS)*; and third, *that terrorism in Southeast Asia is best understood as pathological or evil* which results in narrowly conceived state-responses to behaviours understood to be irrational, rather than political.

8 *Introduction*

Contesting each of these claims from a critical security perspective allows us to see that conventional expertise around counter-terrorism (CT) and countering violence and extremism (CVE) in Southeast Asia contributes twofold to increasing insecurity. On the one hand, much of the existing expertise in the areas of CVE and counter-terrorism in Southeast Asia renders a vast territory and its people as a contingent, emergent threat, homogenously transformed into epistemic objects by the knowledges that seek to govern their potential for becoming dangerous. As a result, large populations of people who pose no specific threat are themselves rendered insecure through the risk management policies and pre-emptive security practices of the state (Lacher 2008). Second, and related to the previous point, counter-terrorism discourses and CVE rationalities can be easily utilized by the state security apparatus in service to a variety of manoeuvres and practices designed to consolidate the political power of ruling elites rather than address the problem of terrorism per se. In fact, counter-terrorism measures and CVE policies may, in some instances, hasten radicalization and the formation of anti-establishment or revolutionary Islamist identities. Hence, these "epistemic objects," and the potential threat they pose may *come out of* problematizations of security and not the other way around.

Picking up on that theme, Chapter 5 utilizes critical feminist and post-structuralist methods of analysis to ask after the gendered implications of regional security politics in Southeast Asia in the context of the ongoing War on Terror. After 9/11 there was a concerted re-establishment of a regional US military presence as well as a discursive re-framing of US relations in Asia more generally. The resulting security narratives allowed for significant shifts to occur in the security logics and practices of governing regimes in the region. This contributed to an escalation of gendered insecurities around regional military architecture; re-configurations of post-colonial constructions of national identity; and a discernible rise in state repression due to the coupling of counter-terror security policies with statist notions of "national resilience." Chapter 5 explains how the War on Terror itself is not unique in creating these insecurities but provided a felicitous scenario for the renewed continuation of American imperial formations in Southeast Asia. Further, these heightened gendered and post-colonial insecurities intersect with and bring forth complex questions relating to expressions of sovereignty and identity in the region.

Chapter 6 is concerned with questions around the overlapping and unsettled iterations of what the "region" of (South) East Asia looks like. What sort of impact did the War on Terror have on regional identities and on related notions of regional security after 9/11? How did 9/11 and the War on Terror affect regional configurations, if at all? Have the War on Terror security narratives affected trade and economic relations in the region? In exploring these questions, Chapter 6 first looks at the evolution of regionalism and regionalization efforts in (South) East Asia,[10] and especially those related to security. Second, Chapter 6 is curious about how the security narratives of the War on Terror affected articulations of regional security and identity, if at all. It further examines the "securitization" of economic relations between the US and the region under the

Introduction 9

Bush Doctrine (Higgott 2004) and examines regional approaches to terrorism after 9/11. Finally, it looks at how War on Terror security narratives have reinforced an "ASEAN-way" of "comprehensive security" as the means by which the concepts of "regional resilience" and "national resilience" are deployed by governing elites in order to maintain *regime* security in a variety of repressive ways (Burke and McDonald 2007; Noor 2006).

Finally, because this project and the questions it asks are focused primarily on the decade immediately after 9/11, Chapter 7 points us towards questions that have emerged relating to the ongoing effects of US foreign policy in East and Southeast Asia in the years beyond the Bush administration. Barack Obama became the 44th President of the United States and took office in 2009, serving two terms until the election of the 45th and current president of the United States, Donald Trump, who took office in 2017. Chapter 7 focuses on Obama's approach to foreign policy in the region, as well as the early days of the Trump administration and what both can tell us about the continuities and changes in security discourses and practices relating to the threat of terrorism in (South) East Asia (Bentley and Holland 2016). It asks the following questions using the same critical security approach outlined in the rest of the book: Did we witness a change in the understanding and practices of security in East and Southeast Asia in a post-Bush era? Or did we see a continuation of familiar security discourses that marked the region? More importantly, what can a critical security analysis of these questions tell us about how American security policy continues to influence actors in the region? Ultimately, Chapter 7 argues that we can observe a continuing retrenchment, and in many cases escalation, of the same types of security practices observable under the Bush administration. This leads into a discussion about the impact of discursive sedimentation, possibilities for discursive transformation, and the different ways that security discourses continue to make certain material security practices possible.

The Conclusion pulls together the significance of the book's arguments, empirical examples, and theoretical contributions to both the critical security and South Asian security literatures. Significantly, it explains how it would have been difficult to arrive at the conclusions drawn without deploying the particular critical security approach that is utilized in the book. This is a critical security approach with post-structuralist underpinnings but is an approach that demurs from strawman "postmodern" tendencies to eschew any and all foundational assumptions. Instead, I reiterate my deployment of a method of critique that calls for a thoughtful engagement with complex security questions using a case-based examination of empirical problems. This exercise is about contingently situating one's theorizations of security in response to *particular cases* and in *particular contexts*. This creates opportunities to engage in the types of foundational ontologizing that is required to cope with the political and ethical problematics of security, but to do so in ways that avoid reifying or essentializing any particular security structure. It is only then that a successful immanent critique can begin – one where the role of the scholar goes beyond simply reproducing the same knowledge and power structures that are constitutive of various insecurities.

10 *Introduction*

Quite simply, we will never be able to answer the questions that we don't take the time to ask. As such, this analysis of the many-layered critical security effects of the War on Terror in Southeast Asia is predicated on the presupposition that it is not only desirable, but necessary, to situate critical security perspectives within particular empirical contexts – historical, geographical, and discursive.

Notes

1 Jackson (2005) has argued that the term "9/11" is now deployed as a tidy concept that "erase[s] the history and context of the events and turn[s] their representation into a cultural-political icon where the meaning of the date becomes both assumed and open to manipulation" (7). With this in mind, this book will use the short-form "9/11" with reflexive acknowledgement of its discursive significance, which is very much a part of what this book is about.

2 This is a tendency that Foucault (1980) called "eventalism."

3 I would argue for a gradual and historically situated emergence of such discourses, informed by previously-held cultural and institutionalized beliefs about the Virtuous Western Self and the Evil Muslim Other (Said 1993).

4 The term "mainstream" will be defined more clearly in Chapter 2 but refers generally to conventionally realist approaches to security in the field of International Relations.

5 It is important to note at this juncture that "East Asia" is a largely arbitrary designation that refers to the Western rim of the Pacific, from the Koreas, down to Indonesia. "Southeast Asia" refers more specifically to the members of ASEAN – Indonesia, Malaysia, Singapore, Thailand, the Philippines, Laos, Cambodia, Vietnam, and Myanmar/Burma. This book is primarily interested in Southeast Asia, but it is often impossible to talk about Southeast Asian issues without bringing China, Japan or Korea into the picture. The term "East Asia" will be used in this book to refer to the larger area, and "Southeast Asia" will be used to talk about that specific part of the region. The term "(South) East Asia" will be used to refer broadly to overlapping regional ideas and institutions that include Southeast Asia and East Asia.

6 *Critical security in the Asia-Pacific*, the 2007 volume edited by Burke and MacDonald, is one of the only texts, currently published, that specifically contains *critical* security analyses as applied to East and Southeast Asia. Hamilton-Hart (2005, 2009) and Foot (2005) are both Asia scholars who have produced work that is critical of the conventional security discourses in East Asia. Capie (2004) has specifically looked at the effects of the US War on Terror on Southeast Asia, including its contributions to the anti-democratic tendencies of governments in the region. However, his analysis is largely constructivist, state-focused, and concerned with more traditional balance-of-power matters. Beeson and Bellamy examine security reform in Southeast Asia (2012) but again, not from the type of critical security perspective this book advances. And, as mentioned, Jackson (2005) has produced some really engaging critical security analyses of the US War on Terror but has not focused specifically on its effects in Asia. Nevertheless, as distinguishable from a Welsh School "human security" perspective like Caballero-Anthony's (2005) work, we are seeing the emergence of some critical security work on Southeast Asia emerging such as that produced by Tan (2013) and Chan (2018).

7 A representative cross-section of this type of mainstream analysis of terrorism in East Asia can be found in the 2003 volume, *Terrorism in the Asia Pacific: Threat and response*, edited by Gunaratna.

8 For example, see the 2003 volume, *Asian security order: Instrumental and normative features*, edited by Alagappa.

Introduction 11

9 See White's various works on "weak ontology" in White (2000; 2003; 2005; and 2009).
10 As mentioned, the term "(South) East Asia" is used to refer broadly to the overlapping regional ideas and institutions that include Southeast Asia *and* East Asia.

References

Alagappa, Muthiah (Ed.). 2003. *Asian security order: Instrumental and normative features*. Stanford, CA: Stanford University Press.

Ba, Alice D. 2014. Asia's regional security institutions. In Evelyn Goh, Saadia Pekkanen, John Ravenhill, and Rosemary Foot (Eds) *The Oxford handbook of the international relations of Asia*. Oxford: Oxford University Press, pp. 667–689.

Beeson, Mark and Alex Bellamy. 2012. *Securing Southeast Asia: The politics of security sector reform*. London: Routledge.

Bentley, Michelle and Jack Holland (Eds). 2016. *The Obama Doctrine: A legacy of continuity in US foreign policy?*. London: Routledge.

Bogain, Ariane. 2018. Terrorism and the discursive construction of national identity in France. *National Identities*: 1–25.

Burke, Anthony and Matt McDonald (Eds). 2007. *Critical security in the Asia-Pacific*. Manchester: Manchester University Press.

Caballero-Anthony, Mely. 2005. *Regional security in Southeast Asia: Beyond the ASEAN way*. Singapore: Institute of Southeast Asian Studies.

Campbell, David. 1998. *Writing security: US foreign policy and the politics of identity*. Manchester: Manchester University Press.

Capie, David. 2004. Between a hegemon and a hard place: The "war on terror" and US–Southeast Asian relations. *The Pacific Review* 17(2): 223–248.

Chan, Nicholas. 2018. The Malaysian "Islamic" state versus the Islamic State (IS): Evolving definitions of "terror" in an "Islamising" nation-state. *Critical Studies on Terrorism*: 1–23.

Chowdhry, Geeta. 2007. Edward Said and contrapuntal reading: Implications for critical interventions in international relations. *Millennium* 36(1): 101–116.

Falk, Richard. 2003. A worldwide religious resurgence in an era of globalization and apocalyptic terrorism. In Fabio Petito and Pavlos Hatzopoulos (Eds) *Religion in international relations*. Palgrave Macmillan: New York, pp. 181–208.

Foot, Rosemary. 2005. Torture: The struggle over a peremptory norm in a counter-terrorist era. *International Relations* 20(2): 131–151.

Foucault, Michel. 1980. *Power/knowledge: Selected interviews & other writings 1972–1977*. Colin Gordon (Ed.). New York: Pantheon Books.

Friedman, Jonathan. 2002. Globalization, dis-integration, re-organization: The transformations of violence. In J. Friedman (Ed.) *Globalization, the state and violence*. Boston, MA: Altamira Press, pp. 1–34.

Fukuyama, Francis. 1992. *The end of history and the last man*. New York: Simon and Schuster.

Geertz, Clifford. 1973. *The interpretation of cultures*. New York: Basic Books.

George, Cherian. 2015. Islamic radicalisation: Questioning the security lens. *Media Asia* 42(1–2): 5–20.

Gunaratna, Rohan (Ed.). 2003. *Terrorism in the Asia-Pacific: Threat and response*. Singapore: Eastern Universities Press.

Gusterson, Hugh. 1999. Missing the end of the Cold War in international security. In Jutta Weldes, Mark Laffey, Hugh Gusterson, and Raymond Duvall (Eds) *Cultures of*

12 *Introduction*

insecurity: States, communities, and the production of danger. Minneapolis, MN: University of Minnesota Press.

Hamilton-Hart, Natasha. 2005. Terrorism in Southeast Asia: Expert analysis, myopia and fantasy. *The Pacific Review* 18(3): 303–325.

Hamilton-Hart, Natasha. 2009. War and other insecurities in East Asia: What the security studies field does and does not tell us. *The Pacific Review* 22(1): 49–71.

Hellwig, Timothy and Abdulkader Sinno. 2017. Different groups, different threats: Public attitudes towards immigrants. *Journal of Ethnic and Migration Studies* 43(3): 339–358.

Higgott, Richard. 2004. After neoliberal globalization: The "securitization" of US foreign economic policy in East Asia. *Critical Asian Studies* 36(3): 425–444.

Holland, Jack. 2012. *Selling the war on terror: Foreign policy discourses after 9/11.* New York: Routledge.

Huntington, Samuel. 1993. The clash of civilizations? *Foreign Affairs* 72(3): 22–49.

Jackson, Richard. 2005. *Writing the war on terrorism: Language politics and counter-terrorism.* Manchester: Manchester University Press.

Jarvis, Lee and Jack Holland. 2014. *Security: A critical introduction.* London: Palgrave Macmillan.

Kaplan, Lawrence F., William Kristol, and Robert Whitfield. 2003. *The war over Iraq: Saddam's tyranny and America's mission.* San Francisco, CA: Encounter Books.

Krauthammer, Charles. 2002. The unipolar moment revisited. *The National Interest* 70: 5–18.

Lacher, Wolfram. 2008. Actually existing security: The political economy of the Saharan threat. *Security Dialogue* 39(4): 383–405.

Mustapha, Jennifer. 2013. Ontological theorizations in critical security studies: Making the case for a (modified) post-structuralist approach. *Critical Studies on Security* 1(1): 64–82.

Noor, Farish. 2006. How Washington's "War on Terror" became everyone's: Islamophobia and the impact of September 11 on the political terrain of South and Southeast Asia. *Human Architecture: Journal of the Sociology of Self-Knowledge* 5(1): 29–50.

Said, Edward. 1993, 2012. *Culture and imperialism.* London: Vintage.

Schmidt, Vivien. 2017. Britain-out and Trump-in: A discursive institutionalist analysis of the British referendum on the EU and the US presidential election. *Review of International Political Economy* 24(2): 248–269.

Tan, See Seng. 2013. *The making of the Asia Pacific: Knowledge brokers and the politics of representation.* Amsterdam: Amsterdam University Press.

Walt, Stephen M. 2002. Beyond bin Laden: Reshaping US foreign policy. *International Security* 26(3): 56–78.

White, Stephen K. 2000. *Sustaining affirmation: The strengths of weak ontology.* Princeton, NJ: Princeton University Press.

White, Stephen K. 2003. After critique: Affirming subjectivity in contemporary social theory. *European Journal of Political Theory* 2(2): 209–226.

White, Stephen K. 2005. Weak ontology: Geneology and critical issues. *The Hedgehog Review* 7(2): 11–25.

White, Stephen K. 2009. Violence, weak ontology and late modernity. *Political Theory* 37(6): 808–816.

Wyn-Jones, Richard. 1999. *Security, strategy, and critical theory.* London: Lynne Rienner.

2 The politics and ethics of critical approaches to security

This book advances a critical disposition towards knowledge that emphasizes the power of discourse and sees the War on Terror operating as a powerful hegemonic security narrative within which the beliefs, interests, and actions of actors take shape. Academic "bodies of literature" in the field of International Relations (IR) can also be understood as narratives: discursive frameworks within which the theory and practice of IR operate. Approaching academic bodies of literature this way allows us to recognize that these are not homogenous or monolithic areas of inquiry, as each contain unique and sometimes competing representations of the subjects to which they pertain. Further, within academic literatures there are dominant perspectives as well as sites of contestation, and the dominance of some perspectives tends to reflect the extent to which they are in accord with the hegemonic narratives of the day. It is important then, to critically engage with these literatures in ways that recognize which perspectives are privileged and which perspectives struggle to gain traction.

This chapter focuses on several interrelated bodies of literature and areas of scholarship within IR and security studies that seek to explain and understand questions of "security," both generally and within the specific regional context of East and Southeast Asia. First, it introduces the emergence and relevance of "critical" approaches to security studies, and puts forth some of my own contributions (Mustapha 2013) to articulating a critical security approach that functions at both the level of politics and of ethics. As such, some of the ideas advanced in this chapter originate from ideas that I first explored in a piece for the *Critical Studies on Security* journal in 2013. This chapter does not go into those in full detail, but the main arguments outlined here build upon the approach to security explained in that article and form the basis for the critical security methods used in this book. Following this, the chapter explores the question of how security in East and Southeast Asia has been conventionally explained and understood. Here, a tour of a representative sampling of the security-related literature pertaining to the region allows us to observe some important trends and commonalities, as well as identify analytical gaps that exist.

14 *Critical approaches to security*

Critical security studies and the question of ontology

Over the years, critically minded scholars of security have been actively engaged in explorations of disciplinary boundaries. There have been definitional debates about what it means to be critical with respect to the study of security and discussions around the emerging problematics that arise in critical projects and in concerted attempts to articulate the politics and the ethics of a critical security studies.[1] A notable effort was made by the self-described C.A.S.E.[2] Collective (2006) to "collectively assess the evolution of critical views of security studies in Europe, discuss their theoretical premises, examine how they coalesce around different issues, and investigate their present – and possibly future – intellectual ramifications" (C.A.S.E. Collective 2006, 443). Browning and McDonald (2011) once asked: what is the future of critical security studies, and what are the promises and limitations of the "Welsh School," the "Copenhagen School"[3] and the politics and ethics of both? Waever (2011) has delved into the politics of his own theories of "securitization." Buzan and Hansen (2009) have mapped the "evolution" of security studies, revealing the challenges of an ingrained Western-centrism following Hansen's (2000) critique of the sexism inherent in the Copenhagen School. Booth (2007) and others like Nyman and Burke (2016) have moved towards articulating a constructed and contingent understanding of the "good" or the ethical in their critical understanding of security. What these interventions share is a broad interest in defining the boundaries of the "critical" in security studies. They also share an interest in exploring both the politics and the ethics of theorizing security.

In my own contribution to this discussion (2013), I have argued for the need to move *beyond* critical post-structuralist deconstruction in order to engage with the (contingent) realities of actually occurring security problems, but without simply re-producing an unproblematic deference to foundational claims, liberal or otherwise. In my original exploration of these topics, I addressed the inclination within post-structuralism, and particularly within postmodernism, to defer engagement with this conundrum and noted that this is deeply troubling for those of us who wish to avoid the ethical and political hazards of being unable to *make claims*. Utilizing Stephen K. White's (2000, 2003, 2005, 2009) arguments for the viability of "weak ontologies," I argued that a post-structurally inclined critical security studies does not require a wholesale rejection of making foundational claims, nor does it necessitate a paralytic disjuncture from the "real world" or the real people who reside there.

Ultimately, I continue to assert that maintaining critical commitments in theorizing security can mean "being reflexive about the claims that are ultimately made, but also of being accountable to them" (Mustapha 2013, 64). This "weak ontology" understanding of critical security studies proves compatible with the type of "immanent critique" method that Wyn-Jones (1999) and Browning and McDonald (2011) advocate for in their support for the practical application of theory. Informed by a weak ontology, methods of critique that examine particular security logics in ways that recognize their historical, geographical, and ideational contingencies become possible. In other words, my own contribution to the critical security literature articulates a method of critique that calls for an empirically rooted examination of *actually-occurring* insecurities in order to move beyond *de*construction towards a *re*constructive exercise of engaging with existing, but always contingently constructed, security logics. Further, it addresses the weaknesses of the aspects of critical security studies that have proven to be ill-equipped to grapple with the politics and ethics of security practices. This general concern is now echoed in work emerging in what is now called the "post-critical" space in security studies and IR that seeks to "ask not [just] what comes after critique, but what should come with critique in order to make it more effective in but also beyond academia" (Tallis 2017, 7).

At this juncture, it is useful to (carefully) make a distinction between "conventional" and "critical" approaches to IR and security studies in order to illustrate these points. For our purposes, conventional (or mainstream/traditional/orthodox) approaches to IR and security tend to have a "modernist" disposition that relies on foundationalist claims to make assertions about how the world works. Conventional approaches rely on an understanding of knowledge that is both positivist and objectivist, and are characterized by an adherence to "the epistemology, ontology and normative implications of traditional (realist) approaches to security that continue to privilege the state as the referent object of security and the 'threat and use of force' (Walt 1991) as the subject of security" (Browning and McDonald 2011, 2). It is important to note that "traditional realism" here refers to the type of (neo)realism articulated by theorists like Waltz (1979) and Mearsheimer (2001). Admittedly, as in the work on "reflexive realism" spearheaded by Williams (2005a, 2005b, 2006, 2013), there have been ongoing projects that seek to re-visit our readings of classical realism, which have resulted in more sophisticated treatments of its formulation. However, projects of critical security in particular, and IR theory in general, continue to be constructed around and against a more mainstream study of security as articulated by conventional theories of realism. The use of neorealism as a foil is not meant to ignore recent theoretical developments within realist thought, nor is it meant to simplistically caricature "realism" writ large. Rather, this more conventional reading of realism is significant because it represents well the use of strong ontology in theorizations of security, and also because it continues to hold such a central place in the conventional study and practice of security (Mustapha 2013).

Traditional realist approaches overwhelmingly possess what White (2000, 2003, 2005, 2009) would call "strong ontologies," in that their ontological commitments are framed unreflexively and there is little, if any, acknowledgement of their essentially contestable nature (Mustapha 2013). White characterizes as "strong" those ontologies

> that claim to show us "the way the world is," or how God's being stands to human being, or what human nature is. It is by reference to this external ground that ethical and political life gain their sense of what is right;

16 *Critical approaches to security*

> moreover, this foundation's validity is unchanging and of universal reach … strong [ontologies] carry an underlying assumption of certainty that guides the whole problem of moving from the ontological level to the moral-political.
>
> (2000, 6–7)

However, White cautions that unquestioned assumptions about what *is* and what *can be known* comprise a double-move that ignores the limits of knowledge production and downplays the inevitable confines of our discursive abilities to think and communicate our ideas (Mustapha 2013). In efforts to respond to these shortcomings of modernist thinking, there has been an "ontological turn" perceptible in what White calls "late-modern" thinking, in which we see "a growing propensity to interrogate more carefully those 'entities' presupposed by our typical ways of seeing and doing in the modern world" (White 2000, 4). In other words, there is a growing recognition of *the contingency and indeterminacy of what is known and how it is known* and as such, the divisions within security studies can be better understood (Mustapha 2013) using this helpful distinction between the strong ontology of modernity and the late-modern "ontological turn," which highlights the significant contributions and "strengths of *weak* ontology" (White 2000, 4).

White's (2000) concept of "weak ontology does not so much name a doctrine as gesture toward a thicket of philosophical issues" (11) and refers to an acknowledgement of the contestability of any theory's ontological commitments. This is distinguishable from the *anti-foundationalism* of Rorty (1996) or Rorty and Vattimo (2007), which rests on a philosophy of history that casts foundationalism as "violent in its essence [and]… irredeemably destined for annihilation" (White 2009, 811). Rather, the concept of weak ontology aims to emphasize the changeable processes and practices of arriving at one's ontological commitments (Mustapha 2013), where "at issue is not where but *how* you carry your most basic commitments, theistic or otherwise" (White 2000, 7, emphasis in original).

A weak ontology approach further recognizes that rejecting any and all ontological commitments, as Rorty and Vattimo's (2007) anti-foundationalist approaches might do, is also undesirable (Mustapha 2013). Instead, weak ontologies respond to two basic concerns. First, there is acceptance that all fundamental conceptualizations of self, other, and world are contestable … and second,

> there is the sense that such conceptualizations are nevertheless necessary or unavoidable for an adequately reflective ethical and political life … the latter insight demands from us an affirmative gesture of constructing foundations, the former prevents us from carrying out this task in a traditional fashion.
>
> (White 2000, 8, emphasis added)

This "affirmative gesture of constructing foundations"[4] is crucial to debunking the simplistic reconstructive/deconstructive and modern/postmodern binaries as

Critical approaches to security   17

they are often evoked (Mustapha 2013). Such labels, along with their connotations, delimit discussion and are too often used in "disciplinary mud-slinging matches, which can close down discussion and inquiry before a close reading of specific arguments or consideration of the issues involved" (Fierke 2007, 3). The strong/weak ontology distinction is also useful because it illustrates a fundamental divergence in approaches to knowledge production and simultaneously cautions against the conflation of weak ontologies with anti-foundationalism. Further, this strong/weak ontology division is helpful because it can, and often does, cross the otherwise rigid boundaries of disciplinary gate-keeping.[5]

I have articulated the usefulness of White's "weak ontology" for a critical security studies in the context of a growing awareness that "conventional" notions of security are of limited relevance in a post-Cold War and post-9/11 context (Mustapha 2013). Consequently, security can now be theorized in a variety of different ways that challenge the ontological footing of a conventional security studies by challenging the realist formulations of concepts like power and sovereignty (Edkins and Pin-Fat 2004; Muppidi 2004; Walker 1993). Without going into great detail about how the various critiques of traditional realism gave rise to new theorizations of security,[6] it is possible to highlight common threads emerging from these interventions, all of which reveal the limitations of a security studies grounded in "strong" ontology.

In the realist conception of security outlined above,[7] the referent object of security is the state, which can be linked to the deployment of strong ontology in realist theorizing. As the Cold War drew to a close, critiques of this orthodox view began to emerge. For example, Booth's (1979) observations from within realism critiqued its innate ethnocentrism, and its attendant conjuring of "enemy images" to serve psychological, sociological and political functions (Booth 1979, 25). This kind of critique raised epistemological questions around the ability to separate subject and object in security studies. Coming at the height of the Cold War, this was a bold theme of critique that ushered in important challenges to orthodox modes of understanding security (Mustapha 2013).

Other critical voices in IR and security also emerged around this same time, including feminist critiques of realist security,[8] which highlighted how the state itself is often complicit in an array of exploitative and gendered power relations embedded within the very precepts of state security and related practices of sovereign exception (Chatterjee 2005). As Edkins and Pin-Fat (2004) and Peterson (1992) have noted, such states of sovereign exception indicate the ways that state violence is "legitimately" directed towards its own subjects "both literally – such as with corporal punishment in the justice system – and structurally – such as with complicity in gendered domestic power relations" (Mustapha 2013, 68). Critical IR theorists engaged with discourse, like Cohn (1987) and Gusterson (1999), demonstrated how realist orthodoxy was simply unable to anticipate or account for significant developments that were increasingly obvious from other perspectives, a notable example being the end of the Cold War. And as mentioned, Campbell (1998) significantly asserted the importance of security and foreign policy discourses, where state identity and perceived threats to that

18 *Critical approaches to security*

identity do not exist independently of the ways that we talk about them. Such themes of critique acknowledge the problems with theory *as* practice, revealing how conventional discourses of security both construct and reinforce the common sense of the defence establishment, and raise questions about how security narratives are constitutive of the *material* practices of security as well (Mustapha 2013).

All of this leads us to ask: what *is* security? How can we reconcile an onto-logically critical understanding of security with the fact that there are millions of people who face literal dangers to their corporeal survival every day? A critical security studies approach requires that we move forward from simply decon-structing the orthodoxy towards meaningful engagement with alternative security logics. But is it possible to do so without simply replacing one orthodoxy with another? This question further highlights the importance of ontology in under-standing security studies (Mustapha 2013). As I have argued elsewhere, critical approaches to security can and do raise interesting questions about how security is practised, how security is studied, and what security *is*. Notably, there is a wide variety of critical approaches to security, all of which have different ideas about what constitutes security; what the referent object of security is; where threats come from; and what any "alternative security futures" should look like (Burke and McDonald 2007). "Security" then, is an *essentially contested concept* (Buzan 1983/1991; see also Fierke 2007, 33–35), and a "critical" disposition towards security "can refer to an emancipatory project, to epistemological inter-rogation, to ontological deconstruction, or to some combination of all three" (Mustapha 2013, 69).

As Peoples and Vaughan-Williams (2010) have also pointed out, one could be forgiven for "wondering what security *is* and what it means to adopt a critical approach to it" (1). Jarvis and Holland (2014) ask if "security" is even possible, or if seeking security is actually desirable if it can end up being the cause of so much harm. As Burke and McDonald (2007) note however,

> we can [still] talk about *a* critical security approach … [which] shares dis-satisfaction with the analytical and normative implications of traditional security studies with its predominant focus on the territorial preservation of the nation-state from external military threat … there is clearly a need for such a broad-based definition in order to open the door to the range of ways of conceptualizing, understanding and potentially redressing human suffer-ing and insecurity.
>
> (5–6)

Hence, critical security studies approaches share overlapping concerns that in one way or another reflect dissatisfaction with conventional security approaches. *How* the different approaches critique this realist orthodoxy and what they seek to do with these critiques are significant questions. In my own analytical review of critical security approaches, I highlighted three successive modes of division (Mustapha 2013). I will not go into detail about them here, but going through the

Critical approaches to security 19

divisions demonstrated how there are some useful and promising weak onto-logical reconstructive approaches that get ignored or misunderstood due to "a tendency to assume that all *re*constructive efforts can occur only in the light of strong ontologies ... [while] on the flip side, there is a corresponding assumption that all *de*constructivist efforts are necessarily synonymous with anti-foundationalism" (Mustapha 2013, 70).

My perspective instead advocated for the promise of a *re*constructive approach that utilizes a weak ontology for the critical analysis of security. This is a broadly post-structuralist approach, which can bring in post-modern, post-colonial, and post-positivist feminist analyses among others, but does not need to descend into what Connolly (1989) calls a "post-ponism," which "links the inability to establish secure ontological ground for a theory with the obligation to defer infinitely the construction of general theories of ... politics" (336). Ulti-mately, I argue that a post-structuralist approach to critical security is not inevit-ably doomed to this "post-ponism" if, and when, a *weak* ontology is deployed to establish the basis for alternative security logics. These approaches already exist and are the ones where deconstruction is part of an analytical disposition towards the way the world currently *is*. In this regard, security (and insecurity) is under-stood to be constructed, yes, but also tangibly experienced. Such theorizing also challenges the basic presuppositions of a traditional realism. It understands that material and discursive security practices warrant critique that is undertaken for the purposes of not only revealing, but also and remedying, sources of insecurity (Mustapha 2013).

Although it can be difficult to do, engaging with actually occurring security logics is necessary in order to address forms of insecurity. And this is because

> weak-ontology approaches take seriously the poststructuralist assertion that reification and essentialism should be avoided in the making of ontological claims. For this reason, any ontological claims that are made must always remain open to interrogation. In other words, weak ontology theorizing allows the theorist to make claims, but this must be done reflexively. These are tentative claims about what *might be*, as opposed to unreflexive claims about what *is*.
>
> (Mustapha 2013, 74–75)

These are the weak ontologies, which "demand from us an affirmative gesture of constructing foundations," but which nevertheless prevent us "from carrying out this task in a traditional fashion" (White 2000, 8).

Relatedly, the notion of weak ontology can help to articulate a reconstruc-tive role for a (modified) post-structuralist critical security studies as it pertains to a (modified) *immanent critique* (Wyn-Jones 1999). This is because in security studies, in general, and in critical security studies, in particular, there has been a tendency to work with both "universalizing security logics and under-theorized or limited conceptualizations of progress" (Browning and McDonald 2011, 3). In other words, addressing the politics and ethics of

20 *Critical approaches to security*

security requires the recognition of the "various ways in which security is conceptualized and practiced in different social, historical and political contexts" (Browning and McDonald 2011, 3). Hence, what this requires is

> a method of [immanent] critique concerned with locating possibilities for progressive change *in existing social and political orders* … [where there is a need] to develop understandings of the politics of security that are *context specific*; that recognize and interrogate the role of *different security discourses* and their effects in *different settings*; and that come to terms with sedimented meanings *without endorsing these as timeless and inevitable.*
>
> (Browning and McDonald 2011, 14, emphases added)

I have argued that this is ultimately an articulation of the need for a weak ontology approach to critical security projects. And that the whole exercise is about contingently situating one's theorizations of security in response to *particular cases* and in *particular contexts* (Mustapha 2013).

The notion of "immanent critique" itself is underutilized in post-structuralist critical security studies because of its close association with the Frankfurt School of Critical Theory and its promise of "emancipation" rooted in the Gramscian idea of *Praxis*. Harkening back to the theories of Adorno and Horkheimer, immanent critique seeks to examine an existing order from within it, rather than relying on an ahistorical and foundationalist external point of reference (Fierke 2007). So, in immanent critique

> the critique involves an analysis of the criteria set by the actors themselves, pointing out the contradictions within this context and its emancipatory potential … the assumptions of immanent critique contrast with those of problem-solving theory [which] in assuming that the present order reflects a timeless pattern … legitimizes the existing order and reproduces the pattern.
>
> (Fierke 2007, 167)

This key point helps to explain why post-structuralist critical security theorists can sometimes demur from the idea that there are "security problems" that must be solved. However, while solving a problem of insecurity does not, by definition, *require* that one legitimize or reproduce existing social orders it almost always requires operating within them. In rejecting the "strong ontology" of the Frankfurt School, post-structuralists can miss the epistemological and methodological value of critiquing an existing order *from within*. Further, because immanent critique gestures towards a strong ontological understanding of "emancipation," a post-structuralist perspective might miss the point that the task of remedying actually-occurring insecurities can take many possible forms. Immanent critique also allows us to conceptualize the role of the theorist "towards the end of challenging prevailing hegemonic discourses" (Fierke 2007, 168), but does not necessarily require the theorist to sign on to a single strong-ontological Frankfurt School understanding of emancipation.

Critical approaches to security 21

Fortunately, there are already movements from within post-structuralist critical security studies that gesture towards a weak ontology approach, although they may not always be expressed as such.[9] As mentioned earlier, in his critique of Richard Ashley, William Connolly (1989) identifies a tendency within the postmodern formulation of issuing

> an interwoven set of self-restrictions [that reduce] "post-structuralism" to one perpetual assignment to "invert hierarchies" maintained in other theories. One might call this recipe for theoretical self-restriction "post-ponism." It links the inability to establish secure ontological ground for a theory with the obligation to defer infinitely the construction of general theories of global politics.
>
> (336)

Instead, Connolly resists these simple binary oppositions as a recipe for self-restriction (Mustapha 2013). Rather, he points out that Foucault (1980) himself, despite engaging in deconstructivist critique and despite being oft-evoked in strawmen depictions of "postmodernism," refused the label "deconstructionist" and argued that "there is nothing in the structural imperatives of a 'post-structuralist' or 'postmodern' problematic *requiring* perpetual 'post-ponism' at the level of theory construction and contestation" (Connolly 1989, 337).

Connolly's admonition, coming from a perspective sympathetic to post-structuralism, brings to light two important and interconnected points that provide the theoretical underpinnings of the critical security approach and the analytical methods that are utilized in this project. They are,

> First, that acts of reconstruction can be critical in the most fundamental ontological sense, and they do not always have to look like the "strong ontologies" of either modernist-traditionalist theories, or the alternative critical security theories that appeal unproblematically to external grounds to make their claims [and] Second ... that acts of reconstruction *can* emanate directly from post-structuralist commitments, where deconstruction is seen as both a first step and as an ethic to bring to engagement with the status-quo of existing power-relations. This engagement is necessary if we are serious about avoiding a paralytic disjuncture from the "real world," where millions face corporeal insecurity every day. Rather, maintaining critical commitments can mean being reflexive about the inter-subjectivity and indeterminacy of the claims that *are* ultimately made, and of being accountable to them.
>
> (Mustapha 2013, 77–78)

This book's analysis of the many-layered critical security effects of the War on Terror in (South) East Asia is predicated on the presupposition that it is not only desirable, but necessary, to situate critical security perspectives within particular empirical contexts – historical, geographical, and discursive. This is the key to

22 *Critical approaches to security*

bridging the divide between a postmodern post-ponism that is disengaged from the "realities" of security and insecurity and the pragmatic need to move from deconstruction towards a practical engagement with the world in the hopes of re-visioning alternative security futures contingent upon the empirical realities of specific places and times.

In other words, a politically and ethically consistent post-structuralist critical security approach

> is not about trying to operate without ever making ontological claims, but rather being very careful not to naturalize particular security logics as being timeless and inevitable ... [which] creates opportunities to still engage in the types of foundational ontologizing that is required to cope with the political and ethical problematics of security.
>
> (Mustapha 2013, 76)

This book seeks to do just that. By approaching security problematics in Southeast Asia with a critical post-structuralist sensibility while still recognizing the importance of historical, social, and geographic contingencies, we can realize opportunities to not only identify (using post-structuralist methods of inquiry) a set of security logics that might be otherwise invisible through a realist lens; but we also realize opportunities to engage with the possibilities of remedying insecurity in tangible terms. Arguably, operationalizing a weak ontology approach can also be helpful (and perhaps necessary) for navigating the *intra*-disciplinary exclusions that are too often invoked in what Mutimer (2009) calls the "broad church" of critical security studies, where

> by speaking for some we necessarily speak against others ... [and] ... while we cannot avoid effecting exclusions in our work, we can resist the temptation to effect them *a priori*. Rather, we need to turn our critical gazes constantly on ourselves to ask if, at each time and in each place, we are theorizing for those most in need. Doing so acknowledges that other outsiders will be excluded by our choices, but has at least the benefit of doing so in a limited and contingent fashion.
>
> (20)

This is yet another gesture towards weak ontology in critical security. And it is a weak ontology that "eschews disciplinary foreclosures and allows us to consider any question, with the corrective that all conceptualizations of self, other, and world are contestable" (Mustapha 2013, 76).

Campbell (1998) recognized this in *Writing security*, when his exploration of American foreign policy meant that he would obviously have to engage with the idea of "the state" as the primary producer of security discourses and one of many significant sites of security politics (Mustapha 2013). To ignore this fact in a discussion of threat construction in American foreign policy would be to miss opportunities for change, whatever that might look like. This should not be confused with continued attention to the state *in the same way that the state is understood from a traditional realist perspective*, but instead requires "a re-visioning of the state (or of any factor) in security studies through the epistemological commitments of a post-structuralist ethic, without making the mistake of creating new blind-spots in analysis" (Mustapha 2013, 77) or of simply replacing an old orthodoxy with a new one.

The scope and meaning of "security" in (South) East Asia

This next section examines how the concept of "security" in East and Southeast Asia is broadly defined within the existing scholarly literature. It further outlines the issues that, according to this literature, fall under the umbrella of "security." In other words, what is the scope and meaning of security according to the conventional security studies approaches that relate to East and Southeast Asia? Traditional realism, as outlined earlier in the chapter, and constructivism, each dominant in turn, are identified as the two leading scholarly approaches to security in the region. Hence, this section sketches out the two "images" of security that are developed through the realist and constructivist lenses respectively. Following this, critiques of both approaches are explored and the degree to which "critical" approaches to security have emerged within the literature on Southeast Asian security is briefly assessed. Finally, this chapter concludes with a summary of the gaps in the existing literature and elaborates further upon the theoretical contributions offered by this book.

To understand how security in East and Southeast Asia is explained and understood, the following related questions are asked: *Who* defines security in East and Southeast Asia? *Which theoretical approaches* dominate the study of security in the region? *What variables* are considered to be important when analyzing security in the region? And, finally, *which actors* are privileged in discussions on East and Southeast Asian security? As outlined in the previous section, an increasingly multifaceted security studies literature that includes more critical perspectives has emerged since the end of the Cold War. Decisions made about how to define security inform choices about which issues are placed under the umbrella of security. And because security studies is widely considered to be a policy relevant field, this means that conceptualizations of security by the "experts" have practical implications for real people and real situations. Accordingly, a focus on questions of ontology is useful for unpacking and deconstructing the specific nuances of a "critical" security studies. Drawing on earlier work (Mustapha 2013), I characterized as "ontologically critical," those theoretical approaches that are reflexive about their foundational assumptions. The delineation between "strong" and "weak" ontologies, as outlined by Stephen K. White (2000), allows us to further home in on these questions.

While the broader field of IR has demonstrated a growing affinity for criticality, the prevailing literature on Southeast Asian security has not tended to reflect this to any considerable degree. As will be demonstrated shortly, this is not to say that critical voices are wholly absent. But a survey of IR security literature

24   *Critical approaches to security*

as it pertains to East and Southeast Asia reveals a continued reliance upon tradition-ally conventional theoretical approaches that continue to reify a state-centric under-standing of security (Kang 2003). Further, the scope of *what* constitutes security and what counts as a security issue has continued to be dictated by a narrow focus on inter-state conflict and military security (Hamilton-Hart 2009, 2012).

Traditional realist approaches have enjoyed a long history and established position in East Asian security studies. Up until at least the 1980s it was the dominant, if not the only, approach to scholarship in the field. Arguably, this reflected the fact that inter-state conflict was seen as the main security issue dominating the attention of regional scholars and policy makers during most of the twentieth century. Southeast Asia alone saw three major wars: the First (1945–1954), Second (1965–1973) and Third (1978–1989) Indo-China Wars respectively; and it was the US involvement in the Second Indo-China War in particular that generated a large body of related security literature in the aca-demic fields of IR and security studies (Peou 2001). Although there were some attempts made by Kantian liberals and neo-liberal institutionalists to offer their perspectives in the study of East Asian security during the same period, the undisputed prevailing scholarship of the time was being undertaken by realists (Peou 2001).

Not surprisingly, following the collapse of the Soviet Union and the end of the Cold War in the 1990s, realist security scholarship offered a particularly pessimistic prognosis for the region. Two widely read pieces in the 1993/1994 Winter Volume of *International Security* characterized the region as "ripe for rivalry" and bound for instability and military uncertainty due to the new real-ities of a now multipolar world (Friedberg 1993; Betts 1993). These predictions were based on a variety of factors and included the wide disparities in economic and military power in the region; the vast differences in political systems among East Asian states; longstanding and pre-existing historical animosities between regional actors; and the widespread perception that the region was lacking in robust institutions (Kang 2003).

For Friedberg, the end of the Cold War and the bipolar international system meant that the region

> will not lack for crises, whether they are handled well or poorly, in the years just ahead. To the south, disputes over borders and resources (especially oil and natural gas) could engage the interests of Japan, China, and India, as well as the members of ASEAN. The relationship between China and Taiwan may yet be resolved through the use of force. To the north, the future shape of Korea and the manner in which it is determined will be matters of intense concern to Japan, China, Russia, and perhaps the United States, to say nothing of the Korean people themselves.
>
> (1993, 31)

Friedberg also predicted an inevitable arms race, as he expected the US role in the region to greatly diminish. Related to that prediction, he posited that Japan

Critical approaches to security 25

would re-militarize, which would cause security dilemma anxieties among its immediate neighbours as well as the ASEAN members who relied upon US power to balance Japan's.

Betts (1993) held similar concerns about the status of security in a post-Cold War East Asia. He emphasized the continued importance of balance-of-power politics, which he felt was "up for grabs" with the end of the bipolar Cold War system but he was also worried about the high costs of maintaining US dominance in the region (35). For Betts, US strategic commitments in a post-Cold War East Asia were "dangerously vague" and were "sure to invite miscalculation by Asian adversaries and allies" (Betts 1993, 37). This problem would be exacerbated by China, which in Betts' view would surely pose a threat to regional equilibrium in a variety of ways. A particularly interesting feature of Betts' analysis was his contention that a "truncated end of history" in East Asia, ushering in "an era of economic liberalization decoupled from democratization," could actually have a destabilizing effect on the region (Betts 1993, 36). He argued from a realist perspective that a trajectory of "normal" economic and political development following a linear pattern of East Asian modernization, "is not necessarily something to be desired from an American perspective" (Betts 1993, 55). In other words, Betts was concerned that Western-style economic liberalism and prosperity in East Asia would run against US interests and would be likely to threaten the political and military stability of the region. He postulated that

> by realist criteria, a China and a Japan unleashed from Cold War discipline could not help but become problems ... Japan is powerful by virtue of its prosperity ... which creates political friction with competitors ... China evokes the structural theory of the German Problem; even without evil designs, the country's search for security will abrade the security of surrounding countries ... Individually, countries on the mainland cannot hope to deter or defeat China in any bilateral test of strength; collectively, they cannot help but worry China if they were to seem united in hostility. If China becomes highly developed economically, the problem would change. Asia would be stable but unhappy, because a rich China would be the clear hegemonic power in the region ... and perhaps in the world.
>
> (Betts 1993, 61)

This type of cynical analysis was characteristic of the realist security studies literature on East Asia in the 1990s (Kang 2003; Goh 2008; Hamilton-Hart 2009, 2012).

As the Friedberg and Betts contributions to this conversation suggest, the realist security literature at the time also paid a disproportionate amount of attention to the role of the US in the region *from the point of view of US security interests*. This is not very surprising considering that we are talking about a predominantly American-produced security literature meant for American policy and academic audiences. But this is the crux of the "bodies of literature *as* discourses and narratives" idea. *Who* "security" is defined by and for holds deep

26 Critical approaches to security

significance for any analysis of security. On an ontological level, it shapes the most basic ideas about what "security" itself is understood to be (Hamilton-Hart 2005, 2012).

Notwithstanding the prevailing dominance of realism, a growing discontent with its narrow vision of East Asian security emerged during this same period. In response to the gloomy predictions of realists "a newer set of more sophisticated counter-arguments were put forward" (Hamilton-Hart 2009, 54). These counter-arguments focused on three key dimensions or issues of concern. The first two concerns did not depart significantly from realist preoccupations, specifically those surrounding American security alliance commitments in the region, and concerns surrounding China as a rising economic and military power (Hamilton-Hart 2009). Notable however, was the third issue of concern, which called attention to *the nature and role of regional institutions*, and it was this dimension that ensured that the first two issues would come to be seen in fresh ways. As such, this shifted theoretical focus starting in the mid-1990s was instrumental to the emergence of a more social constructivist[10] approach to East Asian security studies, which then went on to become the new dominant approach to the study of security in the region. While realists' analysis dismissed the importance of institutional arrangements,[11] "the most developed critiques of [realist] arguments ... revolve[d] around claims regarding regional institutions and cooperation patterns" (Hamilton-Hart 2009, 58).

Notably, East and Southeast Asian regional institutions and arrangements continue to be of particular interest to IR scholars. The disproportionate scholarly attention that continues to be paid to regional institutions is arguably due to what sets them apart from their counterparts in Europe and North America. For example, East and Southeast Asian security and economic regional institutions have historically operated in a relatively informal manner. Despite this lack of "rules," these institutions continue to exist and evolve and, in many cases, such as with ASEAN and the ASEAN Regional Forum (ARF), still play an important role in moderating regional security relations (Stubbs and Mustapha 2014; Stubbs 2018). This fact erodes the realist dismissal of non-robust institutions and instead lends weight to the social constructivist emphasis on the importance of norms and ideas (Wendt 1992; Stubbs and Mustapha 2014). ASEAN's institutional character, for example, has been built on norms of consensus-building and diplomatic cooperation, much of which takes place under the rubric of informal "Track II" diplomacy (Stubbs and Reed 2005). Furthermore, ASEAN's core guiding principle is a commitment to member-states' sovereignty through a strict adherence to the norm of non-interference in each other's internal affairs.

It is interesting then, that realist predictions of an inevitable and widespread breakdown in East Asian regional security following the Cold War never came to pass (Peou 2001; Kang 2003; Hamilton-Hart 2009, 2012). The trend towards continued regional stability and the uniqueness of regional institutions thus necessarily introduced questions around ideas, institutional norms, and regional identity. This has highlighted the usefulness of a social constructivist focus on institutional relationships among East and Southeast Asian states. This is why a

Critical approaches to security 27

survey of the literature on regional security after the late 1990s reveals an increasing pervasiveness of social constructivist ideas alongside realist ones, largely due to new attention paid to regional institutions. This is what created the space for constructivist approaches to vie for prominence in East Asian security studies.

It is not controversial then, to say that the IR literature on East and Southeast Asian security has been historically dominated by realist and (social) constructivist approaches. Both of these approaches can be understood as ontologically conventional in the sense that they assert a state-centric view of security in terms of both the referent object and the use of force as the main source of threat. While realist scholarship was the norm for the study of regional security after World War II, a constructivist turn that emphasized the importance of institutions and ideas, began gaining prominence in the mid-1990s (Peou 2001; Acharya and Stubbs 2006; Eaton and Stubbs 2006). It is possible then, to sketch out two prevailing "images" of regional security as represented by realist and social constructivist scholarship respectively. Both of these images frame security (and insecurity) in specific ways. Each considers certain factors to be important when analyzing security in the region, and each privileges particular actors in analysis. As with all categorizations however, there is much overlap among and between these two approaches and there is no neat delineation between them.

Realism and the "hub and spokes" model

As Burke and McDonald (2007) have pointed out, the region can be divided into two "distinct – but interconnected security paradigms that are governed by differing normative and structural frameworks and differing levels of great power influence and involvement" (10). They are the "hub and spokes" model of security and the "comprehensive security community" model respectively. The main feature of a realist understanding of East Asian security is an emphasis on strategic inter-state relationships. For realists, security in East Asia is defined in terms of the material power and interests of regional state actors, and the focus is on "great power politicking and military manoeuvring to create a stable regional balance of power" (Eaton and Stubbs 2006, 139). This realist image of security in East Asia corresponds to the so-called "hub and spokes" model of regional stability. This is a security structure of bilateral alliances between the US and East Asian states, dating from the security machinations of the Cold War, that is "focused upon realist frameworks of military deterrence and US strategic power projection" (Burke and McDonald 2007, 10).

Evoking the image of a bicycle wheel, the "hub and spokes" model is so named due to the idea that the regional security structure relies on the US (the hub) projecting its strategic interests outward along the lines of its bilateral security alliances in the region (the spokes). Clearly the image of a bicycle wheel places the US at the centre of the East Asian security model and prioritizes the exercise of US power and interests for the maintenance of stability in the region.

28 *Critical approaches to security*

Regional security is thus seen to be synonymous with regional stability based on the power and position of the US, understood to be the most important security actor in the region. This realist image of security prioritizes the role of the US in East Asia even as it identifies Japan and China as two great regional powers. From this perspective "stability in the broader region is ... in large part a function of the behaviour of, and the relationships among, these three major powers" (Ikenberry and Mastanduno 2003, 3).

Again, the core aspect of this image is the idea that the basic premise of regional security *is* stability, "defined broadly as *the absence of serious military, economic or political conflict among nation-states*" (Ikenberry and Mastanduno 2003, 3, emphasis added). Ikenberry and Mastanduno's (2003) edited volume, *International relations theory and the Asia-Pacific*, was actually meant as a rejoinder to the aforementioned 1994 Friedberg article. The volume acknowledges that a realist emphasis on structure alone is not enough to gain a thorough understanding of the security challenges in the region, and acknowledges that liberal and constructivist theorizations of regional security can be useful for drawing attention to the ways that a US hegemonic order might be made "more acceptable to China and other states in the region" (Ikenberry and Mastanduno 2003, 437). Nevertheless, the ultimate conclusion that they draw is that the key security priority for the region continues to be the maintenance of a US-based hegemonic order (Ikenberry and Mastanduno 2003, 436–437). This was true for realist scholars then, and in the context of contemporary concerns around the Korean Peninsula and new dynamics emerging in the East Asian security landscape, remains largely true today (Tan 2013; Bentley and Holland 2013; Stubbs 2018). In other words, a realist approach to East Asian security sees the continuation and maintenance of American geopolitical hegemony as the lynchpin of regional stability.

A realist approach to East Asian security also tends to eschew regional multilateral security organizations such as the ASEAN Regional Forum (ARF), characterizing such efforts as ineffective and irrelevant. Realist analysts of East Asian security have often rejected the importance of multilateral regional institutions outright, especially in the context of the Cold War (Leifer 1999; da Cunha 1996; Solomon and Drennan 2001). Others have used a more "eclectic approach" to analyze East Asian security "by conceding to the constructivist position that East Asia is more than the story of competing great power relations" (Eaton and Stubbs 2006, 139). However, even the more nuanced takes on regional security (see Hill and Tow 2002; Ikenberry and Tsuchiyama 2002; Alagappa 2003; Buzan 2003; Tow 2004) generally uphold the view that competing great power relations, predicated on state hierarchy as determined by military power, is "always prior to alternative forms of order based on more peaceful, less combative principles" (Eaton and Stubbs 2006) through multilateral organizations.

Hence, we can sketch out this first realist image of security in East and Southeast Asia. For realists, security in East and Southeast Asia is defined *as* stability, specified as the absence of any major military conflict between states in the region. This condition of security is derived from a stable balance of power as

Critical approaches to security 29

determined by the continued presence of an American-based hegemonic security order rooted in the "hub and spokes" model of bilateral security alliances between the US and other actors in the region. China and Japan are also seen as secondary great powers, and relations between the US and these two states are instrumental to the maintenance of security and stability in the East Asian region. Regional institutions, while perhaps relevant insofar as they can make American hegemony seem more "palatable" to China, are seen as largely ineffectual and irrelevant to core questions around competing great power interests. The realist image of security in East and Southeast Asia, prevailed as the dominant view of the region from the end of the World War II until the end of the Cold War, and to a considerable degree, continues to endure into the present (Stubbs 2018).

In the late 1980s and early 1990s, however, we saw a theoretical shift away from realism and towards a constructivist view of the region (Acharya and Stubbs 2006). During this period, students of East and Southeast Asian relations diversified their theoretical perspectives and moved towards constructivism as a means to explain and understand the region. This was partly a reaction to a series of historical events that called into question the validity of relying solely on realist approaches. These events included Vietnam's withdrawal from Cambodia and the dismantling of the Communist Party of Malaysia in 1989, neither of which could be readily explained by a realist analysis; as well as ASEAN's launch of the ARF and the expansion of ASEAN's membership to include controversial member-states like Myanmar, all of which confound realist models of security cooperation (Stubbs and Mustapha 2014). None of these developments were easily explained by a realist focus on material forces, military balancing, and great power alliances as the sole determinants of regional security and stability (Acharya and Stubbs 2006). The problem was not just that realism could not predict these developments, but that its theoretical lens was incapable of even acknowledging them.

The emergence of East and Southeast Asian economic cooperation also brought to the fore the importance of economic considerations. While realists like Betts (1993) had been concerned by the possible destabilizing effects of decoupling economic development from democratic development, it became increasingly apparent that economic relationships between members in the region were having a stabilizing effect. The growing and mutually beneficial economic interdependence between China and its East Asian neighbours appears to have moderated concerns about China posing a military threat (Beeson 2014), bringing into question the realist presupposition that material power is always the most important determinant of regional security.

The Asian financial crisis of 1997/1998 also presented analytical problems for realists (Cheeseman 1999). The widespread domestic disorder that resulted from the financial crisis and its aftermath, some of which involved violent civil unrest and the downfall of sitting governments, forced a re-evaluation of the very concept of "security." According to a realist read, the Asian financial crisis was not a threat to regional security because it did not appear to exacerbate existing inter-state tensions or cause any new inter-state conflicts. Nevertheless, widespread rioting

30 *Critical approaches to security*

and political violence in Indonesia, Thailand, and the Philippines caused by a combination of unemployment, ballooning food prices, International Monetary Fund-imposed austerity measures, and loss of government legitimacy all made a mockery of the idea that "security" is a status limited only to the state in relation to other states. These developments revealed that economic considerations were much more relevant than realists admit. They also highlighted the fact that an absence of inter-state conflict does not mean that populations are free from insecurity or violence. At the very least, the economic crisis "… provided an opportunity for the practice and, to a lesser extent, the theory of regional security to be (re)debated and (re)interpreted" (Cheeseman 1999, 333).

Related to this need to re-debate and re-interpret international relations and security in the face of new contingent realities, the more general proliferation of novel theories of IR contributed to increased theoretical diversity in East and Southeast Asian studies in this period (Acharya and Stubbs 2006). During the 1990s and beyond, theories of realism faced a range of challenges from burgeoning scholarship in constructivism and neo-liberal institutionalism, as well as from critical post-structuralist approaches to understanding the global. As such, a

> ferment of new approaches as well as refinements to the old neo-realist perspectives offered analysts of Southeast Asian relations a wide range of theories from which to choose as they sought to come to grips with the changes that were sweeping across the region.
>
> (Acharya and Stubbs 2006, 127)

Constructivism and the "comprehensive security community" model

Constructivist approaches then, began gaining theoretical ground when a realist understanding of East and Southeast Asia failed to account for the numerous changes that occurred in the region after the end of the Cold War. This was partly attributable to constructivists' ability to account for the importance of institutions which filled a large analytical gap in the realist literature on regional security. As Cheeseman pointed out

> there was, prior to the start of the economic crisis in July 1997, an "emerging consensus" among academics … that: (1) multilateral dialogue and institution-building was security enhancing; (2) the "Asian way" of proceeding by consensus and seeking to build confidence and trust between participants was a more appropriate means to achieving regional security than the more formal and rule-bound approaches that were being advanced by Western scholars and policy-makers; (3) security needed to be seen in comprehensive terms, incorporating non-military as well as traditional politico-military considerations; and (4) … the fledgling multilateral regional security framework needed to be buttressed by continuing bilateral ties and the presence of American military forces.
>
> (1999, 384)

Critical approaches to security 31

Here we see a distinctly constructivist turn in theorizations of East Asian security. While there once was a dearth of scholarship that sought to understand ideational questions relating to East Asian international relations, in the late 1990s we saw the emergence and growth of constructivist readings of the region. As mentioned, this was "the constructivism of Wendt, Katzenstein and so forth, rather than of Onuf and other more critically inclined theorists, that matters for the leading constructivist works on Southeast Asian security" (Tan 2006, 251). Hence, the strand of constructivism employed by most East Asia scholars during this turn is "the one which takes a similar epistemological stance to those of the rationalist IR schools" (Katsumata 2006, 187). In other words, even though a conventional constructivist analysis of East Asia favoured the social construction of regional structures over the causal power of those same structures, it nevertheless still presupposed that the international system was one of anarchy between rational and unitary state actors.

In contrast to realists, constructivist scholars like Acharya (2001)[12] accord greater causal weight to institutions like ASEAN in their assessments of (South) East Asian security. Constructivists credit the region's "state of relative peace to the regulative effect of key ASEAN norms, in particular norms of non-interference, non-use of force and settlement of disputes by peaceful means" (Eaton and Stubbs 2006, 140). In other words, where realists would attribute regional stability to external factors such as the balancing power of the US military, constructivists put much more weight on the regional actors themselves and on the socialization between them. From this perspective, the importance of local actors' agency and the significance of regional institutions should not be viewed as a mere adjunct to a great power balancing act (Acharya and Stubbs 2006, 127). Rather, the conceptions of power that determine the shape of a regional security architecture go beyond a narrow realist understanding of military power. For constructivists, conceptions of power, like all "social facts," do not arise out of an a priori state of anarchy but "are constructed endogenously through socialization processes" (Eaton and Stubbs 2006, 146).

This brings us to the constructivist "image" of security in East Asia, exemplified by the so-called "comprehensive security" model. As outlined earlier, the "hub and spokes model" of security corresponds with a realist image of East and Southeast Asia. This "hub and spokes model" sees the maintenance of an American hegemonic balance of power via bilateral alliances as the hub of East Asian security, defined as an absence of inter-state warfare in the region. For the (conventional) constructivist view however, security is understood as a condition that goes beyond the military dimension, albeit without excluding it (Burke and McDonald 2007). In other words, the constructivists here are ontological *broadeners* when it comes to conceptualizing security (Mustapha 2013). This approach still considers the military dimension to be the most important aspect of security, but *includes* the political, economic and socio-cultural dimensions into a broader conceptualization of security factors. Importantly, this "comprehensive" understanding of security is a core working principle of ASEAN and of regional security cooperation in general. This concept enabled the formation of ASEAN and also led to

32 *Critical approaches to security*

the emergence of a nascent "security community" that challenged some dominant strategic norms. Its first members ... agreed to eschew the use of force to resolve disputes between them, to respect each other's internal sovereignty (the doctrine of "non-interference") and to minimize the intrusion of great power competition ... from the outset ASEAN constituted a combination of liberal norms in interstate strategic relations and statist norms pertaining to the maintenance of "internal security," in which sovereignty ... is paramount, and regime security a dominant objective.

(Burke and McDonald 2007, 12)

In this comprehensive conceptualization of security, which extends beyond the military dimension, the notion of security is closely related to the concept of "national resilience," or the idea that domestic economic, political and socio-cultural stability in combination with a norm of non-interference between states is necessary for maintaining the stability of the region (Stubbs and Mustapha 2014; Stubbs 2018). In other words, stable and happy states make for a stable and happy (or free of military inter-state conflict) region.

In his analysis of the formation of the ASEAN Regional Forum (of ARF), Katsumata (2006) points out that the interests and policies that initiated the forum were "defined by what can be regarded as a norm of security cooperation in Asia ... this norm contains two sets of ideational elements: common security ... [and] the ASEAN Way of diplomacy" (181). The underlying purpose of the regional comprehensive security community is thus defined as the collective commitment to and reinforcement of these norms and ideas. Security communities then, despite being seen as mere talk-shops by realists, can and do have a causal role in the maintenance of security and stability. In the constructivist image of security, it is the social relationships between state actors that allow them to develop sedimented norms like the ASEAN norm of non-interference, which in turn moderates the otherwise unequal and potentially destabilizing power dynamics between state actors that a realist might predict.

Nevertheless, within this type of constructivism, the state is still the referent object of security in that it is the state that is to be secured from instability arising from a multitude of (broad) factors. Constructivism may open the black-box of the "unitary" state and look "inside" it to understand inter-state relations, but this exercise still forecloses too many questions. What we can see is that "... in granting ontological priority to states, constructivism cannot fully transcend [state] reification because its effort to avoid reifying international anarchy or regions comes at the expense of a reified state" (Tan 2006, 254). The enduring rationalist tendency to couple subjectivity with sovereignty means that the realist shortcoming of treating agency as ultimately pre-given remains a feature of constructivism (Tan 2006). As such, the constructivist image of East Asian security remains "tellingly essentialist, particularly [with] concessions to state-centrism and ideational/normative determinism, both due partly to an uncritical emulation of rationalist constructivist perspectives in IR theory" (Tan 2006, 239).

Critical approaches to security 33

The enduring state-centrism of constructivism is significant because, even though constructivist analysis has much to contribute to the study of East Asian security through its emphasis on the significance of multilateralism and ideational norms as they relate to inter-state conflict, constructivist scholarship nevertheless "tends to soft-soap the darker side of the ASEAN-way, and the essentially statist (and internally coercive) character of its norms" (Burke and McDonald 2007, 13). Importantly then, this East Asian concept of comprehensive security, along with the norms of national resilience and non-interference that are incorporated into its structures, are also sources and sites of *in*security. Indeed

> comprehensive security as "resilience," links internal security paradigms preoccupied with the (often violent and repressive) defence of regime security and territorial integrity with regional frameworks that ... extend the internal structures into region-wide paradigms that place a primacy upon sovereign freedom, non-interference and "political stability" ... cooperation in the ASEAN case tends to *strengthen* statist norms and insulate regional governments from scrutiny over their approach to human rights and internal claims to justice, separatism and difference.
>
> (Burke and McDonald 2007, 13)

Hence, if ASEAN is a security community according to this view, it is a community of "economic, political and military elites, and the security that it provides is morally (and conceptually) incoherent, being too often premised on the insecurity of others" (Burke and McDonald 2007, 13).

Conclusion – beyond constructivism in (South) East Asian security

So, where are we now in terms of theoretical approaches to regional security? Acharya and Stubbs (2006) once argued that the early 2000s witnessed the emergence of a much greater "theoretical pluralism" in East and Southeast Asian studies. But this was a generous assertion that understated the continued pervasiveness of state-centric strong ontologies in much of the constructivist scholarship on the region. It also overstated the "critical" nature of English School and neo-liberal institutional approaches, which actually share basic foundational assumptions with the conventional constructivism outlined in their analysis. Nevertheless, their observation of a developing theoretical pluralism in the study of East Asian security did gesture towards the emergence of some fresh perspectives and theories over the last 15 years or so. Notably, these perspectives and theories point to and correspond with developments occurring in (critical) security studies more generally, as outlined at the beginning of this chapter.

As mentioned, realist perspectives see the state as the primary actor *and* the primary referent of security. For realists, it is the state that is to be secured from military threats and instability arising from imbalances in strategic power. Conventional constructivists, in turn, are mostly just "broadeners." Though they

34 *Critical approaches to security*

have been able to bring in institutions, norms, ideas, epistemic communities, and social movements into analysis – which realism is unable to do (see Acharya 2003; Caballero-Anthony 2005) – they still see the state as the chief referent in the East Asian security architecture. From this constructivist perspective the state remains abstracted as a modern, Westphalian construct – as a sovereign and unitary rational actor and as the primary actor in regional security relations. As I have argued here, this type of constructivist analysis was the "critical" edge of the East Asian security literature for a significant period.

One of the most crucial lines of critique that *has* emerged in the newer critical literature on (South) East Asian security is to take to task this ongoing tendency in both realist and constructivist scholarship to over-privilege the state (see Foot 2005; Tan 2006; Burke and McDonald 2007; Hamilton-Hart 2009, 2012). Nevertheless, there are still relatively few examples of epistemologically and/or ontologically critical analyses of regional security. Hence, it is apparent that there is an opening for approaches that utilize critical post-structuralist ways of understanding East and Southeast Asian security – ones that emphasize the importance of intertextuality and inter-subjectivity; that see the constitutive effects of larger security narratives and discourses; and that acknowledge the "insecurities" that exist beyond (and because of) the state. They are starting to emerge, and what is promising about them is that they ask important ontological questions about the concept of "security" itself.[13] Who or what is being "secured" and does a "secure" state necessarily translate into a "secure" population? Can security and insecurity exist simultaneously? What questions have yet to be asked about security and insecurity in East Asia, and what questions are *unable* to be asked under the statist rubric of either realism or constructivism, both of which rely on strong ontological theorizations of security?

A key idea central to the type of critical security analysis deployed in this book, is that the state itself can be a site of, and a cause of, forms of insecurity that neither realism nor constructivism is equipped to recognize. This does not mean that the security of or between states is not relevant in assessments of regional security – rather that it only tells us so much – and may also preclude investigations into other forms of insecurity. So for example, ASEAN may represent a relatively stable and secure region in terms of inter-state conflicts or military concerns, but that particular conceptualization of security and "stability" tells us nothing about the status of those states' democratic apparatuses; the corporeal safety of their populations; their policies on migration; or of levels of gender and racial equality – all of which are dynamics that operate in and across borders and do not easily fit into conventional formulations of what constitutes "security."

As Hamilton-Hart (2009) points out, there has long existed in mainstream security studies of the region a

> "stability bias" … [where] it is commonplace to see security equated with stability, as an extension of the generalization that instability is associated with insecurity … but situations that are "stable" may also be disastrously insecure for many people.

(65)

Critical approaches to security 35

This blind spot means that "threats to security emanating from the state and directed against its own citizens or civilians of another nation" (Hamilton-Hart 2009, 64) are ignored. One of the goals of this book is to not only acknowledge this blind spot, but to also shine a light onto this gap and others like it – to get a picture of what is missing in more conventional mainstream approaches to security, and ultimately, to add to the critical security literature on East and Southeast Asia which is still somehow in its nascent stages.

Notes

1 "Critical" approaches here include a variety of post-structuralist approaches that emphasize discourse, inter-subjectivity, and contingency in analysis. They also refer to approaches that pose meta-theoretical challenges to conventional realist ontology.
2 "Critical Approaches to Security in Europe."
3 The "Welsh School" gets its name from the fact that its original ideas were found in the works of Ken Booth (1979, 1996), Richard Wyn-Jones (1999) and others associated with the Department of International Politics at Aberystwyth University. The "Copenhagen School" and the "Paris School" are similarly named. The "Copenhagen School" of critical security emphasizes the social aspects of securitization originating with the work of Barry Buzan, Ole Waever, and Jaap de Wilde (1998) *et al.* who were working out of the Copenhagen Peace Research Institute. The "Paris School" refers to critical security ideas inspired by the work of Foucault and originally developed by Didier Bigo (2002) *et al.* from *SciencePo* in Paris.
4 It is important to distinguish the "construction of foundations" from the philosophical stance of "foundationalism." The latter presupposes that "foundations" are always immutable and universally true/accessible. This is not the case when contingent foundations are affirmed using a weak ontology approach, which asserts that "foundational claims" are sometimes necessary, but making claims about what foundations are being assumed as the starting point for analysis is not necessarily the same thing as saying that they are always true. White calls this "non-foundationalism," which, again, should not be confused with the "anti-foundationalism" discussed above (Mustapha 2013).
5 White (2000) demonstrates this when he shows how the liberal views of George Kateb, the communitarian views of Charles Taylor, the feminist views of Judith Butler, and the post-structuralist views of William Connolly all deploy weak ontologies in their own ways.
6 This has been done rather well by Fierke (2007), Mutimer (2007), Peoples and Vaughan-Williams (2010), and Jarvis and Holland (2014) among others.
7 This conventional perspective is best exemplified by the field of "strategic studies," with its attention to game theory, nuclear deterrence, and power relations between states based upon material capabilities and military power.
8 Seminal examples include Enloe's (1990) liberal feminist critique and Peterson's (1992) post-positivist feminist critique of IR and security studies.
9 Theories on "securitization" and security discourse are examples that can be joined by the type of work being done in International Political Sociology and the "Paris School" on governmentality, risk, aesthetics, borders and biosecurity (for example, see Leander 2005; Leander and Van Munster 2007; Muller 2011); and potentially work on "ontological security" and identity (see Kinnvall 2004) and work on "reflexive realism" (see Steele 2007) as well. See also examples of comparative "application" of post-structural analysis like Campbell's (2002) work on Bosnia or Burke's (2008) work on Australia. And Linda Åhäll (2016) has explicitly used "weak ontology" in her critical feminist analysis of militarization. It is beyond the purview of this

36 *Critical approaches to security*

chapter to comprehensively list specific examples, but the point is that we can actually see examples of "weak ontology" in critical security theorizing in probably more places than we realize. Notably, any critical security studies analysis that seeks to "engage" with "real world" issues but still coherently maintain an ethic of deconstruction and non-foundationalism would probably require (or already deploys) "weak ontology" in some form.

10 This refers to what is often called *social* constructivism, rather than the *critical* constructivism associated with post-structuralist theorizing. The social constructivism in question is one that many relate back to the ideas of Wendt (1992) even though social constructivists like Johnston (2003) have moved away from Wendt. The emphasis is on the power of ideas, norms, and identity in an otherwise realist-conceived world of nation states operating in a default environment of anarchic relations between self-interested units.

11   The most ambitious institutionalist alternative to relying on balance of power to keep peace, hypothetically, is a genuine collective security arrangement. The idea became vaguely popular again as a result of the end of the Cold War and has been broached in regard to Asia by Soviet and other proposals, but it does not offer much for Asia.

(Betts 1994, 73)

12 Acharya is widely regarded as a kind of godfather of East Asian constructivism.
13 *Critical security in the Asia-Pacific*, the 2007 volume edited by Burke and MacDonald, was the first and still only one of few existing texts that specifically engages in (ontologically) critical security analyses as applied to East and Southeast Asia.

References

Acharya, Amitav. 2001. *Constructing a security community in Southeast Asia: ASEAN and the problem of regional order*. New York: Routledge.
Acharya, Amitav. 2003. Democratisation and the prospects for participatory regionalism in Southeast Asia. *Third World Quarterly* 24(2): 375–390.
Acharya, Amitav and Richard Stubbs. 2006. Theorizing Southeast Asian relations: An introduction. *The Pacific Review* 19(2): 125–134.
Åhäll, Linda. 2016. The dance of militarisation: A feminist security studies take on "the political." *Critical Studies on Security* 4(2): 154–168.
Alagappa, Muthiah (Ed.). 2003. *Asian security order: Instrumental and normative features*. Stanford, CA: Stanford University Press.
Beeson, Mark. 2014. *Regionalism and globalization in East Asia: Politics, security and economic development*. London: Palgrave Macmillan.
Bentley, Michelle and Jack Holland (Eds). 2013. *Obama's foreign policy: Ending the War on Terror*. London: Routledge.
Betts, Richard. 1993. Wealth, power and instability: East Asia and the United States after the Cold War. *International Security* 8(3): 34–77.
Betts, Richard. 1994. *Conflict after the Cold War: Arguments on causes of war and peace*. New York: Macmillan.
Bigo, Didier. 2002. Security and immigration: Toward a critique of the governmentality of unease. *Alternatives* 27(1): 63–92.
Booth, Ken. 1979. *Strategy and ethnocentrism*. London: Croom Helm.
Booth, Ken. 1996. 75 years on. In Steve Smith, Ken Booth, and Marysia Zalewski (Eds) *International theory: Positivism & beyond*. Cambridge: Cambridge University Press, pp. 328–339.

Booth, Ken. 2007. *Theory of world security*. Cambridge: Cambridge University Press.
Browning, Christopher S. and Matt McDonald. 2011. The future of critical security studies: Ethics and politics of security. *European Journal of International Relations* (Online First: October 27, 2011): 1–21.
Burke, Anthony. 2008. *Fear of security: Australia's invasion anxiety*. Cambridge: Cambridge University Press.
Burke, Anthony and Matt McDonald (Eds). 2007. *Critical security in the Asia-Pacific*. Manchester: Manchester University Press.
Buzan, Barry. 1983/1991. *People, states and fear: An agenda for international security studies in the post-Cold War era*. London: Harvester Wheatsheaf.
Buzan, Barry. 2003. Security architecture in Asia: The interplay of regional and global levels. *The Pacific Review* 16(2): 143–173.
Buzan, Barry and Lene Hansen. 2009. *The evolution of international security studies*. Cambridge University Press: Cambridge.
Buzan, Barry, Ole Waever, and Jaap de Wilde. 1998. *Security: A new framework for analysis*. Boulder, CO: Lynne Rienner.
C.A.S.E. Collective. 2006. Critical approaches to security in Europe: A networked manifesto. *Security Dialogue* 37(4): 443–487.
Caballero-Anthony, Mely. 2005. *Regional security in Southeast Asia: Beyond the ASEAN way*. Singapore: Institute of Southeast Asian Studies.
Campbell, David. 1998. *Writing security: US foreign policy and the politics of identity*. Manchester: Manchester University Press.
Campbell, David. 2002. Atrocity, memory, photography: Imaging the concentration camps of Bosnia – The case of ITN versus Living Marxism. *Journal of Human Rights* 1: 1–33.
Chatterjee, Partha. 2005. Sovereign violence and the domain of the political. In Thomas Blom Hansen and Finn Stepputat (Eds) *Sovereign bodies: Citizens, migrants, and states in the postcolonial world*. Princeton, NJ: Princeton University Press. pp. 82–100.
Cheeseman, Graeme. 1999. Asian-Pacific security discourse in the wake of the Asian economic crisis. *The Pacific Review* 12(3): 333–356.
Cohn, Carol. 1987. Sex and death in the rational world of defence intellectuals. *Signs: Journal of Women in Culture and Society* 12: 4.
Connolly, William. 1989. Identity and difference in global politics. In J. Der Derian and M. Shapiro (Eds) *International/intertextual relations: Postmodern readings of world politics*. Toronto: Lexington Books. pp. 323–342.
da Cunha, Derek (Ed.). 1996. *The evolving Pacific power structure*. Singapore: Institute of Southeast Asian Studies.
Der Derian, J. and Michael J. Shapiro (Eds). 1989. *International/intertextual relations: Postmodern readings of world politics*. Toronto: Lexington Books.
Eaton, Sarah and Richard Stubbs. 2006. Is ASEAN powerful? Neo-realist versus constructivist approaches to power in Southeast Asia. *The Pacific Review* 19(2): 135–155.
Edkins, Jenny and Véronique Pin-Fat. 2004. Introduction: Life, power, resistance. In Jenny Edkins, Véronique Pin-Fat, and Michael J. Shapiro (Eds) *Sovereign lives: Power in global politics*. New York: Routledge. pp. 1–19.
Enloe, Cynthia. 1990. *Bananas, beaches, and bases: Making feminist sense of international politics*. Berkeley, CA: University of California Press.
Fierke, Karin M. 2007 *Critical approaches to international security*. Cambridge: Polity Press.
Foot, R. 2005. Collateral damage: Human rights consequences of counterterrorist action in the Asia-Pacific. *International Affairs* 81(2): 411–425.

38 *Critical approaches to security*

Foucault, Michel. 1980. *Power/knowledge: Selected interviews & other writings 1972–1977*. Colin Gordon (Ed.). New York: Pantheon Books.

Friedberg, A. 1993. Ripe for rivalry: Prospects for peace in multipolar Asia. *International Security* 18(3): 5–33.

Goh, Evelyn. 2008. Great powers and hierarchical order in Southeast Asia: Analyzing regional security strategies. *International Security* 32(3): 113–157.

Gusterson, Hugh. 1999. Missing the end of the Cold War in international security. In Jutta Weldes, Mark Laffey, Hugh Gusterson, and Raymond Duvall (Eds) *Cultures of insecurity: States, communities, and the production of danger*. Minneapolis, MN: University of Minnesota Press.

Hamilton-Hart, Natasha. 2005. Terrorism in Southeast Asia: Expert analysis, myopia and fantasy. *The Pacific Review* 18(3): 303–325.

Hamilton-Hart, Natasha. 2009. War and other insecurities in East Asia: What the security studies field does and does not tell us. *The Pacific Review* 22(1): 49–71.

Hamilton-Hart, Natasha. 2012. *Hard interests, soft illusions: Southeast Asia and American power*. Ithaca, NY: Cornell University Press.

Hansen, Lene. 2000. The little mermaid's silent security dilemma and the absence of gender in the Copenhagen School. *Millennium* 29(2): 285–306.

Hill, Cameron J. and William Tow. 2002. The ASEAN regional forum: Material and ideational dynamics. In Mark Beeson (Ed.) *Reconfiguring East Asia: Regional institutions and organizations after the crisis*. London: Routledge Curzon, pp. 161–183.

Ikenberry, G. John and Michael Mastanduno (Eds). 2003. *International relations theory and the Asia-Pacific*. New York: Columbia University Press.

Ikenberry, G. John and Jitsuo Tsuchiyama. 2002. Between balance of power and community: The future of multilateral security co-operation in the Asia-Pacific. *International Relations of the Asia-Pacific* 2(1): 69–94.

Jarvis, Lee and Jack Holland. 2014. *Security: A critical introduction*. London: Palgrave Macmillan.

Johnston, Alistair Iain. 2003. Socialization in international institutions: The ASEAN way and IR theory. In John Ikenberry and Michael Mastanduno (Eds) *International relations theory and the Asia Pacific*. New York: Columbia University Press. pp. 107–162.

Kang, David C. 2003. Getting Asia wrong: The need for new analytical frameworks. *International Security* 27(4): 57–85.

Katsumata, Hiro. 2006. Establishment of the ASEAN regional forum: Constructing a "talking shop" or a "norm brewery." *The Pacific Review* 19(2): 181–198.

Kinnvall, Catherine. 2004. Globalization and religious nationalism: Self, identity, and the search for ontological security. *Political Psychology* 25(5): 741–767.

Leander, Anna. 2005. The power to construct international security: On the significance of private military companies. *Millennium* 33(3): 803–825.

Leander, Anna and Rens Van Munster. 2007. Private security contractors in the debate about Darfur: Reflecting and reinforcing neo-liberal governmentality *International Relations* 21(2): 201–216.

Leifer, Michael. 1999. The ASEAN peace process: A category mistake. *The Pacific Review* 12(1): 25–38.

Mearsheimer, John J. 2001. *The tragedy of great power politics*. New York: W. W. Norton.

Muller, Benjamin. 2011. Risking it all at the biometric border: Mobility, limits, and the persistence of securitisation. *Geopolitics* 16(1): 91–106.

Muppidi, Himadeep. 2004. Colonial and postcolonial global governance. *Power in Global Governance* 98: 273–295.

Critical approaches to security 39

Mustapha, Jennifer. 2013. Ontological theorizations in critical security studies: Making the case for a (modified) post-structuralist approach. *Critical Studies on Security* 1(1): 64–82.

Mutimer, David. 2007. Critical security studies: A schismatic history. In A. Collins (Ed.) *Contemporary security studies*. New York: Oxford University Press, pp. 53–74.

Mutimer, David. 2009. My critique is bigger than yours: Constituting exclusions in critical security studies. *Studies in Social Justice* 3(1): 9–22.

Nyman, Jonna and Anthony Burke (Eds). 2016. *Ethical security studies: A new research agenda*. London: Routledge.

Peoples, C. and N. Vaughan-Williams. 2010. *Critical security studies: An introduction*. New York: Oxford University Press.

Peou, Sorpong. 2001. Realism and constructivism in Southeast Asian security studies today: A review essay. *The Pacific Review* 15(1): 119–138.

Peterson, V. Spike (Ed.). 1992. *Gendered states: Feminist (re)visions of international relations theory*. Boulder, CO: Lynn Rienner Publishers.

Rorty, Richard. 1996. Who are we? Moral universalism and economic triage. *Diogenes* 44(173): 5–15.

Rorty, Richard and Gianni Vattimo. 2007. *The future of religion*. New York: Columbia University Press.

Solomon, Richard and William Drennan. 2001. The United States and Asia in 2000. Forward to the past? *Asian Survey* 41(1): 1–11.

Steele, Brent. 2007. Eavesdropping on honored ghosts: From classical to reflexive realism. *Journal of International Relations and Development* 10(3): 272–300.

Stubbs, Richard. 2018. Order and contestation in the Asia-Pacific region: Liberal vs developmental/non-interventionist approaches. *The International Spectator* 53(1): 138–151.

Stubbs, Richard and Jennifer Mustapha. 2014. Regional economic institutions in Asia: Ideas and institutionalization. In Evelyn Goh, Saadia Pekkanen, John Ravenhill, and Rosemary Foot (Eds) *The Oxford handbook of the international relations of Asia*. London: Oxford, pp. 690–702.

Stubbs, Richard and Austina Reed. 2005. Regionalism and globalization. In Richard Stubbs and Geoffrey R. D. Underhill (Eds) *Political economy and the changing global order 3rd edition*. Toronto: McClelland and Stewart, pp. 289–293.

Tallis, Benjamin, 2017. Mediating estrangements; or, shaking our false senses of (in)security. *New Perspectives* 25(3): 7–14.

Tan, See Seng. 2006. Rescuing constructivism from the constructivists: A critical reading of constructivist interventions in Southeast Asian security. *The Pacific Review* 19(2): 239–260.

Tan, See Seng. 2013. *The making of the Asia Pacific: Knowledge brokers and the politics of representation*. Amsterdam: Amsterdam University Press.

Tow, Shannon. 2004. Southeast Asia in the Sino-US strategic balance. *Contemporary Southeast Asia* 26(3): 434–459.

Waever, Ole. 2011. Politics, security, theory. *Security Dialogue* 42(4–5): 465–480.

Walker, R. B. J. 1993. *Inside/outside: International relations as political theory*. Cambridge: Cambridge University Press.

Walt, Stephen M. 1991. The renaissance of security studies. *International Studies Quarterly* 35(2): 211–239.

Waltz, Kenneth. 1979. *Theory of international politics*. New York: McGraw-Hill.

Wendt, Alexander. 1992. Anarchy is what states make of it: The social construction of power politics. *International Organization* 46(2): 391–425.

40 *Critical approaches to security*

White, Stephen K. 2000. *Sustaining affirmation: The strengths of weak ontology*. Princeton, NJ: Princeton University Press.

White, Stephen K. 2003. After critique: Affirming subjectivity in contemporary social theory. *European Journal of Political Theory* 2(2): 209–226.

White, Stephen K. 2005. Weak ontology: Geneology and critical issues. *The Hedgehog Review* 7(2): 11–25.

White, Stephen K. 2009. Violence, weak ontology and late modernity. *Political Theory* 37(6): 808–816.

Williams, Michael C. 2005a. *The realist tradition and the limits of international relations*. Cambridge: Cambridge University Press.

Williams, Michael C. 2005b. What is the national interest? The neoconservative challenge in IR theory. *European Journal of International Relations* 11(3): 307–338.

Williams, Michael C. (Ed.). 2006. *Realism reconsidered: The legacy of Hans Morgenthau in international relations*. Oxford: Oxford University Press.

Williams, Michael C. 2013. In the beginning: The international relations enlightenment and the ends of international relations theory. *European Journal of International Relations* 19(3): 647–665.

Wyn-Jones, Richard. 1999. *Security, strategy, and critical theory*. London: Lynne Rienner.

3 In search of monsters

US foreign policy in East and Southeast Asia

The absence of inter-state military conflict is not a sufficient definition or measure of security. Rather, there are a variety of state security and foreign policy practices that contribute directly to the *in*security of groups and individuals. Foreign policies also play a significant role in the constitution of identities and the framing of political problems. This chapter delves into the powerful constitutive effects of US foreign policy in East Asia after 9/11 and argues that the so-called Bush Doctrine set the stage for how the War on Terror itself continues to operate as a dominant security narrative in the region. In order to assess how the US-led War on Terror affected regional security after 9/11, we have to go all the way back to the constructions of US foreign policies in the region under the administration of President George W. Bush.

First, this chapter explores the various different ways to define and approach "foreign policy," ultimately arguing for a critical constructivist analysis of foreign policy as informed by Campbell's persuasive call to reorient our understanding of it. Campbell (1998) sees "foreign policy" as performative and constitutive, and as a boundary-producing practice "central to the production and reproduction of the identity in whose name it operates" (68). As such, it is an integral aspect of the narratives of *Self* and *Other* that both construct and define threats and the security practices of states in response to those threats. This chapter then sets out the argument that foreign policies operate, on multiple levels, as discursively constructed "regimes of truth" and that the War on Terror operates as a powerful security narrative. Finally, this chapter sketches out the significant aspects of US foreign policy towards East and Southeast Asia, revealing both its continuities and discontinuities from before 9/11 and into the post-9/11 era. Importantly, a critical security analysis demonstrates the powerful role that ideas, beliefs, and relationships play in the construction of security narratives that directly affect the region and its inhabitants.

What is foreign policy and how can we know it?

In order to discuss how a specific set of foreign policies, during a specific historical period, may or may not operate as a dominant security narrative, it is crucial to establish a few things. A significant first question to ask is: what exactly *is*

42 *In search of monsters*

"foreign policy," and how can we know it? As Hill (2003) points out "... most people ... would have little difficulty in accepting that foreign policy exists and that it consists of what one state does to, or with, other states. To many specialists, however, this conventional wisdom is deeply suspect" (Hill 2003, 1). "Foreign policy," as an element of world politics, has tended to remain under-theorized and inconsistently understood. This is because comparativists, IR scholars, and public intellectuals all seem to have different ideas about what it is and what its significance is, which means that "at best ... debates are conducted at cross-purposes and at worst that in the area of external policy the democratic process is severely compromised" (Hill 2003, 2).

Such an assessment is pessimistic, and perhaps unduly so. Certainly, there are problems with the opaqueness of foreign policy making, as well as with the general lack of public interest in the vagaries of foreign policy. These problems contribute to stunted public discourses around a state's foreign dealings, which can further contribute to a democratic deficit on matters of foreign policy. But in terms of different ways of understanding and analyzing foreign policy, there is no essential problem with theoretical pluralism, nor is it somehow incorrect to acknowledge the ways that "foreign policy," as a concept and practice, operates simultaneously on different levels. In fact, there are advantages to developing a variety of different approaches to understanding foreign policy – especially when we consider that the different theories often correspond to distinct ideas about grand strategy and international relations itself (Schmidt 2012). Theoretical pluralism *can* be confusing and messy, as Hill's lament harkens back to the longstanding assertions of theoretical purists in political science who sought parsimonious explanations for politics (see Rosenau 1966). But theoretical pluralism can also offer a conceptual richness that a rigid adherence to only one theory can never provide. Different approaches to politics also lend insight into the variously labelled *problematiques* in understanding IR such as the problems of structure versus agency (Carlsnaes 1992), inside versus outside (Walker 1993), "high" politics versus "low" politics, and so on.

In fact, the study of foreign policy, as a distinct sub-field and leading up to its more recent incarnations,[1] emerged partly as a reaction to the dominance of structural realism in the study of IR in the mid-twentieth century (Holsti 1989). As Rosenau (1966) observed at the time, in response to a period when the "external behaviour of nations was considered to be exclusively a reaction to external stimuli ... students of foreign policy ... emphasized that the wellsprings of international action are also fed by events and tendencies within societies" (28). But Rosenau was part of what Neack, Hey and Haney (1995) called the "first generation" of foreign policy scholars, and thus saw theoretical pluralism as a problem that needed to be solved. Picking up on the behaviouralist *zeitgeist* of the mid-twentieth century social sciences, which attempted to approach social and political behaviour in ways that mirrored the positivist methods of the natural sciences, Rosenau was concerned with the inability of foreign policy scholars to utilize and draw upon general theories, and their tendency to only "approach the field from a historical, single country perspective" (Rosenau 1966, 35).

In search of monsters 43

Rosenau's first generation of what was then called *comparative foreign policy*, had as one of its main objectives "a desire to move away from noncumulative descriptive case studies and to construct a parsimonious explanation of what drives the foreign policy behaviour of states" (Neack *et al.* 1995, 3). In fact, one might say that Rosenau's search for parsimony was rooted in a need for a strong ontological (Mustapha 2013) understanding of foreign policy analysis.

As we now know, this proved ultimately unsuccessful. Despite the best efforts of the first generation of comparative foreign policy scholars to be systematic, "scientific" and quantitative, and their hopes to eventually construct a generalized theory of foreign policy analysis, it came to pass that "a shared set of theoretical commitments and the central paradigmatic core of the field never came into focus" (Neack *et al.* 1995, 4). This was due to a combination of factors including the general move away from positivism in the social sciences outlined in Chapter 2, as well as concurrent theoretical developments in related fields (Hudson 2005; Holsti 1989; Rowley and Weldes 2012). Competing approaches to understanding foreign policy emerged despite the single-mindedness of first generation comparative foreign policy scholarship, and foreign policy came to be studied in a wide variety of ways including through the lenses of international history, comparative country studies, realism and neo-realism, rational-choice, and post-positivist approaches, among others (Hill 2003, 9). These sorts of different approaches eventually contributed to the emergence of the so-called "second-generation" of foreign policy scholars.

This second generation of scholars, engaged in what came to be known as *foreign policy analysis*, employed "middle-range theories to examine particular areas of human activity such as perception or geopolitics, and [was] sceptical that an overarching single theory of foreign policy can ever be achieved without being bland and tautological" (Hill 2003, 10). This second generation then, was actually a "broad set of approaches bound together by a common focus on studying foreign policy and an eclecticism in theory building" (Neack *et al.* 1995, 2). Hence, not unlike what happened in security studies during the same general period, these newer approaches to understanding foreign policy came to "see any theory of foreign policy as having to be built in a contingent way, focusing on context, informed by empirical analysis ... [and] likely to be conditional and bounded, recognizing that single cause explanations are not sufficient" (Neack *et al.* 1995, 11). Part of what came to be acknowledged was the simple fact that foreign policy is necessarily a complex and multifaceted phenomenon (Rowley and Weldes 2012). Relatedly, there are several different models of foreign policy decision-making (Holsti 1992; Schmidt 2012) and several different ways in which international relations theory pertains to foreign policy (Carlsnaes 1992; Rowley and Weldes 2012; Hudson 2005). Whereas the comparative foreign policy crowd tended to see foreign policy mostly in terms of decision-making, the second generation of foreign policy analysts "extend the subject well-beyond decision-making, and in particular ... ensure that foreign policy is seen not just as a technical exercise but as an important form of political argument" (Hill 2003, 10).

44 *In search of monsters*

And this is where this book comes into a discussion on foreign policy. It is less interested in the specifics of competing theoretical approaches to analyzing foreign policy than in the differently understood aspects of foreign policy itself. That is, in how foreign policy both manifests and influences identities and the framing of political problems. This is because bringing foreign policy into the equation of international politics introduces the important question of *"who acts, for whom, and with what effect?"* (Hill 2003, 2). This evokes three distinct but overlapping images of – or ways of thinking about – foreign policy, each of which provoke our curiosity in different ways.

In the first image, as the comparative foreign policy approach presupposed, we can say that "foreign policy" refers more simply to a *set of official policies*, or "the sum of official external relations conducted by an independent actor (usually a state) in international relations" (Hill 2003, 3). In the second image, we can say that "foreign policy" is a practice by an independent actor (usually a state, but not always), which both reflects and constructs internal identities, values, and interests. In the third image, we can say that "foreign policy" is a set of policies, practices and ideas that are projected outward, influencing other actors in the process: *their* identities, *their* experiences and *their* policies. This book is most concerned with the second and third images, and more specifically with how American foreign policy, beginning with the Bush Doctrine's inception of the War on Terror, acted as a set of policies, practices and ideas that were projected outward with effects felt by actors in East and Southeast Asia: *their* identities, *their* experiences and *their* policies. But it is crucial to first set out the argument that foreign policies are not only narrative constructions, intrinsic to the creation of national identities and values, but that they can also operate as discursively constructed "regimes of truth," which contain powerful political and cultural meaning that come to be through multiple political practices (Jackson 2005).

Foreign policy as the stories we tell

Based on all three ways of thinking about foreign policy outlined in the previous section, we can see that foreign policies enacted by states are obviously bound up with notions of identity. Foreign policies are not merely expressions of a state's interests. They also construct and project an image of a state's identity and disposition towards issues and actors – of what a state's values and motivations might be in pursuit of those interests (Rowley and Weldes 2012). These projected identities are not static, but rather are subject to change over time in response to a variety of factors including the mutually constitutive effects of foreign policies themselves. In other words, existing national identities and interests inform foreign policies, which construct a state's image and behaviours as projected internationally, which in turn inform iterations of national identity and interests, which then go back to informing the creation of foreign policies again.

It is the contingency and fluidity and mutual constitution of these national identities and interests that are often overlooked in a conventional foreign policy analysis. Too often, the interests and identities of state actors are seen to be unchanging and easily predictable, and as a result tend to be approached in an ahistorical manner, presumed to be static over time. Further, state identities are usually thought to be distinct from and always prior to the various practices deployed in their name. However, as David Campbell (1998) argues

> it is not possible to simply understand international relations as the existence of atomized states that are fully fledged intensive entities in which identity is securely grounded and prior to foreign relations. The consequence of this argument is a fundamental reorientation of our understanding of foreign policy ... [it] shifts *from* a concern of relations *between* states that take place *across* ahistorical, frozen, and pregiven boundaries, *to* a concern with *the establishment of boundaries* that constitute, at one and the same time, the "state" and the "international system." Conceptualized in this way, foreign policy comes to be seen as a political practice that makes "foreign" certain events and actors.
>
> (61, emphasis in original)

So, the argument here is not that state identity or threats to a state's interests would not exist at all without the constitutive effects of foreign policy, but that the practices of foreign policy themselves play a key role in the formation of state identity. Thus, foreign policy needs to "be re-theorized as one of the boundary-producing practices central to the production and reproduction of the identity in whose name it operates" (Campbell 1998, 68). Further, the argument is that all of these processes and signifiers of "us" (national identity, political interests, values, foreign policy) come to be through a constitution of difference from "them," where beliefs or ideas about the *Self* can never be fully divorced from beliefs or ideas about the *Other* – and are in fact contingent upon them. In other words, national identity is performative and *requires* the various practices of "foreign policy," which can also be understood as the exercise of making certain events and actors "foreign." Foreign policy itself becomes part of the stories that states tell about themselves.

Risk, pre-emption, and constructions of threat

An examination of any set of foreign policies over time illustrates the importance of foreign policy discourses and narratives to what Campbell (1998) calls the "scripting" of identity. That is, the significance of narratives that help to tell stories about who we are and what we do. These stories of the self contain constitutive properties. They tell us both who we are and who we are not. They also tell us who we should be and who we should fear. As Campbell (1998) observed, the "objectification and externalization of danger that are central to contemporary assessments of security and politics ... need to be understood as the effects of political practices rather than the conditions of their possibility" (16). Thus, it is deeply problematic to accept a conventional understanding of foreign policy as

46   *In search of monsters*

simply a reaction to a priori external threats that emerge from the ether of the international milieu.

Relatedly, Campbell challenges the notion that the construction of foreign policies somehow exists independently from the many different theories formulated to make sense of them. Ultimately, it is by rejecting a "false demarcation of a theory/practice divide so that theory is outside of the world it purports to simply observe," that we can make possible an interpretive and inter-subjective approach that "… sees theory *as* practice: the theory of international relations is one instance of the pervasive cultural practices that serve to discipline ambiguity" (Campbell 1998, 17). It is this "disciplining of ambiguity" that is particularly salient in theorizing the idea that foreign policies call into being grand narratives of *Self* and *Other* that delineate the parameters of identity and the framing of threats. For Campbell then, the so-called common sense that is taken for granted as the foundation for foreign policies are what Foucault (1980) might call "regimes of truth." These regimes of truth have powerful political and cultural meanings. They emerge through "multiple political practices, related as much to the constitution of various subjectivities as to the intentional action of predetermined subjects" (Campbell 1998, 17).

But what does all of this imply? Are Campbell and others who use critical constructivist approaches to foreign policy analysis (see Weldes 1999; Jackson 2005, 2006; Agathangelou and Ling 2004; Zulaika 2009; Bennis 2003; Weber 2006; Croft 2006) suggesting that theorizations of foreign policy are literally the same as the practices that occur? Does this sort of approach discount the existence of tangible, corporeal threats to security, human or otherwise? Does it reduce everything to a question of narrative, thus discounting the multiple and complex sources of a state's identity or interests? The answer to all of these questions is "no." As Campbell (1998) himself cautioned,

> the claim is not that foreign policy constitutes state identity *de novo*; rather it is that foreign policy is concerned with the reproduction of an unstable identity at the level of the state, and the containment challenges to that identity.
>
> (71)

It is just one of the many pervasive cultural practices that exist to discipline ambiguity and as a result solidify the certainty of self. To use the language of strong and weak ontology, this approach rejects a foundationalist, fixed logic (or strong-ontology) understanding of the sources of foreign policy and state identity. Rather, recognizing the contingency and indeterminacy – via weak-ontology – of both allows us to see the vast array of constitutive possibilities that present themselves vis-à-vis the identity politics of foreign policy.

This type of analysis allows us to "see" the weak-ontology of security as well, where security is understood to be more than a condition or a practice. Rather, "security" is a protean concept that is wielded in political discourses and in foreign policy. This is because the meaning of security does not just depend on the specific analytical questions it raises ... "Security" refers also to a wider framework of meaning (symbolic order ... or culture ... or discursive formation) within which we organize particular forms of life.

(Huysmans 1998, 228)

Citing Saussure's ideas of splitting the "sign" into the "signifier" and the "signified,"[2] Huysmans (1998) theorizes security using a "thick signifier" approach, which "focuses on the wider order of meaning which [the word] 'security' articulates" (226). When "security" is understood this way, the story of security "requires the definition of threats, a referent object, and also how it defines our relations to nature, to other human beings and to the self" (Huysmans 1998, 231). Security policy then, like foreign policy writ large, can be seen as a self-referential practice rather than simply as a set of reactions to threat. The signifier of "security" then, serves "a performative rather than a descriptive force ... [and] rather than describing or picturing a condition, it organizes social relations into security relations" (Huysmans 1998, 232).

For the purposes of this book, of particular interest is the notion that the practice of security policy *requires* the definition of threats and organizes and defines our relations to others. Huysmans and Campbell both point out, in slightly different ways, that the logical corollary of such a notion is that the discursive construction of threat becomes essential to the practice of foreign policy and to the formation of state identity. Following this, the articulation and repetition of threat mobilizes fear by identifying and naming who (or what) to fear or not fear. Because this fear is both existential and ontological, "the fear in security stories is a double fear ... it is both the fear of biological death and the fear of uncertainty/the undetermined condition" (Huysmans 1998, 235), which echoes Campbell's point about how there is a pervasiveness of cultural and political practices that exist in order to discipline ambiguity and solidify the certainty of self. This can occur through the mobilization of varying registers of affect in service to the security project of the state (Van Rythoven 2015). It can also occur through the mitigation of risk – or at least by performing the appearance of risk mitigation.

In fact, a common theme that has emerged in foreign policies and security practices relating to the War on Terror is the increasingly central position of uncertainty and risk in the formulation of counter-terrorism and countering extremism and violence (CVE) policies. Threat construction necessarily comes with a desire to "discipline the ambiguity" that arises from the possibilities presented by threat, whether this takes place through a temporal desire to tame a risky and uncertain future (Stockdale 2013, 2015); a spatial and affective desire to govern unease (Bigo 2002) through assemblages that take the shape of "ban-opticons" that seek to govern mobilities both inside and outside the state (Bigo 2014); a risk-assessment approach to airport and border security that attempts to quantify and govern the possibility of emergent threat (Salter 2008); a managerial approach to the risk-related challenges presented by global mobilities and borders that are both permeable and diffuse (Salter 2013; Aradau 2016); and just

48 *In search of monsters*

more generally, through an increasingly risk-based approach to security governance in the context of counter-terrorism that has permeated all levels of society and expressions of state sovereignty to the extent that the pervasiveness of exceptional security practices has come to define contemporary politics – both inside and outside of the state (Aradau and Van Munster 2007, 2008, 2009, 2011). The idea that security governance must address the *risks* posed by *potential* threat, has become a central organizing principle of the state's project of security, and has become a pivotal feature of the narratives and discourses of foreign policy in the context of the War on Terror. This is a theme that links together the empirical cases discussed in this book – that the mapping of emergent threat and the various attempts by the state to govern risk and uncertainty are undertheorized in the context of East and Southeast Asia.

At this juncture, it is worth noting the limitations and boundaries of the concept of "discourse." As explained, foreign policy discourse itself is more than just words. Rather, it refers to documented policies and laws, as well as to the social/cultural/political *practices* of foreign policy. It is also not *wholly* constitutive of the material. With this in mind, one must take very seriously the various warnings about "the potential political [and ethical] consequences of accepting the idea of the materiality of discourse" (Cloud 1994, 142). To be clear, this is not to discount the more "limited claim that discourse is material because it has material effects and serves material interests in the world," but rather, it is a precaution against "a more radical shift [where] discourse not only influences material reality, it *is* that reality … [where] all relations, economic, political, or ideological, are symbolic in nature" (Cloud 1994, 142).

This latter understanding of the "materiality of discourse," resides in the same politically and ethically incomprehensible space as the type of strawman postmodernism that operates only as the "work of thought" (Ashley 1989, 313), and that "cannot claim to offer an alternative position or perspective, because there is no alternative ground upon which it might be established" (Ashley 1989, 278). I argued against such an epistemological and ontological approach in Chapter 2, agreeing with Connolly's (1989) critique that such a position is a form of "'postponism' [that] links the inability to establish secure ontological ground for a theory with the obligation to defer infinitely the construction of general theories of global politics" (336). The problem with this position, along with the consequent idea that discourse (and only discourse) *is* reality, is that it necessitates a paralytic disjuncture from the everyday, where millions of people face actually-occurring insecurity.

Critically assessing US foreign policy in East and Southeast Asia

The nascent days of the War on Terror introduced a set of central narratives that framed the 9/11 attacks in specific ways, ultimately necessitating America's military responses abroad and security practices at home (Jackson 2005, 2006, 2011; Croft 2006; Jarvis 2008; Jervis 2005). The characteristics of the War on

In search of monsters 49

Terror – its narratives, its policies, its irruptions – were informed by a pre-existing pattern of American essentialism and a foreign policy style rooted in founding myths about America's role as the world's foremost superpower. During World War II, President Woodrow Wilson cemented these founding myths by actively promoting the liberal internationalist idea that America would "lose its soul" if it did not go abroad "in search of monsters to destroy," as it had been reluctant to do for so many years (Daalder and Lindsay 2005, 5–6). America's foray into World War II and its active involvement in post-war recovery and reconstruction in both Europe and Asia, marked a distinctive US foreign policy style as being some combination of exceptionalism and [varieties of] liberal internationalism that would follow for decades to come. This manifested itself in different ways under different administrations but suffice to say that exceptionalism and internationalism were the two most notable (and sometimes competing) characteristics of American foreign policy in the post-World War II and Cold War period of international relations (Ruggie 1997; Pederson 2003; Farrell 2005; Deudney and Meiser 2012).

Prior to the 9/11 terrorist attacks, newly elected President Bush's foreign policy outlook was rooted in a continuation of this scripted identity of American exceptionalism and internationalism. Although President Clinton placed more emphasis on multilateralism than both his predecessor and his successor, the same could be said for his administration as well. Clinton's actions in the Balkans, for example, were underwritten by American exceptionalism. For Bush, this exceptionalism found its expression in a more "hegemonist thinking" (Daalder and Lindsay 2005) about America's role in the world, and signalled a renewed tendency for the US to act unilaterally when and if necessary (Deudney and Meiser 2012, 35).

Hence, although the Bush administration tended towards more unilateralism than the Clinton administration, they both had foreign policies rooted in enduring ideas around American exceptionalism and a Wilsonian disposition that caused Washington to face outwards towards the world. And while 9/11 did evince a type of rupture in the landscape of US foreign policy, at a more elemental level 9/11 served to further reinforce the pre-existing scripted identity of an exceptional America. As a result, key elements of what we now call the Bush Doctrine were actually rooted in long-standing foreign policy narratives of American exceptionalism and internationalism, with notable emphasis on the former.

From the Cold War to the War on Terror

The Bush administration's foreign policy responses to the terrorist attacks of 9/11 can be summarized in the following features: a declared belief in the goals of democracy and liberalism at home and the idea that the US has a historical responsibility to restructure and rebuild the world towards what are presumably universal liberal democratic values; the perception that there are great threats to national security that can only be countered by forceful military policies that

50 *In search of monsters*

include pre-emptive strikes and "preventive" war; a willingness to act unilaterally if necessary along with the general conviction that unilateralism can be more effective than multilateralism; and the belief that the US must continue to assert its economic, military and diplomatic hegemony in global politics, whereby "American security, world stability, and the spread of liberalism require the US to act in ways others *can* not and *must* not" (Jervis 2005, 583).

In other words, the Bush Doctrine formed in response to the terrorist attacks of 9/11, and was predicated on a set of beliefs that rested upon two key underlying themes: the role of fear in relation to the perceived threat of terrorism; and an American sense of global responsibility, relating to the liberal internationalism of a latter-day Wilsonian liberalizing mission as outlined above (Jervis 2005; Mustapha 2011). Interestingly, before 9/11, Bush had expressed the opinion that an isolationist foreign policy disposition would result in both the stagnation of American progress and lend to "a savage world," cautioning that "American Foreign Policy cannot be founded on fear ... fear that America will corrupt the world – or be corrupted by it" (Daalder and Lindsay 2005, 36). This refutation of isolationism found its way into the post-9/11 Bush Doctrine and relates to Huysman's understanding of security as a thick signifier. As mentioned, "the fear in security stories is a double fear ... it is both the fear of biological death and the fear of uncertainty/ the undetermined condition" (Huysmans 1998, 235). It is this latter aspect of Huysman's double fear that was particularly observable within the Bush Doctrine (Mustapha 2011). For example, in the *2006 National Security Strategy* (NSS), Bush stated that

> America now faces a choice between the path of fear and the path of confidence ... history teaches that every time American leaders have taken [the path of fear], the challenges have only increased and the missed opportunities have left future generations less secure.
>
> (The White House March 12, 2006)

This is an articulation of a fear *of fear*, and we see themes of fear-based rationalizations for security policies and practices emerge again and again in War on Terror discourses, Bush's policy statements and speeches, and those of his successors into the present.

Building on this theme of fear, the *US National Strategy for Combating Terrorism* under the 2006 NSS managed to successfully conflate terrorism, ballistic missile defence (BMD), and "rogue states" via the threat of weapons of mass destruction (WMD) procurement by terrorist groups. Core elements of Bush's National Security Strategy then, became characterized as preventative or pre-emptive, marking a clear departure from established international norms of warfare and international security governance. The preventive and pre-emptive nature of the Bush Doctrine was illustrated, for example, under Section III of the 2006 NSS, which sought to

> 1) *Prevent* attacks by terrorist networks *before* they occur; 2) *Deny* WMD to rogue states and terrorist allies who *would* use them without hesitation;

3) *Deny* terrorist groups the support and sanctuary of rogue states, and 4) *Deny* the terrorists control of any nation that they *would* use as a base and launching pad for terror.

(The White House March 12, 2006, 12, emphases added)

These persistent appeals against living in fear remind us of Campbell's observation that foreign policies often contain within them a sort of "evangelism of fear" (Campbell 1998, 49). This "evangelism of fear" is a continued fostering of anxiety that becomes instrumental to the organization of a state's project of security and the emerging role that risk-management now plays as a central organizing principle of security governance. In terms of narratives and discourses, threats (or possible threats) are construed and located through and within the "texts"[3] of foreign policy. In the case of the Bush Doctrine, the supposedly imminent danger of *potential* terrorism was linked to Saddam Hussein's regime in Iraq and to the *possible* threats arising out of the so-called "rogue" states of Iran, Syria and North Korea that Bush once referred to as the "axis of evil" (Daalder and Lindsay 2003).

As we now know, foreign policy texts guide national security and relate to the scripting of American identity (Campbell 1998). The fact that the Bush Doctrine collapsed the fear of terrorism into a messianic obligation to restructure the world as part of a vision for a New American Century (Altheide 2007), speaks to the central position of threat and fear in the post-9/11 world. And the same foreign policy discourses, typified by statements like "the greater the threat, the greater the risk of inaction" (The White House March 12, 2006, 18), were linked to oft-stated American aspirations to restructure the world towards freedom and democracy. In other words, American national identity as a global enforcer and upholder of freedom and democracy was at least partially constructed by a discourse rooted in threat and fear (Jackson 2005). Fear and threat became mobilized in the Bush Doctrine as "the backdrop against which the US policy disposition is regularly vindicated" (Loeppky 2005, 87). Further, the Bush Doctrine constructed the image of the terrorist as simultaneously rational and irrational, which appealed to both the citizen's "reasonable logic of possibility" and "their fear of the unknown" (Loeppky 2005, 88–89) and continues to be part of the contemporary "common sense" around terrorism.

State practices of security under the War on Terror thus hinge upon a narrative of fear – both the fear of terrorist threats and of fear itself. As such, the security narratives of the Bush Doctrine *required* that US hegemony and "homeland security" be aggressively maintained. The corollary to this has been an ongoing set of security logics consisting of pre-emptive military action, the utilization of extra-legal detention and prisoner interrogation practices, as well as the systematic erosion and subversion of privacy and civil rights under the guise of counter-terrorism and CVE. Herein lay the greatest *problematique* of the Bush Doctrine and the War on Terror: common items in the security toolbox, such as pre-emptive drone strikes; extraordinary rendition; the use of waterboarding and other forms of prisoner abuse and humiliation; unlawful detentions of "enemy

52 *In search of monsters*

combatants" at Guantanamo Bay and so on, have actually contributed to insecurity in a variety of ways. Insecurity for America and the West, in the sense that these policies provoke the ire of terrorist groups and have aided in recruitment efforts by *Al-Qaeda*, the Islamic State (IS), and other Islamist terror organizations; and insecurity for the communities subject to the security practices of the War on Terror (Stampnitzky 2013; Hamid 2016). A second-order critique of the War on Terror *problematique* questions the ways that the pursuit of security by the state has steadily eroded values that are intrinsic to a historic understanding of Americanness and of liberal values in general – such as freedom from the tyranny of government.[4] All of these developments occurred under the umbrella of counter-terrorism, and have continued to operate as a powerful security narrative that frames these sorts of practices in ways that legitimize and normalize them.

An examination of American security practices over time illustrates another important way that foreign policy discourses do what Campbell calls the scripting of identity: the significance of narratives that help to tell stories about who we are. These stories of *Self* have constitutive properties, and they also tell stories about the *Other*, having constitutive effects as well. American identity is not the only identity being "scripted" by American foreign policy narratives. Rather, American foreign policy and security narratives also play a role in scripting the identities of those various actors that are the subjects of US foreign policy discourses, and they frame what counts as a security problem and who counts as a security threat. Due to the significant influence of US policies in shaping world politics, American foreign policy narratives are uniquely positioned in terms of their impact and effects on the rest of the world. The War on Terror, in particular, has left an indelible mark. As Jackson (2005) observes, right from its onset the discourses of the War on Terror

> prevented the consideration of alternative paradigms and approaches to counter-terrorism; the inbuilt logic of the language, and the privileging of only certain kinds of knowledge ... circumvented the kind of in-depth, rigorous and informed debate that a complex political challenge such as terrorism requires.
>
> (188)

The Bush Doctrine in East and Southeast Asia

During the Cold War, US security policies in East Asia were predicated on establishing successful, liberal, capitalist economies that would "stand as a bulwark against communist expansion, which led [the US] to pour aid and investment into [the region]" (Beeson 2007, 4). As outlined in the last chapter, this integrated foreign policy approach, characterized by a merging of military purpose with economic instruments, was a sort of "hub and spokes" model of bilateral strategic-military-economic relationships meant to contain communism in Asia.[5] As a result, many of Washington's economic policies during the Cold

War were closely tied to American geo-strategic goals. After the end of the Cold War however, Washington's foreign policy disposition turned even more towards economic matters.[6] During the Clinton administration, in particular, US foreign policy in East Asia was characterized by the relative subordination of strategic military interests to liberal economic interests. Clinton's often quoted catch-phrase – "It's the economy, stupid" – described much of his administration's policies both at home and abroad. As a result, American foreign policy during this period "… [was] replete with assumptions about the need to make the world safe for the neoliberal economic enterprise" (Higgott 2004, 429) and rested upon the fact that the US was the world's single, unrivalled military superpower – a distinct historical moment that allowed Washington to pursue their liberal economic goals unhindered by military distractions.

Freed from the geostrategic constraints of the Cold War, US foreign policy towards East Asia during the Clinton era was more "open-textured" and commercially focused (Dittmer 2002) and there was a significant trend away from a strategic-military focus in the region and towards a distinctly liberal economic approach to regional engagement (Acharya 1999; Dibb *et al.* 1998; Rosenberger 2001; Christoffersen 2002; Higgott 2004). The clear focus of US foreign policy during this period was on maintaining a stability in the region that was favourable to American interests and underwritten by policies favouring economic growth and trade liberalization (Christoffersen 2002). As with US foreign policy in general, in East Asia specifically there was "a preponderance of the multilateralisms geared towards neoliberal economic globalization" (Dibb *et al.* 1998, 18). In the late 1990s and following the Asian financial crisis, US foreign policy in the region shifted even further away from strategic-military matters as the US secured unrivalled economic primacy in the global economy, both functionally and ideationally through wide acceptance of the so-called Washington Consensus principles of neoliberal economic globalization (Williamson 2009). Furthermore, even after a post-Cold War period of steady and stable growth in East Asia

> the high tech boom was in full flight and the Asian Economic Miracle had run out of steam across the board. Following sustained stagnation in Japan and financial crisis in other parts of Asia the "miracle" was pronounced dead. The atmospherics of the US–Asia relationship saw Asian hubris of the early 1990s give way to American *schadenfreude* in the late 1990s. US preponderance was firmly established – unipolarity seemed to be more than just a moment.
>
> (Higgott 2004, 428)

It was at this precise moment, an apex of American military, ideational, and economic pre-eminence in the region that the newly elected Bush administration moved into the White House.

Because he was able to, Bush took for granted America's moment as an unrivalled economic superpower. He criticized Clinton's apparent lack of priority

54 In search of monsters

setting and did not approve of the way that the State Department under the Clinton administration had dispatched troops to various areas with no clear benefit to American national interests (Daalder and Lindsay 2005; Deudney and Meiser 2012; Bush 2010). Under Bush's foreign policy, "traditional" security concerns like nuclear proliferation, ballistic missile-defence systems, and strategic balance-of-power matters were re-incorporated into the national security agenda and into policies towards specific regions, including East Asia. For the Bush administration, it was not just about re-prioritizing security. It was also about re-prioritizing an active pursuit of national interest (Bush 2010) as part of the Project for a New American Century (Altheide 2007). Hence, the Bush administration tuned in to China as a potential geo-strategic concern in East Asia and, to a lesser degree, to North Korea as well. In other words, the Bush administration's approach to East Asia prior to 9/11 was characterized primarily by a containment strategy for China's growing strategic power in the region, in tandem with efforts to moderate North Korea's then embryonic nuclear designs.

This pre-9/11 security strategy was highly dependent upon the US–Japan security relationship (Christoffersen 2002), which, as mentioned in the previous chapter, was the lynchpin of US strategic policy in the region under the "hub and spokes" model of security relations in East Asia. The continued importance of the US–Japan relationship was declared on numerous occasions in national security documents, speeches, and policy meetings. For example, a joint statement by President Bush and then Prime Minister Yoshiro Mori on March 16, 2001 asserted that "… the US-Japan alliance is the foundation of peace and stability in the Asia-Pacific region," and the two leaders "reaffirmed the particular importance of maintaining close consultations and coordination regarding North Korea, both bilaterally and trilaterally with the Republic of Korea" (The White House March 16, 2001). On June 30, 2001, President Bush and the newly elected Japanese Prime Minister Junichiro Koizumi issued another joint announcement re-affirming the US–Japan Security Treaty. In that statement, they "… emphasized the importance of encouraging China's constructive role in the international community and … working with the Republic of Korea to achieve peace on the Korean peninsula, furthering non-proliferation efforts around the globe" (The White House June 30, 2001).

Under the activist liberal internationalism of the Clinton administration, the US–China relationship was already relatively strained, mostly due to Clinton's open criticism of China's human rights abuses. After the bombing of the Chinese embassy in Belgrade during the NATO airstrikes in the Balkans, the US–China relationship continued to suffer. Subsequently, the Bush administration's geo-strategic policy changes towards East Asia brought with them an even further deterioration of those relations, exacerbated by the April 2, 2001 incident of a Chinese fighter jet colliding with an American EP-3 spy plane over the South China Sea. The Chinese aircraft and pilot were lost in the incident and the EP-3 was forced to make an emergency landing on an airfield on Hainan Island, China. The members of the EP-3 crew were not immediately returned to American authorities and the Chinese declined all foreign access to the EP-3 plane in

In search of monsters 55

the days immediately following the collision (Slingerland *et al.* 2007). The event precipitated a notable diplomatic crisis between the two countries, which was only resolved 11 days later, upon the return of the crew to the US. Following the incident, President Bush issued a statement admonishing the Chinese government and asserting that

> China's decision to present the return of our crew … is inconsistent with the kind of relationship we have both said we wish to have … We disagree on important basic issues such as human rights and religious freedom … I will always stand squarely for American interests and American values. And those will, no doubt, sometimes cause disagreements with China.
>
> (The White House April 23 2001)

The EP-3 spy-plane incident was followed by declarations of official US support for an independent Taiwan, the re-introduction of a ballistic missile defence plan as part of the US national security agenda, and a gradual rolling-back of US participation in East Asian multilateralism more generally.

In other words, leading up to 9/11 all signs pointed towards a US foreign policy in East Asia that was mostly defined by the passive maintenance of peaceable relations with their "hub and spoke" allies and the more hawkish strategic containment of China and North Korea. On September 4, 2001, just a few days before the 9/11 terrorist attacks, the White House issued a press release announcing that officials from Washington and Beijing would meet "in the coming weeks" to discuss the subject of ballistic missile defence and express official concern about China's plans to develop offensive nuclear forces. This planned meeting was in response to growing apprehensions in both countries that the other may pose an offensive military threat. In the meeting, and in keeping with the pursuit of a containment-focused approach towards Chinese strategic power, US officials were planning to

> make clear that … no one should try to blame … China's offensive nuclear forces on US missile defence efforts. China's ongoing modernization effort was initiated years ago … [US] missile defence is an important element of a broader strategy to combat proliferation of missiles and weapons of mass destruction. The export of Chinese missile technology continues to be a concern, as does the Chinese build-up of short-range ballistic missiles.
>
> (The White House September 4, 2001)

In other words, prior to 9/11 the Bush administration saw China as a potential threat that required management and containment through firm diplomatic pressure and the continued maintenance of the existing East Asian security architecture.

As we now know, just a few days later, *Al-Qaeda* operatives launched a large-scale terrorist attack on New York City and Washington DC on September 11, 2001, using hijacked commercial jetliners and shocking the entire world with

56 *In search of monsters*

the attack's magnitude of destruction and loss of life. The War on Terror that followed 9/11 became the singular focus of US foreign policy around the globe, usually to the detriment of other policy issues. Despite nothing very substantive actually changing in terms of US relations with other states, the ideational rupture of 9/11 meant that a whole host of issues fell to the bottom of the foreign policy agenda or disappeared entirely. Certainly, this was the case for East and Southeast Asia. Notably, the scheduled discussion regarding Chinese missile technology never did take place. Instead, American and Chinese officials finally did meet in October of 2001 to talk mostly about shared concerns about Islamism and terrorism. Missile defence was briefly mentioned in subsequent statements by the two governments, but the promised challenge to China's development of nuclear forces never materialized. Instead, Washington and Beijing declared their allegiance and cooperation as allies in the newly conceived global War on Terror (Cox 2012).

In other words, the events of September 11, 2001 signalled an important shift in the Bush administration's foreign policy priorities and the US national security agenda. Bush's response to 9/11 was to reconfigure US foreign policy attentions towards terrorism. At the same time, the Bush administration took the opportunity to cement a new foreign policy doctrine that reflected and reinforced the longstanding core founding myth of American exceptionalism in new ways. The ensuing *National Security Strategy* and *National Strategy to Combat Terrorism* under the Bush administration crystallized the twin dogmas of unilateralism and pre-emption, and the Bush Doctrine was born.

Conclusion: the War on Terror as a hegemonic security narrative

One of the primary goals of this book is to shed light onto the blind spots that exist in a conventional analysis of security – one that prioritizes narrow state-centric perspectives and ignores the role that the state's pursuit of security can have in the production of *in*security. Consequently, in addressing fundamental (weak) ontological questions about security itself, the analytical and epistemological methods used here seek to undertake a critical security analysis rooted in a reflexive post-structuralist ethic while avoiding the trap of falling into the "post-ponism" cautioned by Connolly (1989) or the discursive reductionism cautioned by Cloud (1994).

With this in mind, this chapter has examined the powerful constitutive effects of US foreign policy in East and Southeast Asia prior to and leading into the War on Terror and explored the idea that the Bush Doctrine formed the basis for a dominant security narrative rooted in the twin notions of exceptionalism and pre-emption. Here we see that the Bush Doctrine operated as a powerful founding narrative for the War on Terror involving

> not just speeches by politicians … but also the symbols they appropriate …, the myths and histories they refer to …, the laws they pass …, the organizational

In search of monsters   57

structures they create ..., the decision-making procedures they follow and the actions they undertake.

(Jackson 2005, 19)

Under Bush and under his successors into the present, we continue to see how exceptionalism and pre-emption have come to define a security narrative that seeks to discipline uncertainty and ambiguity through counter-terror *dispositifs* rooted in notions of managing risk and anticipating emergent threats.

From a conventional security perspective, East and Southeast Asia is a region that appears stable and secure due to the lack of any remarkable inter-state conflict. Both realist and conventional constructivist understandings of the regional security architecture would point to the stabilizing role of the US and its carefully curated bilateral "hub and spokes" alliances. However, the potentially *de*stabilizing effects of US foreign policies at the regional, state, and sub-state levels in East Asia tend to be ignored or under-theorized. While it is often "... commonplace to see security equated with stability, as an extension of the generalization that instability is associated with insecurity, ... situations that are 'stable' may also be disastrously insecure for many people," and this blind spot means that "threats to security emanating from the state and directed against its own citizens or civilians of another nation" are too often invisible or ignored (Hamilton-Hart 2009, 64–65). As Burke and McDonald (2007) have also cautioned, a limited focus on regional and state stability tends to "soft-soap" the darker side of a "secure" and "stable" region.

We now know that the War on Terror operates as a security narrative – a discursive framework within which the definitions and practice of security operate – and as a *hegemonic* security narrative because it has achieved a degree of political and socio-cultural domination in the sense that its "regimes of truth" continue to be taken for granted as the foundation for policy and public debate at this specific historical juncture. The idea that the War on Terror operates as a hegemonic security narrative carries into the arguments made in the following chapters, where I engage in the type of critical security analysis outlined in Chapter 2. This entails examining relevant empirical examples and cases in contingent historical, geographic and social contexts. This is a critical security approach buttressed by ontologizing carefully in ways that seek to ask (and answer) hard questions about "real" places and "real" people: Who or what is being "secured"? Does a secure state necessarily translate into a secure population? Can security and insecurity exist simultaneously? Can the practices of security *cause* insecurity?

The following chapters seek to grapple with these questions. For example, in Southeast Asia, the War on Terror ushered in a renewed concern about Islamist terrorist threats in the region. Notably, although separatist militancy and terrorism have a long history in the region and have not necessarily been linked to Islamism, the historical moment of the post-9/11 security narratives meant that the threat of separatism was interpreted and framed in ways that have actually increased the risk of terrorist attacks occurring (Gershman 2002; Cotton 2003;

58 *In search of monsters*

Hamid 2016). Under the Bush Doctrine, the threat of terrorism in the region also became elevated to a status that seemed incommensurate with its actual potential to do damage (Wright-Neville 2004; Kadir 2004; Hamilton-Hart 2005; Sidel 2008). And the spectre of terrorism and the security politics of the War on Terror provided opportunities for state governments in the region to frame their internal security policies in ways that allow for a host of human rights violations and the suppression of political dissent (Cotton 2003; Noor 2006).

This is partly because US foreign policy in East Asia took on a different cast after 9/11. First, there was a notable and marked American withdrawal from economic multilateralism in the region. This was a significant change that was felt keenly by regional actors and will be discussed further in Chapter 6. Washington also began to actively ignore human rights abuses in Thailand, Indonesia, the Philippines, and Malaysia – issues that had previously held a prominent place on the diplomatic agenda of US envoys to the region. Relatedly, under the guise of counter-terrorism, Washington re-established relations with the Indonesian military, sold them weapons, and began pressuring the Indonesian government to enact extra-judicial measures to crack down on local militant groups. US support for the counter-terror operations of many of the governments in the region meant that local dissident groups of any political stripe could be brutally repressed beyond international reproach, as long as they were officially labelled as terrorists by the relevant government authorities. This is discussed in Chapter 5. In the Philippines, the renewed Visiting Forces Agreement re-established a controversial American military presence in the country, re-opening defunct American military outposts as regional forward operating bases and dispatching American troops to Southern districts to aid the Philippine military in counter-terror operations against Muslim separatist groups. This will be discussed further in the next chapter. Finally, US advocacy for democracy and human rights appeared to fall off the diplomatic agenda, with grave implications for minority populations subject to state repression in the region. These issues, and more, will be discussed in the following chapters.

Notes

1 Of course, studying "foreign policy" is not actually new, for

> as long as there have been political units engaging in relations with other political units, people have thought about and studied the problems of relations with the other or foreign group … new, is the attempt to structure the activities of scholars engaged in the study of foreign policy into a coherent and identifiable field of study.
>
> (Neack *et al.* 1995, 1)

2 Huysmans explains the significance of the distinction between Saussure's "signifier," which is the word, and the "signified," which is a particular *image* that we relate to the word/signifier. Importantly, there is no natural link between the signifier (word) "security" and a particular *understanding or image* of what "security" *is* (the signified). Rather, what is important is that the signifier (word) "security"

> has a history and implies a meaning, a particular signification of social relations … it is not the same to say – "Refugees pose a security question," and to say –

> "Refugees are a human rights question" … The meaning of the refugee question differs according to the register [of meaning] in which it is used. Uttering "security" articulates such a register of meaning … this aspect provides the intelligibility of security – that which makes security *mean something*. This is what "thickness" refers to.
>
> (Huysmans 1998, 228)

3 Texts, both in the literal sense of official foreign policy documentation, and in the non-literal sense of the social/cultural/political practices of foreign policy.
4 The integrity of liberal democratic values and institutions is called into question when unconstitutional practices such as unlawful surveillance of citizens become either ignored or sanctioned by legislative bodies and normalized by the prevailing security culture. What, then, is being defended from the "evildoers?"
5 The "hub and spokes" model is explained in Chapter 2.
6 Recognizing that some of what might be called "conventional" strategic-military concerns continued to have a place in post-Cold War US foreign policy. This was evidenced in the examples of military intervention in the former Yugoslavia and the strong involvement of the Clinton administration in the Oslo Peace Accords regarding Israel–Palestine.

References

Acharya, Amitav. 1999. Realism, institutionalism, and the Asian economic crisis. *Contemporary South East Asia* 21(1)(April): 1–29.

Agathangelou, A. and L. Ling. 2004. Power, borders, security, wealth: Lessons of violence and desire from September 11. *International Studies Quarterly* 48(3): 517–538.

Altheide, David. 2007. The mass media and terrorism. *Discourse & Communication* 1(3): 287–308.

Aradau, Claudia. 2016. Political grammars of mobility, security and subjectivity. *Mobilities* 11(4): 564–574.

Aradau, Claudia and Rens Van Munster. 2007. Governing terrorism through risk: Taking precautions, (un)knowing the future. *European Journal of International Relations* 33(2): 251–277.

Aradau, Claudia and Rens Van Munster. 2008. Insuring terrorism, assuring subjects, ensuring normality: The politics of risk after 9/11. *Alternatives* 33(2): 191–210.

Aradau, Claudia and Rens Van Munster. 2009. Exceptionalism and the "War on Terror" criminology meets international relations. *The British Journal of Criminology* 49(5): 686–701.

Aradau, Claudia and Rens Van Munster. 2011. *Politics of catastrophe: Genealogies of the unknown.* London: Routledge.

Ashley, Richard K. 1989. Living on the border lines: Man, poststructuralism and war. In J. Derderian and M. Shapiro (Eds) *International/intertextual relations: Postmodern readings of world politics.* Toronto: Lexington Books. pp. 259–321.

Beeson, Mark. 2007. The United States and Southeast Asia: Change and continuity in American hegemony. In K. Jayasuria (Ed.) *Crisis and change in regional governance.* London: Routledge. pp. 215–231.

Bennis, P. 2003. *Before and after: US foreign policy and the September 11th crisis.* Moreton-in-Marsh, Gloucestershire: Arris Publishing.

Bigo, Didier. 2002. Security and immigration: Toward a critique of the governmentality of unease. *Alternatives* 27(1): 63–92.

60 In search of monsters

Bigo, Didier. 2014. The (in)securitization practices of the three universes of EU border control: Military/navy-border guards/police-database analysts. *Security Dialogue* 45(3): 209–225.

Burke, Anthony and Matt McDonald (Eds). 2007. *Critical security in the Asia-Pacific*. Manchester: Manchester University Press.

Bush, George W. 2010. *Decision points*. New York: Random House.

Campbell, David. 1998. *Writing security: US foreign policy and the politics of identity*. Manchester: Manchester University Press.

Carlsnaes, Walter. 1992. The agency-structure problem in foreign policy analysis. *International Studies Quarterly* 36(3): 245–270.

Christoffersen, Gaye. 2002. The role of East-Asia in Sino-American relations. *Asian Survey* 42(3): 369–396.

Cloud, Dana L. 1994. The materiality of discourse as oxymoron: A challenge to critical rhetoric. *Western Journal of Communication* 58(Summer): 141–163.

Connolly, William. 1989. Identity and difference in global politics. In J. Der Derian and M. Shapiro (Eds) *International/intertextual relations: Postmodern readings of world politics*. Toronto: Lexington Books. pp. 323–342.

Cotton, James. 2003. Southeast Asia after 11 September. *Terrorism and Political Violence* 15(1): 148–170.

Cox, Michael. 2012. The USA, China and rising Asia. In Michael Cox and Doug Stokes (Eds) *US foreign policy, 2nd edition*. Oxford: Oxford University Press, pp. 259–273.

Croft, Stuart. 2006. *Culture, crisis and America's war on terror*. New York: Cambridge University Press.

Daalder, Ivo H. and James M. Lindsay. 2005. *America unbound: The Bush revolution in foreign policy*. Hoboken: John Wiley and Sons.

Deudney, Daniel and Jeffrey Meiser. 2012. American exceptionalism. In Michael Cox and Doug Stokes (Eds) *US foreign policy, 2nd edition*. Oxford: Oxford University Press. pp. 21–36.

Dibb P., D. Hale, and P. Prince. 1998. The strategic implications of Asia's Economic crisis. *Survival* 40(2): 5–26.

Dittmer, Lowell. 2002. East Asia in the "new era" in world politics. *World Politics* 55(1): 38–65.

Farrell, Theo. 2005. Strategic culture and American empire. *SAIS Review* 25(2): 3–18.

Foucault, Michel (1980). *Power/knowledge: Selected interviews and other writings, 1972–1977*. New York: Pantheon.

Gershman, John. 2002. Is Southeast Asia the second front? *Foreign Affairs* 81(4): 60–74.

Hamid, A. F. A. 2016. *ISIS in Southeast Asia: Internalized wahhabism is a major factor. ISEAS perspectives reports*. Singapore: Yusof Ishak Institute.

Hamilton-Hart, Natasha. 2005. Terrorism in Southeast Asia: Expert analysis, myopia and fantasy. *The Pacific Review* 18(3): 303–325.

Hamilton-Hart, Natasha. 2009. War and other insecurities in East Asia: What the security studies field does and does not tell us. *The Pacific Review* 22(1): 49–71.

Higgott, Richard. 2004. After neoliberal globalization: The "securitization" of US foreign economic policy in East Asia. *Critical Asian Studies* 36(3): 425–444.

Hill, Christopher. 2003. *The changing politics of foreign policy*. New York: Palgrave Macmillan.

Holsti, Ole R. 1989. Models of international relations and foreign policy. *Diplomatic History* 13(1): 15–44.

Holsti, Ole R. 1992. Public opinion and foreign policy: Challenges to the Almond-Lippmann consensus. *International Studies Quarterly* 36(4): 439–466.

Hudson, V. 2005. Foreign policy analysis: Actor-specific theory and the ground of international relations. *Foreign Policy Analysis* 1(1): 1–30.

Huysmans, Jef. 1998. Security! What do you mean? From concept to thick signifier. *European Journal of International Relations* 4(2): 226–255.

Jackson, Richard. 2005. *Writing the war on terrorism: Language politics and counter-terrorism*. New York: Manchester University Press.

Jackson, Richard. 2006. Genealogy, ideology, and counter-terrorism: Writing wars on terrorism from Ronald Reagan to George W. Bush Jr. *Studies in Language & Capitalism* 1(1): 163–193.

Jackson, Richard, Lee Jarvis, Jeroen Gunning, and Marie Breen-Smyth. 2011. *Terrorism: A critical introduction*. Basingstoke: Macmillan International Higher Education.

Jarvis, L. 2008. Times of terror: Writing temporality into the war on terror. *Critical Studies on Terrorism* 1(2): 245–262.

Jervis, Robert. 2005. Understanding the Bush Doctrine. In G. John Ikenberry (Ed.) *American foreign policy: Theoretical essays*. New York: Longman, pp. 576–599.

Kadir, Suzaina. 2004. Mapping Muslim politics in Southeast Asia after September 11. *The Pacific Review* 17(2): 199–222.

Loeppky, Rodney. 2005. "Biomania" and US foreign policy. *Millennium* 34(1): 85–113.

Mustapha, Jennifer. 2011. Threat construction in the Bush administration's post-9/11 foreign policy: (Critical) security implications for Southeast Asia. *The Pacific Review* 4(24): 487–504.

Mustapha, Jennifer. 2013. Ontological theorizations in critical security studies: Making the case for a (modified) post-structuralist approach. *Critical Studies on Security* 1(1): 64–82.

Neack, Laura Jeanne, A. K. Hey, and Patrick J. Haney (Eds). 1995. *Foreign policy analysis – Continuity and change in its second generation*. Englewood Cliffs, NJ: Prentice Hall.

Noor, F. A. 2006. How Washington's "war on terror" became everyone's: Islamophobia and the impact of September 11 on the political terrain of South and Southeast Asia. *Human Architecture: Journal of the Sociology of Self-Knowledge* 5(1): 29–50.

Pederson, V. S. 2003. In search of monsters to destroy? The Liberal American security paradox and a Republican way out. *International Relations* 17(2): 213–232.

Rosenau, J. N. 1966. Pre-theories and theories of foreign policy. In R. B. Farrel (Ed.) *Approaches in comparative and international politics*. Evanston: Northwestern University Press, pp. 18–30.

Rosenberger, Leif. 2001. The changing face of economic security in Asia. In Sheldon W. Simon (Ed.) *The many faces of Asian security*. Latham: Rowan and Littlefield. pp. 115–140.

Rowley, Cynthia and Jutta Weldes. 2012. Identities and US foreign policy. In Michael Cox and Doug Stokes (Eds) *US foreign policy, 2nd edition*. Oxford: Oxford University Press, pp. 178–194.

Ruggie, John G. 1997. The past as prologue?: Interests, identity and American foreign policy. *International Security* 21(4): 89–125.

Salter, Mark. 2008. Securitization and desecuritization: A dramaturgical analysis of the Canadian Air Transport Security Authority. *Journal of International Relations and Development* 11(4): 321–349.

Salter, Mark. 2013. To make move and let stop: Mobility and the assemblage of circulation. *Mobilities* 8(1): 7–19.

62   In search of monsters

Schmidt, Brian. 2012. Theories of US foreign policy. In Michael Cox and Doug Stokes (Eds) *US foreign policy, 2nd edition*. Oxford: Oxford University Press, pp. 5–19.

Sidel, John. 2008. The Islamist threat in South East Asia: Much ado about nothing? *Asian Affairs* 39(3): 339–351.

Slingerland, Edward, Eric M. Blanchard, and L. Y. N. Boyd-Judson. 2007. Collision with China: Conceptual metaphor analysis, somatic marking, and the EP-3 incident. *International Studies Quarterly* 51(1): 53–77.

Stampnitzky, L. 2013. *Disciplining terror: How experts invented "terrorism."* Cambridge: Cambridge University Press.

Stockdale, Liam P. D. 2013. Imagined futures and exceptional presents: A conceptual critique of pre-emptive security. *Global Change, Peace & Security* 25(2): 141–157.

Stockdale, Liam P. D. 2015. *Taming an uncertain future: Temporality, sovereignty, and the politics of anticipatory governance*. London: Rowman and Littlefield.

The White House. March 16, 2001. *Joint statement by President Bush and Prime Minister Yoshiro Mori*, Press Release, Washington DC.

The White House. April 12, 2001. *Remarks by President Bush upon the return of US service members*, Rose Garden Press Conference, Washington DC.

The White House. June 30, 2001. *Joint statement by President Bush and Prime Minister Koizumi*, Press Release, Washington DC.

The White House. September 4, 2001. *US, China to discuss missile defence*, Statement by the White House Press Secretary, Washington DC.

The White House. September 2002. *National strategy for combating terrorism*. Washington DC: The White House.

The White House. March 12, 2006. *National Security Strategy*. Washington DC.

Van Rythoven, Eric. 2015. Learning to feel, learning to fear? Emotions, imaginaries, and limits in the politics of securitization. *Security Dialogue* 46(50): 458–475.

Walker, R. B. J. 1993. *Inside/outside: International relations as political theory*. Cambridge: Cambridge University Press.

Weber, Cynthia. 2006. *Imagining America at war: Morality, politics, and film*. London: Routledge.

Weldes, Jutta. 1999. *Constructing national interests: The United States and the Cuban missile crisis*. Minneapolis: Minneapolis University Press.

Williamson, John. 2009. A short history of the Washington Consensus. *Law & Business Review of the Americas* 15(1): 7.

Wright-Neville, David. 2004. Dangerous dynamics: Activists, militants and terrorists in Southeast Asia. *The Pacific Review* 17(1): 27–46.

Zulaika, Joseba (2009). *Terrorism: The self-fulfilling prophecy*. Chicago, IL: University of Chicago Press.

4 Here be monsters!

"Experts" and the mapping of terror

On early European cartographic records of newly explored territory dating back to the mediaeval period, it was not uncommon to see depictions of dragons and sea serpents on the unknown areas and edges of the mapped world. This "unknown" terrain was, as a matter of course, marked with danger. In the popular imagination, the term *Here Be Monsters* or *Here Be Dragons* is often attributed to these early maps, to connote a region of land or sea that is still uncharted or reputed through folklore or explorer travelogue to be home to dangerous beasts. In fact, illustrated depictions of monsters and serpents have been observed on a wide variety of historical maps, along with inscriptions that specifically reference the presence of scorpions, lions, hippos, elephants, and the like (George 1969; Allen and Griffiths 1979). However, there is only one known cartographic relic where the actual Latin phrase *Hc Svnt Dracones* has been inscribed,[1] and it can be found on the Hunt-Lenox Globe housed in the New York City Library's collection of rare historical artefacts.

Of unknown origin, the Hunt-Lenox Globe was purchased in France in the 1800s and is widely believed to date back to the early 1500s (da Costa 1879). The globe includes illustrations of serpents, large whale-like creatures, and even an image of a drowning man and capsized ship, all of which are depicted as hazards of the ocean. The aforementioned phrase, *Hc Svnt Dracones*, appears as a small inscription on an area of the map that is marked, appropriately enough for our purposes, off the Eastern coast of Asia near what is probably the Indonesian island of Sumatra (da Costa 1879).

The Latin phrase *Hc Svnt Dracones* is often translated to mean "Here Be Dragons" and is sometimes thought to refer to the Komodo lizards of Indonesia. The phrase may also refer to Marco Polo's account of a supposed race of men from the "Kingdom of Dagroian" who according to Polo's travelogues "were a people who once charged against the Irish, feasted upon the dead and picked their bones" (da Costa 1879, 536). Similarly, The Borgia Map (*c.*1430) has a serpent figure in Asia with an inscription that reads "*Hic etiam homines magna cornua habentes longitudine quatuor pedum, et sunt etiam serpentes tante magnitudinis, ut unum bovem comedant integrum*" ("Here also are enormous men having horns four feet long, and there are serpents of such magnitude that they can eat an ox whole").[2]

64 *Here be monsters!*

What is so fascinating about these depictions of the unknown – both as sensationalistic travelogue and uncharted territory where monsters may be lurking – is that the unknown, by definition, is represented as that which must be feared.[3] The unknown, *by virtue of being unknown* and especially as an exotic unknown, is deemed necessarily to hold the potential for danger. And in order to govern (or secure) this danger (or terror), the unknown must be named in order to become known. And this is where the powerful role of "experts" comes in to play. As Dillon (2007) asserts, "you cannot secure anything unless you know what it is ... integral to the problematizations of security are the ways in which people, territory, and things are transformed into epistemic objects" (12). The identification of Southeast Asia as a second front in the War on Terror can be seen as another incarnation of these sorts of Dark Continent discourses, where a vast territory and its inhabitants are viewed through the lens of risk and emergent threat that transforms them into epistemic objects by the expertise that seeks to govern them (Lacher 2008). But as Campbell (1998) reminds us, these epistemic objects and the shape that they take in our imaginations, *come out of* problematizations of security and not just the other way around. And this is precisely why expert discourses deserve our attention as part of a wider set of security narratives that, in the case of the War on Terror, mark bodies as subaltern and as always already dangerous.

This chapter examines constructions of threat in post-9/11 Southeast Asian security politics, in particular the perceived threat posed by political Islam in the region as informed by expert discourses. Chapter 3 explained how the War on Terror operates as a powerful security narrative that has constitutive effects on identity formation of the self, perceptions of the other, the framing of political problems, and the formation of policy responses to those problems. As others have argued as well,[4] I maintain that US foreign policies vis-à-vis the War on Terror have had a pervasive impact on global security politics and on the perception of threats everywhere. In the case of Southeast Asia, the War on Terror brought with it an important discursive shift that has continued to frame security practices within the region.

What is important about this shift, is that the security narratives of the War on Terror have shaped and constructed conceptualizations of existing regional security dynamics in particular ways. This has occurred due to a combination of "common sense" perspectives encouraged by expert discourses framed by these security narratives, and a variety of other factors that relate to regional Southeast Asian security politics. It must be emphasized again that the point of this analysis is not to discount the threat of terrorism in Southeast Asia as far as it does exist. Rather, the point is to ask different sorts of questions about terrorism than ones traditionally asked by the experts, in order to reveal some of the less obvious ways that terrorism, along with state reactions to it, can influence the security and insecurity of groups and individuals.

Expertise and the construction of threat

When we acknowledge that inter-subjectivity always exists in the production of knowledge, the notion of "expertise" brings political and ethical questions into the foreground. There is no denying that expertise is important. Expertise is required to address and understand complex problems, ideally in ways that are empirically sound, that reflect available data, and that are based on verifiable information. In an age where popular discourse increasingly treats ideas of wildly varying quality as equally valid, it is especially important to parse out the difference between facts and opinions. Equally important is knowing the difference between a well-founded opinion and an indefensible one. Being able to rely on valid expertise is part of that. Nevertheless, different types of expertise can be seen as more or less authoritative within different contexts, and there are often epistemological disagreements and well-worn debates even *within* areas of expertise. So, it is always worth paying attention to fault lines of contention within a discipline or area of study. This is because expert discourses play a powerful role in setting policy agendas and framing information.

To paraphrase Cox (1981): *knowledge* is always for someone and for some purpose. Expert knowledge and language can become tools to exclude individuals who can be cast as non-experts, and to exclude ideas that cannot be spoken of in a particular language of expertise (Cohn 1987). Expert discourses often "draw boundaries around themselves by celebrating certain kinds of statements while excommunicating others, which then take on the status of 'subjugated knowledges'" (Gusterson 1999, 326). In the case of security, the nature of expertise is instrumental in constructing the parameters of what counts as a security problem and of constructing particular logics of security in response to those problems. But who are the "experts"? What version of common sense do they put forward? What constitutes "legitimate" knowledge about security and terrorism in the context of the War on Terror, and why?[5]

As with the study of security more generally, there are problems with setting up an exaggerated dichotomy between a conventional terrorism studies and a more critical approach to studying terrorism (Horgon and Boyle 2008; Gunning 2007a, 2007b), or as it is sometimes characterized, a dichotomy between "problem-solving" and "critical" terrorism studies (Gunning 2007a, 2007b; Jackson 2007a, 2007b). It is perhaps better to suggest, as Gunning (2007a) does, that this "dichotomy" between the conventional and the critical is much better conceptualized as a *continuum*. And along this continuum, among the many different experts and scholars who study, theorize, and conceptualize terrorism, there are varying degrees of reflexivity, a variety of methodologies being used, and a host of competing motivations behind the questions being asked. Hence, while this chapter identifies and challenges some of the central themes in the prevailing expert discourses on terrorism in Southeast Asia, it also seeks to actively avoid the construction of a straw man "terrorism expert" while engaging in such critiques. It is also beyond the scope of this chapter to comprehensively engage with all the debates that continue to occur under the umbrella of "Critical Studies on Terrorism."[6]

66 *Here be monsters!*

That being said, it is possible to identify significant common threads that have emerged in conventional expert discourses on post-9/11 terrorism in Southeast Asia. A deconstruction of these common threads reveals a shared reliance on modernist ontological underpinnings to make arguments about how the world works, and a tendency to presuppose the objectivity of the knowledge that is produced. As Gunning (2007a) asserts:

> In its most "uncritical" manifestation … a "problem-solving" approach [to studying terrorism] does not question its framework of reference, its categories, its origins, or the power relations that enable the production of these categories … It is state-centric, takes security to mean the security of the state rather than that of human beings, on the assumption that the former implies the latter, and sees security in narrow military or law-and-order terms, as opposed to the wider conception of human security, as for instance developed by critical security studies … It … ignores social and historical contexts; if it did not, it would have to account for the historical trajectory of the state … The problem-solving approach is positivist and objectivist, and seeks to explain the "terrorist other" from within state-centric paradigms rather than to understand the "other" inter-subjectively using interpretative or ethnographic methods.
>
> (371)

In other words, in the conventional expertise on terrorism, there is a reliance on *strong* ontology – specifically in foundational assumptions regarding the nature of security, which is understood as *stability among states* and the *safety of the state* from existential threats, and regarding the function and nature of the state as the primary actor in the international system.

With this in mind, this chapter challenges three commonly made claims that have emerged out of the post-9/11 security narrative and related expert discourses on Southeast Asian terrorism. These claims are inter-related and flow into one another: first, *that all forms of political Islam necessarily represent an imminent threat of terrorism because Islam itself is seen as the primary, if not the sole, causal factor of terrorist violence*; second, *that there exists a regionally cohesive radical Islamist identity with robust organizational and ideological links to Al-Qaeda and the Islamic State (IS)*; and third, that *terrorism in Southeast Asia is best understood as pathological or evil*, which results in narrowly conceived state-responses to behaviours understood to be irrational, rather than political.

Contesting each of these claims from a critical security perspective allows us to see that conventional expertise around counter-terrorism (CT) and countering violence and extremism (CVE) in Southeast Asia contributes twofold to increasing insecurity.[7] On the one hand, much of the existing expertise in the areas of CT and CVE in Southeast Asia transforms a vast territory and its people into a contingent, emergent threat, always *en route* to becoming dangerous. As a result, risk management policies and pre-emptive security practices of the state exert biopolitical influence on large populations of people, ultimately rendering them less secure. While this is not an aspect of the War on Terror that is unique to Southeast Asia, it manifests in the region in particular ways that are worth exploring. Second, and related to the previous point, counter-terrorism discourses and CVE rationalities can be easily utilized by the state security apparatus in service to a variety of practices designed to consolidate the political power of ruling elites rather than address the problem of terrorism, per se. In fact, counter-terrorism measures and CVE policies, in some instances, hasten radicalization and contribute to the formation of anti-establishment or revolutionary Islamist identities (Noor 2006; Hamid 2016; Chan 2018). Hence, these "epistemic objects," and the potential threat they pose may *come out of* problematizations of security and not the other way around.

This chapter places particular emphasis on the first claim relating to the perceived threat of political Islam in the region. A seemingly devotional adherence to this central claim has meant that the idea of a direct causal relationship between Muslims and terrorism took on the axiomatic status of "common sense" in the War on Terror security narratives in Southeast Asia after 9/11, and to a large degree appears to continue into the present. This sort of "uncritical" approach to security, as Gunning calls it, results in a perspective that is blinkered to the many ways that the securing of the state continues to be implicated in the creation of various forms of insecurity. While separatist militancy and terrorism have long existed in the region in some form or other, this chapter is concerned with how the specific historical moment of the War on Terror has significantly re-framed these threats in ways that have increased various forms of insecurity.

The problem with terrorism experts

Terrorism has an interesting definitional history. The question of what constitutes "terror" varies, and "terrorism" itself largely remains an essentially contested concept. Regardless of its lack of a clear definition, terrorism has long been a problem in search of expertise and the expertise bred in response to terrorism has a traceable genealogy that belies a pervasive desire to discipline and govern the unknown. As Stampnitzky (2013) argues, there have been several clear successive periods of terrorism expertise that reflect difficulties with defining terrorism within specific historical contexts. Thus, even though "terrorism" is central to contemporary political discourse and security politics, it is "not a stable or fixed category" and "neither the problem of 'terrorism' nor the field of terrorism expertise has been fully 'disciplined'" (Stampnitzky 2013, 4, 7).

As Jackson (2005) has noted, after 9/11 counter-terrorism and CVE have become a crucial part of the larger security discourses and narratives of the War on Terror, and a cottage industry of sorts has emerged in the area of terrorism expertise. A review by Cynthia Lum, Leslie Kennedy and Alison Sherley (2006) found that of all scholarly articles relating to terrorism published between 1972 and 2002 *over 54% were published in the brief period after 9/11* (cited by Stampnitzky 2013, 196). Despite – or perhaps because of – the lack of a clear

68 *Here be monsters!*

and agreed-upon definition of terrorism, there has nevertheless been a burgeoning of terrorism expertise in the wake of 9/11. The first notable rise of the "terrorism expert" can be traced back to the 1972 attack by members of the Palestinian nationalist Black September Organization that resulted in the deaths of nine Israeli athletes at the Munich Olympics, after which US President Richard Nixon established the Cabinet Committee to Combat Terrorism (Stampnitzky 2013, 21–28). This ushered in the first decade of official "terrorism expertise," and created momentum that brought together academics and policy makers with knowledge of terrorism. This new era of terrorism expertise sought explicitly to make the problem of terrorism "governable" through three overlapping (but sometimes disparate) modes of knowledge production – international law and diplomacy; crisis response management and simulations; and a desire to rationalize and quantify terrorism using risk management techniques (Stampnitzky 2013, 107).

Indeed, we see these three modes of knowledge production reverberate down into post 9/11 counter-terrorism discourses in different degrees. We also see the overlap and complex interplay of security communities and networks that have constitutive effects on the security practices and policies of counter-terrorism through the epistemic "power to construct international security" that is wielded through expertise (Leander 2005). As I talked about in Chapter 3, Jackson (2005) sees this as part of an organized effort to assert and enforce continued state authority through exceptional security practices. He makes the compelling argument that terrorism expertise plays a crucial role in buttressing particular types of discourses and security rationales in the context of the War on Terror. And while I disagree with Stampnitzky's characterization of Jackson's understanding of terrorism discourses as being "rigid," I do tend to agree with her on the point that both terrorism discourses and terrorism expertise are likely more fluid, less organized, and less stable than Jackson suggests (200–201).

This is because terrorism expertise is itself also constrained by the same discourses it creates through what Stampnitzky calls the "politics of anti-knowledge" that have emerged in the context of the War on Terror. This is because

> counter-terrorism in recent years has not relied upon governing the problem by making it legible. Rather than rely upon the creation of knowledge about terrorism, the dominant approach has rejected the very possibility of knowing terrorists. The conceptualization of terrorism … contains within it a moral "truth": that terrorism is *illegitimate violence*. As a result … once an event, an individual, or an organization has been placed into this category, it is easy to assert – as President Bush frequently did – that all we need to know about them is that they are evil.
>
> (Stampnitzky 2013, 203, emphasis in original)

Compounding the pressures of "anti-knowledge," there is also a bit of a Wild West mentality in the field of counter-terrorism and CVE where those with

Here be monsters! 69

vastly different credentials of vastly different quality nevertheless claim expertise in the same general area and can still be sought after equally as "experts."
This is not to say that there is no good work being done by individuals or organizations working in counter-terrorism or CVE,[8] but rather that the nature and
make-up of the field necessarily lends to conceptual constraints and quality
issues.

Another factor lending to the problems with terrorism expertise is the use of
(often unnamed) state intelligence or security sources. This is because

> not all intelligence organizations are equally reliable and, particularly in
> some countries, can be highly politicized and running agendas for their gov-
> ernments ... [and] intelligence agencies can selectively leak information to
> analysts – or to the media – to influence public debate.
>
> (Wright-Neville quoted in Hugh 2003)

Expertise in policy-areas also often reflects the needs of power-holders to shape
knowledge production (Hamilton-Hart 2012). This all lends to the great irony of
terrorism expertise, which is that even though terrorism is the central security
preoccupation in the context of the War on Terror and despite the power wielded
by its narratives and discourses, there continues to be enormous uncertainty, dis-
crepancy, and incoherence about what terrorism is, how we can know it, and
who can know it – even *within the field of terrorism expertise itself*. An examination of some of the commonly made expert claims with regards to Southeast
Asian terrorism highlights these problems.

Expert claim one: political Islam as imminent threat

A key aspect of post-9/11 terrorism expertise is its general preoccupation with
Islam and Muslims. This is obviously informed by the fact that the perpetrators
of the terrorist attacks of September 11, 2001 were operatives of Osama Bin
Laden's *Al-Qaeda*, a fringe terrorist group openly disavowed by mainstream
Muslim clerics and jurisprudence but nevertheless informed by a particularly
regressive (and aggressive) form of Wahhabi Sunni Islam originating in Saudi
Arabia, and by the subsequent rise of the so called Islamic State (IS) in Syria.
The idea that terrorism is synonymous with Islam did not originate with 9/11
however, and had been percolating for years in the Orientalist social and political imaginaries of what Edward Said (1978) would call the Occident, dating as
far back as the earliest European encounters with Muslim societies necessarily
seen as both exotic and dangerous by virtue of being unknown. Whether
entrenched and influential ideas like that of irreconcilable "civilizations" (Huntington 1993), inevitable "Muslim rage" towards the West (Lewis 1990), or the
dangers of a monolithic "Jihad" to a liberal democratic "McWorld" (Barber
1992) come out of actual historical fact or xenophobic interpretation alone is
almost beside the point. This is because the essentialist association between an
othered "Muslim world" and its supposedly inevitable violent tendencies has

70 *Here be monsters!*

long been made and has carried forward into the common sense of contemporary terrorism expertise.

These long-held perceptions of the so-called Muslim World continue to form the basis for the security narratives of post-9/11 counter-terrorism in the context of the War on Terror (Jackson 2005, 2006; Noor 2006). Under the George W. Bush administration, and despite occasional assertions to the contrary, Islam itself was clearly identified as the primary locus of terrorism. Both in terms of acts, as in: *terrorism is primarily perpetrated by Muslims*; and in terms of causes, as in: *Islam is the primary cause of terrorism* (Mustapha 2011). This is one of the most conspicuous problems with the conventional expertise of the US foreign policy establishment in the context of the War on Terror: its overly simplistic characterization of the religion of Islam and its followers (Hamilton-Hart 2005; Jackson 2005, 2006; Sidel 2008). One may easily infer from conventional counter-terrorism and CVE discourses that terrorism appears primarily to exist on the spectrum of this religion in particular and, as such, "Categories such as *moderate, fundamentalist, militant* and *terrorist* are sometimes presented as potentially progressive stages through which individuals may move" (Hamilton-Hart 2005, 312). The most insidious implication of this assumption is that any Muslim individual is cast as a potential terrorist threat. This is why state security practices have linked the War on Terror to migration and border control, and why CT and CVE strategies like the United Kingdom's have focused on "preventing" the radicalization of Muslims who already reside in Britain.

In other words, the solution to terrorism is simplistically presented as either a task of keeping Muslims "out," or of somehow keeping the Muslims who are already "in" from getting to the terrorist end-point of some supposed Muslim continuum. Hence, the threat of terrorism is seen to emanate directly from the risks posed by Muslim religiosity itself, and a Muslim who is somehow becoming *more* Muslim, whatever that may mean, is seen to represent an increased threat of terrorism. This is especially the case if Muslim identity is somehow politicized. This tendency to presuppose the emergent threat of political Islam, by definition, was observable in much of the conventional academic expertise on Southeast Asian terrorism immediately after 9/11.

Zachary Abuza, for example, is a leading academic expert on terrorism in Southeast Asia and he has served as an advisor to both the US State and Defence departments. He is a "visiting guest lecturer at the Foreign Service Institute, US Department of State and at the Department of Defense's Joint Special Operations University,"[9] and both national and international media consult him often for his commentary on Southeast Asian terrorism. Abuza is a prolific scholar, producing many articles, books, and studies about regional terrorism and its links to both *Al-Qaeda* and the Islamic State since the early 2000s.[10] He is well regarded for conducting perilous fieldwork, garnering access to high-ranking local politicians and religious leaders, and managing to engage with influential organizational Islamists as part of his research, many of whom speak to him anonymously. The jacket of Abuza's ominously titled volume, *Militant Islam in Southeast Asia: Crucible of terror* (2003a), features an endorsement by another oft-quoted regional terrorism expert, Rohan Gunaratna, proclaiming Abuza's willingness to "risk his own life to get "high-quality information" on "Southeast Asia's terror network." This all lends to the credibility of his expertise, and his opinion and policy advice is sought out by foreign policy and intelligence communities in Washington and around the world.

I bring up Abuza specifically because he is a good example of a well-regarded expert whose work often reflects and reinforces entrenched ideas around the role that Islam plays in terrorism in Southeast Asia, reflecting an analytical tendency to conclude that political Islam necessarily represents a threat of terrorism. For example, in *Tentacles of terror: Al-Qaeda's Southeast Asian network* (2002), Abuza refers to a growing threat of what he calls "radical Islamicism" in Southeast Asia, which, as the title suggests, is slowly extending its grip throughout the region. According to Abuza (2002), the radicalization of regional Islam is evidenced and/or caused by a wide array of factors: widespread "economic dispossession"; a lack of political freedom or of outlets for political dissatisfaction; the "spread" of Wahhabi and Salafi Islam; the "failures of secular education"; and the "hundreds of thousands" of Southeast Asian Muslims attending parochial religious schools in Pakistan and universities in the Middle East (428). And while he acknowledges that Wahhabi and Salafi "Islamicists" are a "distinct minority" in Southeast Asia, he, nevertheless, goes on to claim that "in many cases they [Islamicists] have shaped the agenda" (Abuza 2002, 428).

In fact, there has been little indication that this small minority of Muslims influenced by Wahhabi and Salafist teachings, and who make up an insignificant percentage of the region's more than 250 million Muslims, have shaped the political agenda of the region in any meaningful way. On the contrary, this small group of radicals remains a peripheral element in Southeast Asian politics and their societal influence has remained marginal (Gershman 2002; Kadir 2004; Jayasankaran 2002; McKenna 2002; Sidel 2008; Wright-Neville 2004; Poushter 2015). Even following the 2002 Bali bombings in Kuta Beach that killed over 500 people, there was scant indication that Islamist terrorism in Southeast Asia was well organized or state sponsored, and the extreme diversity of Muslims in the region has continued to work against the establishment of a politically violent fundamentalist hegemony by any one group. Despite several (relatively small-scale) terrorist attacks against "Western" targets in the region over the years following the Bali bombings, and Muslim separatist groups' attacks against state targets in Thailand and the Philippines,[11] we have continued to see a decline in the political and social influence of ultra-conservative Islamist political parties and an overall de-escalation in Muslim separatist violence since the early 2000s (Kadir 2004; Sidel 2008; Bruinessen 2015; Malik 2016; Saat 2016).

As far as it is possible to quantify such things, Southeast Asian Muslim support for *Al-Qaeda*, IS and for "Islamist" ideologies, in general, is indicated in low numbers relative to the population (Poushter 2015). As mentioned, there are over 250 million Muslims in the region and yet there have been only 700–1000 individuals from all of Southeast Asia who have travelled to Syria and surrounding areas, representing less than 0.0003% of the Southeast Asian Muslim

72 *Here be monsters!*

population (Barrett *et al.* 2016)[12] of the Muslim population in Malaysia and 4% of the Muslim population in Indonesia voice anything resembling sympathy for the causes being fought for there, as indicated by the various Pew research polls that are regularly cited by analysts of all stripes (Poushter 2015). Interestingly, these same numbers are often cited as proof of the dangers of political Islam, rather than evidence of its peripheral influence.

For example, Hamid (2016) cites Pew research that suggests only 26% of Malaysian Muslims and 20% of Indonesian Muslims are "very worried about Islamist extremism." He sees this as proof that Malaysian and Indonesian Muslims have internalized and normalized extremist views, rather than as an indication that perhaps extremism has not, in fact, taken hold of these societies. Hamid (2016) goes on to rebuke fellow analysts who remain unconcerned by the possible threat posed by Islamist views saying that they have

> sought to downplay the religious factor … in attempts to perhaps absolve Islam of blame for the violent antics of Muslim terrorists [displaying] *a typical social science bias against religion as a mobilizing force by mainly looking at socio-economic conditions and personal motivations as overriding factors* in … Islamist violence. Whichever way we try to explain it, the phenomenon of rising Islamist extremism is cause enough for worry.
>
> (6, emphasis added)

And yet, Hamid (2016) acknowledges that in fact, "actual ISIS networks in Southeast Asia remain weak and haphazard" (6), that "the more extreme tendencies of Wahhabism have been much toned down throughout the years by the Saud ruling dynasty" (8), and that it "would be inaccurate to equate Salafization with Islamization" (9). Nevertheless, he maintains his assertion that Wahhabi and Salafist political Islam are "increasingly defining mainstream Islam in Southeast Asia" (9).

The sheer number and diversity of Muslims in the region, the vast majority of whom share a rejection of political violence and Wahhabi and/or Salafist Islamist ideology (Poushter 2015), remains a blind spot in much of the conventional regional terrorism expertise, especially on the policy side. Efforts to place regional terrorism and Islamism into a more nuanced or proportional perspective is disregarded by these experts as naïveté and/or apologia, and the hard silos between the terrorism experts who drive policy and the analysts who show "social science bias" remain. This blind spot reflects an entrenched view of political Islam as always radical – somehow both fringe and ubiquitous; amorphous but organized; not everywhere and yet potentially anywhere. In other words, political Islam's perceived links to terrorism becomes a particularly protean relationship, its significance varying depending on how it is framed (Sidel 2007, 2008).[13]

This reminds us of Stampnitzky's (2013) observation that the "politics of anti-knowledge" make terrorism into an unknowable concept precisely because something characterized as both evil and irrational can never be legible. Hence, we see the tendency within the expert perspectives on terrorism in Southeast

Asia to both over-simplify political manifestations of Islam and to presuppose the threat posed by it. In fact, it is arguable that

> the dynamics of state–society relations within the Muslim world, and its impact on domestic as well as international security, are not new … scholars were already debating on the compatibility of Islam and democratic practice long before the events of 9/11.
>
> (Kadir 2004, 202)

Viewing the dynamics of Muslim politics solely through the lens of 9/11 and the War on Terror thus produces a limited and ahistorical reading of the complex and rich terrain of religion and politics in Southeast Asia (or elsewhere for that matter). This is because

> Muslim politics in Southeast Asia … is increasingly … complex and dynamic. It has been affected by forces of development, globalization and Islamization. Development and globalization has allowed for the flowering of Islam in the region but also of different versions and competing strands of the religion vis-à-vis one another. In the process, there have been contests for legitimacy and authority but also growing awareness and insecurity regarding religious identity … Muslim politics has also been shaped by more explicit political dynamics including the nature of state–society inter-action between the regime and the Muslim community.
>
> (Kadir 2004, 219)

Kadir's main point here is that the politics of Islam in the region are far more complex than a more conventional understanding that sees "Islamization" as both necessarily dangerous and as a singular, linear force. As such, rather than signalling a simple movement towards an inevitable end-point on the imagined continuum of Islam from moderation to extremism, Kadir points out that "Islamization [is] not the simple process of return to the golden age of the religion, or towards fundamentalism, per se … [but rather], it introduces increasingly complex strands, ranging from liberal interpretations to fundamentalist discourses and practices" (Kadir 2004, 210).

JAKIM, the Malaysian government body officially in charge of state matters relating to Islam, issued a *fatwa* (a scholarly opinion of religious jurisprudence) against Wahhabi and Salafist teachings, and mainstream Sunni jurisprudence in the country agrees (Hamid 2016). But with regards Kadir's point, there is still a lot of variation in the practice and beliefs of Muslims in Southeast Asia, illustrating "increasingly complex strands" of Islam in the region. It is a fact that some Islamist groups hold views that are at odds with Western-style liberal values on a variety of social, political and economic issues – which is worth paying attention to for a variety of reasons – but this does not mean that they are necessarily also terrorist groups. Nor does an adherence to religious identity necessarily signal a rejection of existing, ostensibly liberal, democratic structures.

74 *Here be monsters!*

One such example is the longstanding *Parti Islam se-Malaysia*, or PAS, a key opposition political party in Malaysia whose membership and organizational principles are based on Muslim religious affiliation. PAS has occasionally been lumped in with and tenuously linked to illegal militant and terrorist groups such as *Jemaah Islamiyah* (JI), *Kumpulan Mujahidin Malaysia* (KMM) and *Abu Sayyaf*, and several PAS members have been investigated or arrested for suspected militant activities even prior to 9/11 (Aslam 2009; Hamid 2016; Chan 2018; Noor 2006). And while PAS' leadership has expressed some support for puritanical Wahhabi ideas around "authenticity" in Islam, the party stalwarts themselves have nevertheless continuously rejected political violence and terrorism (Noor 2003). Despite fiery and divisive populist rhetoric, PAS has consistently followed electoral norms and conventions, accepting defeat in local and federal elections and peacefully transitioning in and out of power. In the recent 2018 Malaysian Federal Election, PAS suffered substantial losses in many of their stronghold parliamentary constituencies, especially in the northern states, without incident. Overly-simplistic characterizations of "political Islam" in the region fail to capture the nuances of specific groups and their specific contexts.

Another example of a widely misunderstood "Islamist" group is *Nadhatul Ulama* (NU), which has been the main independent Islamist organization in Indonesia since 1926, currently boasting over 40 million followers. The group was created in response both to fundamentalist Wahhabist ideas coming out of Saudi Arabia into Indonesia, and to the rise in "modernist" influences by secularist Muslim movements like Turkish Kemalism. NU sought to carve out a distinctively Sunni-based set of religious ideas that would chart a path of moderation in comparison to what they viewed as the opposite extremes of Wahhabist puritanism and modernist secularization. The organization itself is diverse, with some members seeking a more traditionalist conservative role for religion in society, and others advocating the idea of *Islam Nusantara*, which seeks to articulate a distinctive Southeast Asian style of "moderate" Islam in the context of socio-cultural conditions in Indonesia as a counter to an Arab-centric understanding of Islam (Athyal 2015).

Importantly, NU has specifically denounced terrorism and mass casualty violence, decrying such acts as counter to Islamic principles and jurisprudence (Gershman 2002; Noor 2006). Although they have a clear religious mandate, the organization has consistently supported the Indonesian constitutional ideal of *Pancasila* which requires religious pluralism in government; they have remained committed to democratic processes; and they have rejected outright the idea of imposing Shariah law on Indonesian society (Kadir 2004; Noor 2006). Accordingly, as a counter to conventional expert narratives around the linkages between terrorism and Southeast Asian Islam, other analysts were wary of the immediate characterization of Southeast Asia as a "key-theater for terrorist activity" after 9/11 (Wright-Neville 2004, 27) or as a "second front" in the War on Terror (Noor 2006). As a result, "the bulk of [conventional] terrorism-related research consists mainly of a cataloguing of individual terrorists and the organizations and networks to which they belong," with little, if any, "understanding of the complex inter-play of cultural, economic, political and economic social forces that lay behind it" (Wright-Neville 2004, 29).

In response to the "exaggerated sense of threat that rests largely on a failure to account for nuanced differences in the nature of Islamist politics in the region" (27), Wright-Neville offered a typology of Islamist organizations in the region after 9/11, illustrating the varying degrees to which an oppositional Islamist political group can or should be classified as a terrorist group while clearly contesting the implication that all such groups reside along the afore-mentioned sliding scale of Islamist violence, from "moderate" to "terrorist." Instead, his typology was meant to indicate that in trying to understand the wide variances in behaviours and propensities towards political violence among the different groups, it is necessary to recognize and understand that these are groups with different (and in many cases completely disparate) beliefs about the role that violence can or should play in political opposition (Wright-Neville 2004, 32). As he notes, it is true that in Southeast Asia "*some* activists have become militants and *some* militants have become terrorists" (Wright-Neville 2004, 42). But "Islamist" political groups like PAS in Malaysia, NU in Indonesia, and even separatist groups who do have violent militant histories, like the Moro Islamic Liberation Front (MILF) in the Philippines, have not engaged in the type of wholesale rejection of democratic state authority held by avowedly terrorist organizations like JI, KMM and *Abu Sayaaf.*

Instead, a variety of "Islamist" groups have in fact indicated that they are "… clearly uncomfortable on religious and other grounds with the dehumanizing logic that inspires JI's embrace of mass casualty terrorism" (Wright-Neville 2004, 42). These sorts of distinctions are important because they cast serious doubt onto the claim that all Muslims – and especially politicized Muslims – are always already in danger of becoming terrorists, especially when we consider the fact that

> the overwhelming majority of Islamic political organizations in Southeast Asia fall within a category described as "activist." Such groups are dedicated to altering or replacing the political hierarchy and its policies and to infuse national politics with a more Islamic flavour, but they do not seek to change the principles that underpin existing political and/or democratic frameworks … Activists prefer to work "with the system," agitating within existing legal and political norms.
>
> (Wright-Neville, 2004, 32)

Furthermore, a more nuanced understanding of political Islam in the region can help to avoid clumsy policy recommendations that include calls for "more inclusive American diplomacy and outreach to 'moderate' Muslims, as if the problem was largely a Public Relations bungle" (Hamilton-Hart 2005, 314). Such characterizations of political Islam also undermine the legitimate opposition to long-standing suppression by local governments, which will be discussed in the next chapter. This, too often, serves to unfairly marginalize legitimate organizations

76 *Here be monsters!*

who actually have democratic political support among local populations (Cotton 2003; Noor 2006; Chan 2018).

Expert claim two: regional Islamism with global linkages

Related to the claim that political Islam necessarily portends an imminent threat of terrorism, conventional expertise also tends to portray terrorist groups in Southeast Asia as forming a cohesive regional network that is linked globally to *Al-Qaeda* and/or IS. This occurs easily when verified terrorist organizations and groups are lumped together with all *activist* Muslim groups and organizations due to the reasons outlined in the previous section. As commonly occurs, a questionable picture of a vast and unified terror network emerges. This depiction of Southeast Asian "Islamism" suggests that violent manifestations of political Islam with linkages to *Al-Qaeda* and IS lurk ominously around every corner (Collier 2006; Cruz-De Castro 2004; Hamilton-Hart 2005; Noor 2006). A general survey of Southeast Asian terrorism expertise could easily support a picture of the region as a dangerous and violent hotbed of militant Islamist fervour, where the threat of terrorism is ever-growing and always imminent.

It seems natural to view Islam as a threat when terrorism is assumed to come out of the potential of any Muslim to become violent. So, for conventional terrorism experts, despite the minority status of a Muslim sect or group that exhorts violence in the name of its religion, its existence nevertheless implies the possibility that more and more Muslims are in danger of falling under its influence. This is because when such radical groups are seen as an endpoint on a continuum, as opposed to a distinct belief system that is altogether separate (Wright-Neville 2004; Kadir 2004; Kratochwil 2005), it follows that *any* evidence of increased religiosity in the larger mainstream group – such as increased attendance at Islamic universities or increasing numbers of Muslim women donning the hijab – is viewed with suspicion.

For example, Gunaratna (2003) suggests that as Muslims get to know more about their religion, they are more likely to become violent, asserting that

> with more news in the media about Islam, the Muslim public's awareness of Islam will increase. The number of Muslims directly supporting violence will remain very small, but there will be more support for a Muslim way of life, especially the implementation of Shariah ... furthermore, the need to wage *jihad* in support of their suffering brethren will rise among the politicized and radicalized segments of the Muslim community.
>
> (158–159)

Despite the assertion that only a small number of Muslims will support violence, Gunaratna nevertheless also claims that more awareness of Islam will lead to a desire for Shariah governance and to violent jihad among the "politicized and radicalized segments" of the general Muslim population. As mentioned, the main problem with this sort of analysis is that terrorism becomes defined in terms of

Here be monsters! 77

Islamic religiosity, rather than also in terms of the political, historical and social context of violent Islamist groups, and so *any* Muslim – by definition – is in danger of becoming "politicized and radicalized." As Sidel (2008) notes, this leads to an analytical tendency to not only equate Islam with the threat of violence, but also to equate *descriptions* of terrorist activity with *explanations* of terrorist activity in the region where "the over-arching tendency has been to assume that simply by pointing the finger at [a group like *Jemaah Islamiyah*] an adequate explanation has already been provided" (342). Coupled with a tendency to view Islam as a singular, homogenous entity, it is also common to claim the existence of strong connections among and between otherwise disparate groups.

Gunaratna (2003) suggested after 9/11 that *Al-Qaeda*, through what he calls "physical and intellectual contact" with Islamist groups in Southeast Asia, had "created a mission and a vision for the Islamists to create a caliphate comprising Malaysia, Singapore, Brunei, Indonesia, Cambodia and Mindanao" (145). To illustrate this alarming contention, he catalogues known violent acts committed by regional Islamist groups[14] alongside reports of planned but unsuccessful large-scale attacks,[15] as well as the presumption of future attacks against various "Western" targets in the region (Gunaratna 2003, 146–153). Rather than illustrate an organized regional network of terror groups linked to global Islamism, Gunaratna's (2003) "threat trajectory analysis" of what he then called a "network of Al-Qaeda's associate groups in Southeast Asia" (147) functions more like an index of who went where, who spoke to whom, who went to the same religious schools, who lived in the same country at the same time; and so on. This sort of analysis is an example of Sidel's, Hart's, and Wright-Neville's shared observation that descriptions of Islamist groups are often presented as explanations for their actions, with little demonstrated acknowledgement or "understanding of the complex inter-play of cultural, economic, political and social forces that lay behind it" (Wright-Neville 2004, 29).

A critical examination of the trends among active terrorist groups in Southeast Asia reveals that linkages with transnational terror networks, as they are understood in conventional "expert" discourses, tend to be overstated. Local, regional and transnational terror groups do have linkages to one another, but they are rarely as cohesive, as ideologically homogenous, or as well organized as they are often portrayed in the common sense of both regional terrorism expertise and media coverage.[16] For example, the fairly large scale terrorist attacks in Bali, in 2002 and 2005 respectively, were conducted by individuals and groups claiming JI affiliation. But subsequent investigations have shown that they were not carried out by anyone operating within the larger JI hierarchy nor were they executed in the well-coordinated and organized fashion that might be expected from an *Al-Qaeda*-affiliated operation (Collier 2006, 28).

However, more recent terror attacks on several police stations and "Western" targets (including a Starbucks and a Burger King) in Jakarta in 2016 were conducted by an IS-affiliated group in a more coordinated fashion than previous attacks, and Indonesian authorities believe that the masterminded behind them was Bahrun Naim, an Indonesian member of IS living in Syria.[17] The perpetrators were

78   *Here be monsters!*

also reportedly involved in a regional network with IS affiliated individuals in neighbouring Malaysia (Malik 2016).[18] So we know that there are linkages between local, regional and transnational Islamist terror (Napps and Enders 2015; Weintraub 2017), but an important question remains: to what degree?

Again, the point here is not to discount the threat of terrorism as far as it does exist but to critique the pervasive tendency within conventional terrorism expertise to assume a much higher degree of regional linkages to *Al-Qaeda* and IS than what the evidence provides for. On the flip side, there is also an emerging "Lone Wolf" discourse that allows the assumed existence of strong organizational Islamist networks to remain unchallenged when smaller scale attacks that can't be directly traced to IS or *Al-Qaeda* do occur (George 2015; Clarke and Amarasingam November 1, 2017). As Sidel has (2008) noted, if the conventional expert characterization of a tight and organized network of transnationally linked regional terror groups was accurate, we would likely have seen (and would continue to see) far more coordinated terrorist attacks in the region. And the existence of "Lone Wolf" attacks that don't fit into this mould of coordinated terror networks becomes mobilized as proof of the emergent threat posed by Islam and Muslims.

All of this contributes greatly to the powerful role of fear in War on Terror security discourses. A sense of urgency and imminent threat is created, not only by actual incidences of terrorism itself, but also by the repetitive claims by the security establishment that Southeast Asian terrorism is rising in strength and fervour. Part of this "common sense" is that Southeast Asian terror is no longer primarily about local groups with localized grievances and localized goals but has instead acquired a more threatening international dimension via a web of highly organized linkages with global Islamism (Hamilton-Hart 2005, 305). Compounding this, security practices of the state are based on the idea that the risk of an attack should always be assumed. And yet, from a logistical perspective there is very little ability to accurately predict violent outbursts by various groups or individuals who claim to be working towards an Islamist cause (Lacher 2008). This is because common sense regarding global terrorism stresses "the very certainty of its radical uncertainty" (Dillon 2007, 9). Through the War on Terror security practices of states, both material and discursive, we are persistently reminded that "we do not know when terrorists may strike, we do not know how they will strike, and we do not know with what terrifying effect … we only know for sure that they will strike" (Dillon 2007, 9).

This is key to understanding an observable move in security practices instantiated by the War on Terror – where a "toxic combination of [geopolitics and biopolitics]" (Dillon 2007, 10) means that there is a need to govern and fear the "emergent lives [that] are capable of moving out of phase with themselves and becoming other than they were" (14). This is when

> it is not what a body is that makes it biopolitically a threat, then, but what a body *might potentially become*. Pluripotent, we simply do not know, because we have not yet seen an end, to what body of any description –

Here be monsters! 79

individual, collective, cellular or machinic – might become. Hence the hypersecurity of *becoming-dangerous*.

(Dillon 2007, 24, emphasis added)

This is reinforced by the "discursive power of consecutive 'what if?' statements," that have the effect of equating potential threats with imminent ones (Loeppky 2005, 91), and services an ongoing security rationale based on pre-emption and the management of risk. Importantly, it can be useful, both for state actors and for groups who are prepared to use terrorist tactics, to claim the existence of robust organizational linkages between regional Islamism and the global networks of *Al-Qaeda* and IS. For regional state actors, we see that a variety of security practices designed to quell dissent and consolidate the power of ruling elites can be easily rationalized under the language of security (Noor, quoted in George 2015). Further, by attributing global importance and scope to localized terrorist groups, this central narrative of War on Terror security discourses becomes currency for localized terrorist groups and contributes to their ability to invoke fear through the perceived imminent likelihood of their bodies "becoming-dangerous."

Expert claim three: terrorism as pathology

As Stampnitzky (2013) has noted, the common sense of terrorism expertise can create a "politics of anti-knowledge" that necessarily precludes attempts to contextualize or situate the motivations of terrorists, because all that we really need to know about them is that they are evil. This also serves to portray the phenomenon of terrorism primarily in pathological terms, and by definition, disconnects it from social, historical, or political contexts. In terms of theorizing motivations, the emphasis is placed on their supposedly irrational or pathological nature and thus terrorism comes to be seen mainly as "a mental disease propagated by demonic preachers" (Hamilton-Hart, 2005, 317). When War on Terror security narratives paint the enemy in this way, terrorism becomes not only opaque and unknowable, but

> the terrorists – "enemy aliens" – [are] created as evildoers, savages and barbarians, cruel and inhuman, while Americans [are] constructed as innocent, decent, kind, loving, peaceful, united and heroic. The function of this language is to establish clear boundary markers between "them" and "us" – between citizens and aliens, foreign and domestic, inside and outside ... it functions to demonise and dehumanise the enemy to such an extent that any counter-violence towards them appears acceptable and proportionate.
>
> (Jackson 2005, 5)

Pathologizing terrorism serves the dual purpose of stripping humanity from the enemy, and in the process reinforcing "our" own humanity. It also prevents any serious engagement with the political, social, and historical contexts of radicalized groups.

80 *Here be monsters!*

Hence, a lot of terrorism expertise around the threat of "Islam" reinforces it as being an inherently dangerous religion and one that is necessarily incompatible with "the West." As discussed in the previous sections, this casts all Muslims as possible terrorists, by definition, and casts Islam and Muslims as fundamentally at odds with Western liberal *humanity*. Further, the use of dehumanizing "infestation" and "contagion" language that so easily creeps into security discourses imbues the Muslim *Other* with a sort of diseased agency based in irrational hatred, which is similar to something observable during the Cold War, where the Soviet *Other* became increasingly dehumanized in the discourses of American foreign policy (Campbell 1998). We also see in the governing of terror, a vacillation and tension between understanding terrorism as evil but also an illness with the "widespread medicalization of security discourse and practices from asymptomatically ill beings and preventative medicine to asymptomatically dangerous beings and preventative war" (Dillon 2007, 26). Such characterizations suggest that the prevention of terrorism requires that any potential threat of terrorism is something that needs to be contained, quarantined, or simply exterminated. At the level of politics, there is no room for engagement with the Muslim *Other* because their very existence is a threat. Such depictions of terrorism create blind spots in the analytical literature and in the proposed solutions to terrorism outlined in official policies. When the primary cause of terrorism is understood in terms of unknowable pathology, what follows is a wilful ignorance of the politics surrounding both terrorism and responses to terrorism (Collier 2006).

Relatedly, within the security narratives of the War on Terror, America is portrayed as a benevolent world leader and a victim of hatred, rather than also as a source of foreign policies that provoke reactions in different parts of the world or have consequences that continue to reverberate into the present. For example, immediately after 9/11 the funding and support that the US government and military provided to Mujahideen groups in Afghanistan in the 1980s was a taboo topic in media commentary and relevant expert literature on the origins of *Al-Qaeda*. Nor was much attention paid to the ways that US security and economic policies have negatively affected many different parts of the world (Hamilton-Hart 2005, 314; Sidel 2008). Scholarly efforts to explore the potential *causal* effects of US foreign policy in fuelling anti-American sentiment and political disenfranchisement still risks being seen as anti-American or, even worse, as sympathizing with or apologizing for terrorists (Jackson 2005). Which brings us back to the politics of "anti-knowledge" (Stampnitzky 2013).

An absolute disavowal of the idea that US foreign policy itself might play a role in the formation of political violence was notable in the official policy documents outlining the inception of the War on Terror. President George W. Bush's articulations of US security policies after 9/11 dismissed outright the possibility that terrorist groups could have been motivated by American hegemony, or by the perception of American empire. As section III of the 2006 *National Security Strategy* 2006 NSS stated, the official position of the Bush administration was that Americans "… must be clear-eyed about what does and does not give rise to terrorism" (The White House March 12, 2006, 9). The 2006 NSS clearly specified that terrorism was not to be "explained" by global poverty; by US policies in Iraq; or by the US' unwavering support of Israel in the context of Arab–Israeli relations and the Palestinian question. The 2006 NSS also strongly denied the possibility that the ongoing War on Terror, and the security practices undertaken in its name, may itself be contributing to ongoing violence and conflict, because

> terrorism is not simply a response to our efforts to prevent terror attacks. The al-Qaida [*sic*] network targeted the United States long before the United States targeted al-Qaida. Indeed, the terrorists are emboldened more by perceptions of weakness than by demonstrations of resolve. Terrorists lure recruits by telling them that we are decadent and easily intimidated and will retreat if attacked.
>
> (The White House March 12, 2006, 10)

Among the things that *do* cause terrorism, according to the 2006 NSS, are a lack of democratic governments; a victimology in "the Muslim world" of "blaming others for problems"; political rhetoric that is bent on "keeping old wounds fresh and raw"; and, of course, religious ideologies and beliefs that justify the murder of innocents (The White House March 12, 2006).

In other words, the primary policy literature of the War on Terror contends that the causes of terrorism, and explanations for it, are completely exogenous to the US and its foreign policies. Furthermore, meaningful attempts to understand the historical and political complaints that inform political violence become bracketed out and excluded from the security narratives of the War on Terror. That is because terrorist violence is not seen as political violence. It is seen as an irrational form of violence borne of diseased minds, hatred, and evil which – by definition – can never be understood. Those that may be prone to this evil must be met with suspicion and destruction. In place of deeper engagements with the politics of terror, the presiding force informing the security practices of the War on Terror is, quite simply, fear of the contingent threat posed by life. Hence, we can observe that "the more effort that is put into governing terror, the more terror comes to govern the governors" (Dillon 2007, 8).

Conclusion – the making of monsters

Immediately after 9/11 there was an "intensifying US involvement in Southeast Asia that reflect[ed] a somewhat hysterical tone ... about the strength and scope of the terrorist threat there" (Gershman 2002, 61). This contributed to an obfuscation of a variety of social and political issues that local populations continue to grapple with, sometimes in opposition to their own governments. Within this context, this chapter scrutinized the "common sense" understanding of the relationships between terrorism and political Islam in the region and challenged three commonly made expert claims that have emerged out of post-9/11 CT and CVE security narratives. First, this chapter showed that not all forms of political

82   *Here be monsters!*

Islam necessarily represent an imminent threat of terrorism. The tendency to conflate political Islam with terrorism paints a simplistically homogenous and ominous picture of what is actually a very complex and rich terrain of religion and politics in Southeast Asia. Although regional Islamist groups who use terrorism do exist, the use of mass casualty violence is overwhelmingly rejected by the majority of Southeast Asian Muslims, regardless if their levels of religiosity or the degree to which their faith is politicized.

Second, this chapter showed that despite the dire predictions made about Southeast Asia immediately after 9/11, we have yet to see the emergence of a regionally unified violent Islamist identity with robust linkages to a transnational network of global Islamism. Instead, the terrorist incidents that do occur take on a Rorschach-like quality of reflecting pre-existing assumptions held about the relationships between Islam and terrorism, whatever they may be. Third, this chapter put into question the claim that terrorist violence in the region is best understood primarily as irrational and evil behaviour linked to particularistic religious ideas. Rather, the tendency to pathologize terrorism is part of an increasingly hegemonic security discourse that removes the political agency from terrorism and in doing so, allows for an apolitical reading of terrorism where the "generative principle" of the formation of security is contingency and fear (Dillon 2007, 9). Governing terror then, becomes an impossible effort to govern the unknown, where the unknown is always dangerous, and its danger is always imminent.

Contesting each of these claims from a critical security perspective introduced the idea that conventional expertise around counter-terrorism and countering violence and extremism in Southeast Asia can actually lead to increasing insecurity. This is because "the more dangerous and uncertain terrorism becomes, the more extreme the modes of governance that arise in response" (Stampnitzky 2013, 108). Much of the existing expertise in the areas of CT and CVE in Southeast Asia renders a vast territory and its people as a contingent, emergent threat, homogenously transformed into epistemic objects by the knowledges that seek to govern their potential for becoming dangerous. As a result, large populations of people who pose no specific threat are themselves rendered insecure through the risk management policies and pre-emptive security practices of the state (Lacher 2008). The "monsters" that lurk in the unknown become monsters, in part, because they are unknown. The very act of attempting to classify and name them through a risk mitigation lens that necessarily sees the unknown as dangerous, turns monitor lizards into fire breathing dragons, deep-water pacific squid into ship-eating sea leviathans, unfamiliar indigenous tribes into fierce cannibals, and a variety of religious political movements that reject Western forms of secularism into evil, irrational terrorists.

Notes

1 www.geog.ucsb.edu/events/department-news/891/inhuman-geography-here-there-be-dragons/.
2 http://cartographic-images.net/Cartographic_Images/237_The_Borgia_World_Map.html.

Here be monsters! 83

3 Susan Strange's (1982) well known piece "Cave! Hic Dragones: A Critique of Regime Analysis" comes to mind with this phrase. Notably, it was so called because the article was meant to warn readers of the unknown "dragons" that we must "watch out for" (479), which are lurking in the study of regimes.

4 For example, see Beeson (2007); Burke and McDonald (2007); Burke (2003); Capie (2004); Croft (2006); Foot (2005); Gershman (2002); Goh (2008); Hamilton-Hart (2005, 2009); Higgott (2004); Jackson (2005, 2006, 2007a, 2007b, 2007c, 2011); Jarvis (2008); Jervis (2005); Mueller (2006); Noor (2006); Sidel (2008); Wright-Neville (2004); Zulaika (2009).

5 The scare-quotes that pepper this paragraph are used self-consciously. They are meant to connote the contestability of these terms and concepts.

6 There is a comprehensive research program and academic journal specifically dedicated to this very task: Routledge's "Critical Studies on Terrorism" journal, which was founded in 2008.

7 Counter-terrorism (CT) generally refers to policies operationalized at the governmental, military and law enforcement agency levels, whereas countering violence and extremism (CVE) generally refers to policies that are operationalized as the community level. This is the difference between say, state surveillance of potential terrorist cells (CT) versus community outreach under something like the UK's Prevent policies to counsel young people who have shown signs of radical Islamism (CVE).

8 In the Canadian context, for example, terrorism experts like Amarasingam (2017) manage to produce nuanced, sophisticated, and empirically robust work and commentary on CT and CVE based on a combination of field intelligence, high level access to both government and terror networks, academic prowess, and a healthy scepticism of the politicized nature of his field.

9 Abuza's faculty profile, Simmons College Department of Political Science and International Relations, www.simmons.edu/undergraduate/academics/departments/political-science/faculty/abuza.php.

10 See Abuza 2002, 2003a, 2003b, 2003c, 2005, 2006, 2007a, 2007b, 2009a, 2009b, 2010, 2011, 2012a, 2012b, 2015a, 2015b, 2016a, 2016b, and his frequent contributions to the Jamestown Foundation's publication, *Terrorism Monitor*.

11 There have been several attacks and bombings against "Western" targets in Indonesia by JI including attacks on the Jakarta Airport (2003), Bali again (2005), the Marriot and Ritz-Carlton hotels in Jakarta (2009). IS has claimed responsibility for attacks on police and "Western" targets in Jakarta in both 2016 and 2017 as well. In the Philippines and Thailand, longstanding separatist violence by Muslim groups have continued to take place in the southern districts of both countries.

12 In contrast, North America and Western Europe have together been the source of over 5,200 foreign fighters to Syria and Iraq (Barrett *et al*. 2016).

13 To be very clear, this is not meant to be an *ad hominim* indictment against Abuza or Hamid or any other regional terrorism expert, nor is it meant to imply that any research or analyses has been conducted in bad faith. Rather, it is meant to show how even empirical evidence and quantitative data regarding political Islam in the region can take on a sort of Rorschach-like quality, reflecting and reinforcing the pre-existing ideas of those interpreting the information. As expressed in Chapter 2, all social and political knowledge is inter-subjective and necessarily situated. What makes some of the expert work on regional terrorism frustrating to read is not so much that it lacks objectivity or positivist scientific rigor. Rather, it is that it often *commands authority on the very basis* of its supposed objectivity and positivist rigor – when, in fact, a remarkable amount of inter-subjective understanding and interpretive analysis informs this area of expertise. Here again, we see the folly of a "strong ontology" approach to knowledge production.

14 Gunaratna mentions the 2002 Bali and Marriott bombings; the 1994 bombing of a Philippine Airlines flight to Tokyo, which killed one and injured 11 passengers; as

84 *Here be monsters!*

well as a number of smaller-scale church bombings, kidnappings in Indonesia and elsewhere by a variety of disparate groups.

15 Gunaratna points to disrupted plans to assassinate Pope John Paul II and President Clinton during their visits to the region; as well as disrupted plans to execute a simultaneous bombing of 11 airliners in the Asia Pacific in 1995. All three of these plans were meant to have happened well before 9/11 and were not the plans of a single terrorist group.

16 As discussed by Beeson 2007; Collier 2006; Gershman 2002; Hamilton-Hart 2005; Jackson 2005; Sidel 2008; Wright-Neville 2004; Barrett *et al.* 2016; George 2015; Chan 2018.

17 Jakarta attacks: Profile of suspect Bahrun Naim, BBC News (January 14, 2016) www.bbc.com/news/world-asia-35316915.

18 www.abc.net.au/news/2016-01-27/jakarta-terror-attack-and-malaysia-suspect-link/7116136.

References

Abuza, Zachary. 2002. Tentacles of terror: Al-Qaeda's Southeast Asian network. *Contemporary Southeast Asia* 24(3)(December): 427–465.

Abuza, Zachary. 2003a. *Militant Islam in Southeast Asia: Crucible of terror.* Boulder, CO: Lynne Rienner.

Abuza, Zachary. 2003b. Funding terrorism in Southeast Asia: The financial network of Al-Qaeda and Jemaah Islamiya. *Contemporary Southeast Asia* 25(2)(August): 169–199.

Abuza, Zachary. 2003c. The war on terrorism in Southeast Asia. *Strategic Asia* 4: 321–363.

Abuza, Zachary. 2005. The Moro Islamic Liberation Front at 20: State of the revolution. *Studies in Conflict and Terrorism* 28: 453–479.

Abuza, Zachary. 2006. *Political Islam and violence in Indonesia.* London: Routledge.

Abuza, Zachary. 2007a. The social organization of terror in Southeast Asia: The case of Jemaah Islamiyah. In Thomas J. Biersteker and Sue E. Eckert (Eds) *Countering the financing of terrorism.* London: Routledge, pp. 79–106.

Abuza, Zachary. 2007b. The role of foreign trainers in southern Thailand's insurgency. *Terrorism Monitor* 5(11): 7.

Abuza, Zachary. 2010. Indonesian counter-terrorism: The great leap forward. *Terrorism Monitor* 8(2): 6–8.

Abuza, Zachary. 2011. *The ongoing insurgency in Southern Thailand: Trends in violence, counterinsurgency operations, and the impact of national politics (no. 6).* Washington, DC: National Defense University Press.

Abuza, Zachary. 2012a. The Southern Thailand insurgency in the wake of the March 2012 bombings. *CTC Sentinel* 5(6).

Abuza, Zachary. 2012b. Philippines: Internal and external security challenges. *Australian Strategic Policy Institute.*

Abuza, Zachary. 2015a. The smoldering Thai insurgency. *CTC Sentinel* 8(6): 8–11.

Abuza, Zachary 2015b. Joining the new caravan: ISIS and the regeneration of terrorism in Southeast Asia. *Strategic Studies Institute* (25)(June).

Abuza, Zachary. 2016a. The strategic and tactical implications of the Islamic State on Southeast Asia's militant groups. *Georgetown Journal of Asian Affairs* 3(1): 20–30.

Abuza, Zachary. 2016b. Beyond bombings: The Islamic state in Southeast Asia. *The Diplomat.*

Acharya, Amitav and Richard Stubbs. 2006. Theorizing Southeast Asian relations: An introduction. *The Pacific Review* 19(2): 125–134.

Here be monsters! 85

Allen, Judy and Jeanne Griffiths. 1979. *The book of the dragon*. London: Chartwell Books.

Aslam, M.M. 2009. The thirteen radical groups: Preliminary research in understanding the evolution of militancy in Malaysia. *JATI: Journal of Southeast Asian Studies* 14: 145–161.

Athyal, Jesudas (Ed.). 2015. *Religion in Southeast Asia: An encyclopedia of faiths and cultures*. Santa Barbara: ABC-CLIO.

Barber, Benjamin. 1992. *Jihad vs McWorld*. New York: Random House.

Barrett, Richard, Jack Berger, Lila Ghosh, Daniel Schoenfeld, Mohamed el Shawesh, Patrick M. Skinner, Susan Sim, and Ali Soufan. 2016. *Foreign fighters: An updated assessment of the flow of foreign fighters into Syria and Iraq*. New York: The Soufan Group.

Beeson, Mark. 2007. *Bush and Asia: America's evolving relations with East Asia*. London: Routledge.

Bruinessen, Martin van. 2015. Ghazwul Fikri or Arabization? Indonesian Muslim responses to globalization. In Ken Miichi and Omar Farouk (Eds) *Southeast Asian Muslims in the era of globalization*. Basingstoke: Palgrave Macmillan, pp. 61–85.

Burke, Anthony and Matt McDonald. 2007. *Critical security in the Asia-Pacific*. Manchester: Manchester University Press.

Burke, Jason. 2003. *Al-Qaeda, casting a shadow of terror*. London: I. B. Tauris.

Campbell, David. 1998. *Writing security: US Foreign policy and the politics of identity*. Manchester: Manchester University Press.

Capie, David. 2004. Between a hegemon and a hard place: The "war on terror" and US–Southeast Asian relations. *The Pacific Review* 17(2): 223–248.

Chan, Nicholas. 2018. The Malaysian "Islamic" state versus the Islamic State (IS): Evolving definitions of "terror" in an "Islamising" nation-state. *Critical Studies on Terrorism*: 1–23.

Clarke, Colin P. and Amarnath Amarasingam. November 1, 2017. Terrorism fatigue: ISIS attacks are losing their ability to terrify. Slate.com.

Cohn, Carol. 1987. Sex and death in the rational world of defence intellectuals. *Signs: Journal of Women in Culture and Society* 12(4): 687–718.

Collier, Kit. 2006. Terrorism: Evolving regional alliances and state failure in Mindanao. In Daljit Singh and Lorraine C. Salazar (Eds) *Southeast Asian affairs*. Singapore: ISEAS, pp. 26–38.

Cotton, James. 2003. Southeast Asia after 11 September. *Terrorism and Political Violence* 15(1): 148–170.

Cox, Robert. 1981. Social forces, states and world orders: Beyond international relations theory. *Millennium* 10(2): 126–155.

Croft, Stuart. 2006. *Culture, crisis and America's war on terror*. New York: Cambridge University Press.

Cruz-De Castro, Renato. 2004. Addressing international terrorism in Southeast Asia: A matter of strategic or functional approach? *Contemporary Southeast Asia* 26(2): 193–217.

da Costa, B.F. 1879. The Lenox globe. *The Magazine of American History* 3(9): 529–540.

Dillon, Michael. 2007. Governing terror: The state of emergency of biopolitical emergence. *International Political Sociology* 1(1): 7–28.

Foot, R., 2005. Collateral damage: Human rights consequences of counterterrorist action in the Asia-Pacific. *International Affairs* 81(2): 411–425.

86 *Here be monsters!*

George, Cherian. 2015. Islamic radicalisation: Questioning the security lens. *Media Asia* 42(1–2): 5–20.

George, Wilma. 1969. *Animals and maps*. Berkeley, CA: University of California Press.

Gershman, John. 2002. Is Southeast Asia the second front? *Foreign Affairs* 81(4): 60–74.

Goh, Evelyn. 2008. Great powers and hierarchical order in Southeast Asia: Analyzing regional security strategies. *International Security* 32(3): 113–157.

Gunaratna, Rohan (Ed.). 2003. *Terrorism in the Asia-Pacific: Threat and response.* Singapore: Eastern Universities Press.

Gunning, Jereon. 2007a. A case for critical terrorism studies? *Government and Opposition* 42(3): 363–393.

Gunning, Jereon. 2007b. Babies and bathwaters: Reflecting on the pitfalls of critical terrorism studies. *European Political Science* 6(3): 236–243.

Gusterson, Hugh. 1999. Missing the end of the Cold War in international security. In Jutta Weldes, Mark Laffey, Hugh Gusterson, and Raymond Duvall (Eds) *Cultures of insecurity: States, communities, and the production of danger*. Minneapolis, MN: University of Minnesota Press, pp. 319–345.

Hamid, A. F. A. 2016. *ISIS in Southeast Asia: Internalized wahhabism is a major factor. ISEAS perspective, 16*. Singapore: Yusof Ishak Institute.

Hamilton-Hart, Natasha. 2005. Terrorism in Southeast Asia: Expert analysis, myopia and fantasy. *The Pacific Review* 18(3): 303–325.

Hamilton-Hart, Natasha. 2009. War and other insecurities in East Asia: What the security studies field does and does not tell us. *The Pacific Review* 22(1): 49–71.

Hamilton-Hart, Natasha. 2012. *Hard interests, soft illusions: Southeast Asia and American power*. Ithaca, NY: Cornell University Press.

Higgott, Richard. 2004. After neoliberal globalization: The "securitization" of US foreign economic policy in East Asia. *Critical Asian Studies* 36(3): 425–444.

Hugh, Gary. 2003. Analyse this: Whenever a comment has been needed about Al-Qaeda or terrorism, Rohan Gunaratna has been there to supply it. Who is he? *The Age, Australia* July 20. www.theage.com.au/articles/2003/07/20/1058545648013.html.

Huntington, Samuel. 1993. The clash of civilizations? *Foreign Affairs* 72(3): 22–49.

Jackson, Richard. 2005. *Writing the War on Terrorism: Language politics and counter-terrorism*. New York: Manchester University Press.

Jackson, Richard. 2006. Genealogy, ideology, and counter-terrorism: Writing wars on terrorism from Ronald Reagan to George W. Bush Jr. *Studies in Language & Capitalism* 1(1): 163–193.

Jackson, Richard. 2007a. Constructing enemies: "Islamic terrorism" in political and academic discourse. *Government and Opposition* 42(3): 394–426.

Jackson, Richard. 2007b. Symposium: Introduction: The case for critical terrorism studies. *European Political Science* 6(3): 225–227.

Jackson, Richard. 2007c. The core commitments of critical terrorism studies. *European Political Science* 6(3): 244–251.

Jackson, Richard. 2011. Culture, identity and hegemony: Continuity and (the lack of) change in US counter-terrorism policy from Bush to Obama. *International Politics* 48(2/3): 390–411.

Jarvis, L. 2008. Times of terror: Writing temporality into the war on terror. *Critical Studies on Terrorism* 1(2): 245–262.

Jayasankaran, S. 2002. Malaysia – Lost ground: The rise of the Islamic opposition may have been stunted by world events and messy politics. *Far Eastern Economic Review* 19(March 21).

Jervis, Robert. 2005. Understanding the Bush Doctrine. In G. John Ikenberry (Ed.) *American foreign policy: Theoretical essay*. New York: Longman, pp. 576–599.

Kadir, Suzaina. 2004. Mapping Muslim politics in Southeast Asia after September 11. *The Pacific Review* 17(2): 199–222.

Kratochwil, Friedrich. 2005. Religion in (inter)national politics: On the heuristics of identities, structures, and agents. *Alternatives* 30: 113–140.

Lacher, Wolfram. 2008. Actually existing security: The political economy of the Saharan threat. *Security Dialogue* 39(4): 383–405.

Leander, A. 2005. The power to construct international security: On the significance of private military companies. *Millennium – Journal of International Studies* 33(3): 803–826.

Lewis, Bernard. 1990. The roots of Muslim rage. *The Atlantic Monthly* 266(3): 47–60.

Loeppky, Rodney. 2005. "Biomania" and US foreign policy. *Millennium* 34(1): 85–113.

Lum, Cynthia, Leslie W. Kennedy, and Alison Sherley. 2006. Are counter-terrorism strategies effective? The results of the Campbell systematic review on counter-terrorism evaluation research. *Journal of Experimental Criminology* 2(4): 489–516.

Malik, Maszlee. 2016. ISIS in Malaysia: A case study. Discussion Paper for ISEAS Yusof Ishak Institute Regional Outlook Forum 2016, January 12, 2016, Shangri-La Hotel Singapore.

McKenna, Tom. 2002. Saints, scholars and the idealized past in Philippines Muslim separatism. *The Pacific Review* 15(4): 539–553.

Mueller, John. 2006. *Overblown: How politicians and the terrorism industry inflate national security threats and why we believe them*. New York: Simon and Schuster.

Mustapha, Jennifer. 2011. Threat construction in the Bush administration's post-9/11 foreign policy: (Critical) security implications for Southeast Asia. *The Pacific Review* 24(4): 487–504.

Napps, Cameron and Walter Enders. 2015. A regional investigation of the interrelationships between domestic and transnational terrorism: A time series analysis. *Defence and Peace Economics* 26(2): 133–151.

Noor, Farish. 2003. Blood, sweat and jihad: The radicalization of the political discourse of the Pan-Malaysian Islamic Party (PAS) from 1982 onwards. *Contemporary Southeast Asia* 25(2): 200–232.

Noor, Farish. 2006. How Washington's "War on Terror" became everyone's: Islamophobia and the impact of September 11 on the political terrain of South and Southeast Asia. *Human Architecture: Journal of the Sociology of Self-Knowledge* 5(1): 29–50.

Poushter, Jacob. 2015. In nations with significant Muslim populations, much disdain for ISIS, Pew Research Center Factank, November 17. www.pewresearch.org/factank/2015/11/17/in-nations-with-significant-muslim-populations-much-disdain-for-isis/.

Saat, Norshahril. 2016. Terrorism should not be viewed through religious lenses. TODAY Online January 15. www.todayonline.com/commentary/terrorism-should-not-be-viewed-through-religious-lenses.

Said, Edward. 1978. *Orientalism: Western representations of the Orient*. New York: Pantheon.

Sidel, John. 2007. Book review of "Political Islam and Violence in Indonesia" by Zachary Abuza. *Journal of Islamic Studies* 18(3): 449–452.

Sidel, John. 2008. The Islamist threat in South East Asia: Much ado about nothing? *Asian Affairs* 39(3): 339–351.

Stampnitzky, L. 2013. *Disciplining terror: How experts invented "terrorism."* Cambridge: Cambridge University Press.

88   *Here be monsters!*

Strange, Susan. 1982. Cave! Hic dragones: A critique of regime analysis. *International Organization* 36(2): 479–496.

The White House. March 12, 2006. *National Security Strategy*. Washington DC: The White House.

Weintraub, Jonathan. 2017. *Factors influencing the movement of Southeast Asian fighters to ISIS: A comparison of Indonesia and Malaysia*. Doctoral dissertation: Cornell University.

Wright-Neville, David. 2004. Dangerous dynamics: Activists, militants and terrorists in Southeast Asia. *The Pacific Review* 17(1): 27–46.

Zulaika, Joseba. 2009. *Terrorism: The self-fulfilling prophecy*. Chicago, IL: The University of Chicago Press.

5 Irruptions of the War on Terror in Southeast Asia

Gender, sovereignty, and constructions of insecurity

After 9/11 there was a noticeable uptick in the regional US military presence; increased security collaboration with key regional state actors; and a discursive re-framing of US relations in Asia more generally. These developments were heavily influenced by the Bush administration's increasing pre-occupation with terrorism, and other important political and economic interests were pushed down the priority list in short order. The previous chapter interrogated some of the common claims made by conventional counter-terrorism and CVE expertise in Southeast Asia and looked at how those claims remain central to War on Terror security discourses into the present. This chapter considers some of the *irruptions* (Aradau and Van Munster 2007) that the War on Terror and its security narratives have had for and on the region. In terms of the relevance of a weak ontology approach, "seeing" these irruptions requires the use of critical security methods of critique. Broadly speaking, it is through critical feminist and post-structuralist methods that we are able to see that the state itself can be a source of, and site of, insecurity within the context of the War on Terror. These approaches allow us to engage with contingent sets of circumstances, forms of state power, and security logics without essentializing any of them.

Utilizing critical feminist and post-structuralist methods of analysis, this chapter first asks after the gendered implications of regional security politics in Southeast Asia in the context of the ongoing War on Terror. After 9/11 there was a concerted re-establishment of a regional US military presence as well as a discursive re-framing of US relations in Asia more generally. The resulting security narratives allowed for significant shifts to occur in the security logics and practices of governing regimes in the region. This contributed to an escalation of gendered insecurities around the US military architecture; re-configurations of post-colonial constructions of national identity; and a discernible rise in state repression due to the coupling of counter-terror security policies with statist notions of "national resilience." The War on Terror itself is not unique in creating these insecurities but is notable in this respect because it provided a felicitous scenario for a renewed continuation of American imperial formations in Southeast Asia. Further, these heightened gendered and post-colonial insecurities intersect with and bring forth complex questions relating to expressions of sovereignty and identity in the region.

90 *Gender, sovereignty, and insecurity*

First, this chapter examines the impacts of the renewed US military presence in Southeast Asia after 9/11, and particularly in the Philippines. The advent of the War on Terror brought with it a reversal of what had been, up until that point, a growing trend of US military withdrawal from the region. As a result of this reversal, the War on Terror ended up re-entrenching gendered insecurities experienced by populations living around US military bases. It also reignited complex debates and questions around national sovereignties and identities as the increased US military presence triggered a variety of post-colonial anxieties that contributed to the steady rise in populist nationalism in the country, culminating in the 2016 election of Philippine President Rodrigo Duterte. This chapter also examines the impact of rising anti-American sentiment resulting from the War on Terror, and the ways that it has contributed to terrorist violence aimed at "Western" targets in the region. It demonstrates how the War on Terror security narratives have become a convenient discourse under which local governments clamp down on political opposition. In other words, this chapter is concerned with the ways that local insecurities became amplified under War on Terror discourses that triggered more US military presence in the region and provided a convenient discourse now mobilized by local regimes against their own populations under the guise of strong state "national resilience."

Gendered insecurities

As outlined in Chapter 3, the "hub and spokes" model of US East Asian security policy remained largely in place after 9/11. This meant that there was a continued political commitment to a model of regional stability based on state-to-state bilateral security arrangements between the US and regional state actors. This was true from the American perspective, as well as from the perspectives of regional state actors who continued to "look to Washington to play a stabilizing role in regional security" (Capie 2004, 24; see also Cruz De Castro 2004). From a realist, state-centric perspective, this meant that nothing much changed in the larger East Asian regional security architecture after 9/11. However, important changes were, in fact, occurring, most notably at the bilateral level in the area of US military relations with key Southeast Asian states identified as the "second front" in the War on Terror. This was especially so in the Philippines and to a lesser degree in Indonesia, Singapore, Malaysia, and Thailand (Cruz De Castro 2004; Velasco 2015).

Under the Clinton administration, the force structure of US military defence strategy had already shifted away from Cold War manifestations towards more of an emphasis on "lightly armed rapid reaction forces and a reappraisal of the world wide system of US bases" (Camroux and Okfen 2004, 166). This was in keeping with the so-called Revolution in Military Affairs or RMA, and the attention paid to the emergence of "new threats" in the international system like sub-state warfare and terrorism. Under Bush however, East Asia saw a "gradual repositioning of forces" even before 9/11, with no major new base development but a definite increase in "virtual bases" through joint military activity (Camroux

Gender, sovereignty, and insecurity 91

and Okfen 2004, 166), and the provision of targeted military aid seen to benefit efforts to combat terrorism in the region (Velasco 2015).

While the election of the Bush administration ushered in an era of US foreign policy that tended more generally to use "militarization as [its] preponderant policy tool" (Pempel 2008a, 557), it was the perceived threat of terrorism that ultimately led to the noticeable uptick in American military presence in Southeast Asia after 9/11 (Cruz De Castro 2004). Importantly, 9/11 did not suddenly introduce the threat of terrorism into Southeast Asia, and Washington's renewed interest in terrorism in the region had been preceded by long held domestic and regional concerns. Malaysia (then Malaya) and Singapore have both had a lengthy history with terrorism (Cruz De Castro 2004; Velasco 2015; Chan 2018), dating as far back as the 1940s during the Malayan Emergency (1946–1960), where British Commonwealth forces and local law enforcement engaged in counter-insurgency against the guerrilla tactics of the Malayan National Liberation Army (MNLA), which was the militant wing of the Malayan Communist Party). Malaya and Singapore had also faced low-intensity warfare and terror during the *Konfrontasi* with Indonesia in the 1960s. Singaporean civilians were the victims of terrorism when Japan's Red Army hijacked a passenger ferry in 1974 (Tan 2003). Looking even further back, the archipelago that went on to become the Philippines has seen violent unrest among secessionist Muslim populations in the South since the Spanish occupation in the 1500s (Rogers 2004). Central governing authorities in Thailand and Indonesia have also faced the challenges of various secessionist movements, many of whom have used guerrilla and terrorist tactics at different points in history and some of which continue to do so into the present (Cruz De Castro 2004; Velasco 2015).

In other words, a variety of different groups for a variety of different aims and goals have used terrorism in Southeast Asia in a variety of different historical contexts. The context of a long and varied history of regional terrorism is important because it provides a reference point for any understanding of how so-called "Islamist" terrorism fits into the regional security picture after 9/11 (Chan 2018). It also allows us to better appreciate how the problem of terrorism in Southeast Asia has been re-framed within the context of the War on Terror and continues to be a notable factor in understanding American relations with regional state actors (Jackson 2011; Bentley and Holland 2017). This, in spite of the fact that "most narratives of Southeast Asia's place in the War on Terror begin with the arrests of individuals in Singapore, Malaysia and the Philippines suspected of links with Al-Qaeda" (Cotton 2003, 148). In the immediate aftermath of 9/11 there were a number of confirmed arrests and detentions of suspected terrorists who were charged with having links to Osama bin Laden and *Al-Qaeda*. These included 25 alleged members of *Kumpulan Mujahidin Malaysia* (KMM) in Malaysia; 15 alleged members of *Jemaah Islamiyah* (JI) in Singapore;[1] several Arab nationals alleged to be a terrorist sleeper cell in the Philippines; 25 foreign nationals under suspicion of terrorism in Thailand; and in September of 2002, the further arrests of 19 suspected members of JI in Singapore (Chan 2018).

92 *Gender, sovereignty, and insecurity*

Indeed, the conventional security focus tends to be on these specific instances and groups, and conventional terrorism experts such as those reviewed in Chapter 4 tend to speak of terrorism in the region solely in terms of a post-9/11 War on Terror context and in terms of Islamist threats to American and Western interests. To the extent that pre-9/11 terrorist activity is considered in security analyses (as in the case of the arrests in June 2001 of 25 alleged members of KMM in Malaysia), it tends to serve the teleological purpose of "proving" that Southeast Asian Islamists would necessarily become part of a wider *Al-Qaeda –* and now IS – network and agenda (see Abuza 2005; Gunaratna 2003; Liow 2015; Arianti and Singh 2015; Parameswaran 2015). Hence, there is forgetfulness and erasure of the uniquely situated circumstances and histories of the various non-state groups that use violence in the region.

At the same time, the security narratives of the War on Terror have contributed to a general re-framing of state responses to terrorism in Southeast Asia, and of bilateral security and military relations between local governments and Washington. Prior to 9/11, terrorism in the region was largely viewed as a crime rather than an act of war, and one that required a law-enforcement response rather than a state security and/or military one (Rogers 2004, 16). Further, regional governments were performatively chided by previous US administrations for using anti-democratic practices in the face of anti-government opposition – Islamist or otherwise. For example, in 1998 US Vice President Al Gore drew ire from regional observers when at the APEC summit in Kuala Lumpur he publicly denounced the Malaysian government's treatment of then former Deputy Prime Minister Anwar Ibrahim. At particular issue was Anwar Ibrahim's extra-judicial detention under the draconian measures of the Malaysian Internal Security Act (ISA), which is the same act that was subsequently applauded by the Bush administration as an effective counter-terrorism tool after 9/11 (Noor 2003).[2] The 1990s also saw wide-spread criticism from the West of what has sometimes been called the "Singapore School" of soft-authoritarianism, which prioritizes economic growth and the maintenance of domestic political order over the civil and human rights of individuals (Noor 2006). With this in mind, it is interesting to note the changes in US–Southeast Asian military and security relations after 9/11, and in particular the boosted America military presence in the region (Cruz De Castro 2004).

US–Philippines military relations

In the case of the increasing US military presence in Southeast Asia, a focus on the Philippines is warranted in this respect. The US–Philippines military relationship underwent a remarkable renaissance as a result of the post-9/11 moment. It is a relationship that continued to strengthen well into the Obama administration, bringing with it stories of security and sovereignty that relate to constructions of post-colonial national identity and the profoundly gendered implications of militarization. *Operation Enduring Freedom*, the defence "stability and support" collaboration between the US armed forces and the armed forces of the

Gender, sovereignty, and insecurity 93

Philippines, began in 2002 (Swain 2010) until its official end in 2015. It was a sustained collaboration and quite the accomplishment considering the fraught history between the Philippines and its former colonizer, the substantial cooling of US–Philippine relations in the 1990s, as well as considering the fact that under the Philippine constitution there are stringent prohibitions against US military operations on Philippine soil (Capie 2004; Camroux and Okfen 2004; Rogers 2004; Swain 2010; Cruz De Castro 2004; Velasco 2015). Notably, the closure of the Clark and Subic US military bases in 1991 and 1992 respectively, and the subsequent withdrawal of American troops and American military aid from the Philippines once made a close collaboration like *Operation Enduring Freedom* seem highly unlikely (Velasco 2015).

It was significant then, that in January 2002, the Bush administration deployed 660 US troops and personnel to the Mindanao region in the southern Philippines with the full support of the Philippine Senate (Rogers 2004). The US Special Operations Command Pacific formed this *Joint Operations Task Force-510* to assist the 4,000 members of the local military in hostage rescue and counter-terrorist operations against *Abu Sayyaf*, a militant Islamist separatist group operating out of Jolo and Basilan (Swain 2010). *Abu Sayyaf* had recently escalated its hostage-taking operations and terrorist activity in the area, including the kidnapping of 21 hostages, 10 of whom were Western tourists, from a Malaysian resort on the island of Sipadan. After the initial support operation was launched, the Bush administration went on to provide over US$100 million in military and development aid to the Philippines (Capie 2004; Cruz De Castro 2004), in contrast to the relatively paltry US$1 million or so a year that had been directed towards the country's armed forces during the 1990s (Rogers 2004; Cruz De Castro 2004; Simbulan 2010; Swain 2010; Winter 2011). This included, specifically, US$29.5 million in "Excess Defense Articles" in the form of "15000 M-16A1 rifles, 35 M35 trucks, three night capable UH-1 helicopters, a Cyclone Class patrol boat and … 10 million USD in Anti-Terrorist Assistance" (Cruz De Castro 2004, 202).

The renewed security friendship between the US and the Philippines became well established within months after this first of many post-9/11 "joint operations task force" exercises, euphemistically called *Balikatan* ("shoulder to shoulder") operations in efforts to assuage domestic concerns around US forces re-establishing military bases and putting combat troops on the ground, both of which contravene the constitution of the Philippines and in the eyes of many critics, represented a threat to national sovereignty (Simbulan 2010; Winter 2011; Velasco 2015). Hence, the joint exercises, training, and the provision of military aid in combating terrorism in the Southern Philippines were all carefully framed as cooperation between two allies in the War on Terror rather than as an American infringement against Philippine sovereignty (Swain 2010; Velasco 2015). As additional reinforcement of the renewed friendship, President Bush formally addressed the Philippine Congress on October 18, 2003 and stated that their countries were "bound by the strongest ties two nations can share" (Rogers 2004, 15), going on to declare the Philippines a "major Non-NATO Ally"

94   *Gender, sovereignty, and insecurity*

(Swain 2010, 7). This was an important signal that the Philippines had become the US' key Southeast Asian military ally in the War on Terror, and the remarkable longevity of *Operation Enduring Freedom* until its official end in 2015 indicated how the War on Terror was an important catalyst for the re-kindling of their bilateral military relationship.[3]

In order to appreciate the significance of how the War on Terror revitalized the US–Philippine security relationship, it is important to place these developments within a larger historical context. In doing so, it becomes possible to see the peculiar opportunity presented by 9/11 and the War on Terror, especially considering the degree to which (opposition to) American military presence in the Republic has long been intimately linked to expressions of Philippine national identity and sovereignty (Winter 2011; Velasco 2015). The Clark and Subic Bay Naval Bases were the first and second largest overseas US military installations during their time and Washington has long-held strategic interests in maintaining a military presence in the Philippines. The Subic Bay Naval Base, in particular, played a key role in several notable military operations in modern US history, including the Spanish–American War, World War I, World War II, the Korean War and the Vietnam War (Anderson 2006). Some might argue that for Americans there is an added emotional attachment to the Philippines due to the central role that it played in one of the bloodiest theatres of World War II. Indeed, after the fall of the Philippines to the Japanese in 1941, General MacArthur made the recapturing of the Philippines in 1944 one of the central strategic objectives of the US military operations in the Pacific, famously uttering the promise "I shall return!" (Masuda 2012).

The protection of shipping routes along the Pacific Rim of Asia is also of great logistical benefit to US interests – both in security and trade. And the ongoing diplomatic, economic, and security challenges posed by China and North Korea further reinforce the need felt by Washington to secure a physical presence in the strategically favourable conditions of the Philippine islands. But US military presence in the archipelago in the late twentieth century became eroded by a growing sense within the Philippines that the presence of US military bases in the republic was an affront to national sovereignty, leading ultimately to the formal expulsion of the US military in the early 1990s (Felix 2005; Velasco 2015). Prior to this, American military presence in the Philippines can be traced all the way back to the US capture of the islands from Spain during the Spanish–American War in 1898 (Rogers 2004). From then until the Philippines was granted independence in 1946, the archipelago remained a US colony – a period that included a bloody five-year Philippine–American War, which ended badly for the Philippine revolutionaries and entrenched deep mistrust and hostility among Filipinos towards their American colonizers.

After Philippine independence and the end of World War II, US–Philippine military relations fell under the purview of the *Military Bases Agreement* (MBA) of 1947 and the *Mutual Defence Agreement* (MDA) of 1951. The MBA originally granted the US a 99-year lease to establish, maintain, and operate US military bases under full American control on Philippine soil. Due to growing

Gender, sovereignty, and insecurity 95

national sentiment that the presence of US bases was an affront to national sovereignty, the lease period was subsequently shortened in 1966 with the Ramos–Rusk Agreement. The re-negotiated MBA was set to expire in 1991. Leading up to its expiration, the MBA was subject to renewal negotiations between the US and the Philippines under Presidents George H. W. Bush and Corazon Aquino respectively. An initial agreement was struck to extend the lease for ten more years, but strong opposition to the proposed renewal ultimately led the Philippine Senate to refuse to ratify the new agreement and it was subsequently rejected. Following extensive damage to the Clark Air Base from the eruption of Mount Pinatubo in June of 1991 and the failure to renew the lease under the MBA, the agreement was officially terminated on December 21, 1992 and the Americans left the Clark and Subic bases (Swain 2010; Velasco 2015). This signalled a significant downturn in the US–Philippines military and security relationship, which endured throughout most of the 1990s. With the termination of the MBA and what was effectively the expulsion of the American military from the two bases, the only legal framework that remained to govern the bilateral security relationship was the Mutual Defense Treaty of 1951. But that treaty was based on the assumption that the US would have a physical presence in the Philippines. Without their significant military facilities at the Clark and Subic Bay bases, the US announced that they could no longer commit to protecting the Philippines from external aggression, further cementing their downgraded bilateral security relations (Cruz De Castro 2004; Velasco 2015).

However, this nadir in bilateral relations did not drag on into the new millennium and was followed by a tentative rapprochement fairly soon after. During the late 1990s, China had become bolder and more assertive in its maritime territorial disputes with neighbouring countries, including the Philippines. Some speculate that the security threat posed by China was the main catalyst for then President Josef Estrada, who was known to be pro-American, to sign the new *Visiting Forces Agreement* (VFA) with the US in 1998 (Felix 2005). The VFA and its later-conceived cousin, the *Mutual Logistics Support Agreement* (MLSA) of 2002 were controversial from their inception because they were seen as executive level attempts to legally bind the Philippines to a restored US military presence, allowing for an increase in military cooperation and the resumption of unconstitutional combined military exercises involving US troops (Swain 2010). The VFA remains in effect and is itself a document that is much maligned by a variety of groups ranging from right-leaning Philippine republican nationalists who see the VFA as a fundamental infringement on national sovereignty; to organized feminist movements who see the VFA as creating insecurity for Philippine women; and to disparate groups on the left who voice their opposition largely in terms of resisting what they regard as US imperialism and the human rights abuses associated with US military presence in the Philippines (Simbulan 2010; Winter 2011; Lacsamana 2011; Velasco 2015).

One of the most contentious aspects of the VFA is that it allows for the US government to retain a measure of jurisdiction over American military personnel accused of committing crimes while in the Philippines, and further exempts

96 *Gender, sovereignty, and insecurity*

American military personnel from local visa and passport regulations. These aspects of the VFA are meant to remain in place except in "cases of particular importance to the Philippines" (VFA Article 5, section 3(d)). However, this exception is on a case-by-case basis and can only be invoked by Philippine authorities within a brief 20-day period after a crime has allegedly been committed. On balance then, the VFA grants expansive extra-judicial authority to US military personnel while on Philippine soil, with only a few very difficult-to-enact exceptions (Simbulan 2010; Winter 2011; Lacsamana 2011).

Further, there are good arguments to be made that the VFA, the MSLA and the annual *Balikatan* exercises operate in a contentious grey area of what is constitutionally permitted by the existing laws of the Philippines. The permitted "activities" of US forces are ill-defined and open-ended in the agreement, and the VFA does not specify the duration of US "activities" or the number of US military personnel allowed in the country at any one time (Simbulan 2010, 154). These problems were highlighted in 2009 following the high-profile protest resignation of Philippines Navy Lt Senior Grade Gadian. In her testimony to the Philippine Senate's Legislation Oversight Committee on the VFA, Gadian corroborated suspicions that the US had been involved in military operations that were outside of the confines of both the Philippine Constitution and the VFA itself (Simbulan 2010).

Article XVIII, Section 25, of the Philippine Constitution expressly prohibits foreign military bases, facilities, or foreign troops "except under a treaty duly concurred by the Senate," which in the case of the VFA and according to the Philippine Supreme Court must be strictly for joint military and training. Yet, in Gadian's sworn affidavit and testimony in front of the Philippine Senate, she alleged the existence of secret US facilities operating *inside* Philippine army bases in Mindanao

> foremost among them is Camp Navarro … [where] the US Joint Special Operations Task Force is based, with two permanent structures that are guarded by US Marines, and into which Filipino officers cannot simply enter or have access. This is considered a principal "forward operating base" of the US forces in the Philippines, although the US government does not officially acknowledge its existence.
>
> (Simbulan 2010, 153)

These secret or unacknowledged "bases within bases" are significant to a critical security analysis of US military presence in the Philippines and Southeast Asia, particularly with regards to the materially constitutive role that security narratives play in the post-colonial politics of sovereignty and identity.

Sexual violence and privileged exemption

Such zones of indeterminate jurisdiction, geographic and discursive, are liminal spaces that can be interpreted as part of what Anna Stoler (2006) calls the "imperial formations" of the United States (128); that are the

Gender, sovereignty, and insecurity   97

macropolitics whose technologies of rule thrive on the productions of exceptions and their uneven and changing proliferation. Critical features of imperial formations include harboring and building on territorial ambiguity, redefining legal categories of belonging and quasi-membership, and shifting the geographic and demographic zone of partially suspended rights ... imperial formations give rise both to zones of exclusion and new sites of – and social groups with – privileged exemption.

(128)

As such, the bilateral security agreements between the US and the Philippines, along with the "unofficial forward operating bases" that come into being because of them, are aspects of these imperial formations, where zones of territorial and procedural ambiguity have created both legal and geographic spaces for the "privileged exemption" of US soldiers. Basaran (2008) might call these spaces "zones of exception" both because they are exceptional spaces that exist outside of conventional or typical geographies, revealing the complicated relationships between sovereignty, the law, people and geographic spaces; and also because these spaces constitute people as either subjects (with rights) or objects (without rights) in relation to the sovereign power being exercised there.

The implications of this were brought into sharp relief by the highly publicized alleged sexual assault of a local woman by US marines near the Subic naval base in 2005. In November of that year, Suzette Nicolas, a young woman with a business and accounting background who ran a family canteen in Zamboanga, reported to the police that she had been attacked and sexually assaulted by a group of US Marines in Olongapo City near Subic Bay. Nicolas, or "Nicole" as she was publicly known during the trial, had been out with a female cousin along with several US servicemen. The soldiers were identified as members of the 31st Marine Expeditionary Force who were stationed in Okinawa. The four soldiers in question were in the Philippines because they had just completed *Balikatan* exercises in the South with the AFP, and they were on leave at the time of the alleged rape (Lacsamana 2011, 206). The subsequent events are subject to varying accounts but there were some known facts of the evening that were subsequently corroborated by multiple witnesses.[4]

Ultimately, the courts decided that there was enough evidence to prosecute the US servicemen under domestic rape laws. The case of the *People of the Philippines vs. Chad Carpenter, Dominic Duplantis, Keith Silkwood, and Daniel Smith*, or the "Subic Bay rape case" as it came to be known, went on to become a flashpoint for the ongoing debate on the legitimacy of the VFA and the wide-reaching implications of the US presence in the Philippines. The case was especially significant because it highlighted and drew attention to the gendered insecurities that arise in local populations due to an increased US military presence. The Subic Bay rape case, and cases like it, continue to reveal the "privileged exemption" that the VFA effectively grants to US soldiers that are accused of violent crimes while in the Philippines.

98   *Gender, sovereignty, and insecurity*

With respect to the debate on Philippine sovereignty and the constitutional legitimacy of the terms of the VFA, the Subic Bay Rape Case highlighted one of the most contentious aspects of the VFA – specifically the provisions that allow for US servicemen to remain under US jurisdiction except in "cases of particular importance to the Philippines." In fact, after the initial arrests, the US argued that the accused marines should be held in custody at the US embassy as per the default provisions of the VFA. Further, "the VFA, combined with a rumoured offer of an US$80 million aid package, put the Philippine government under considerable pressure not to prosecute" (Winter 2011, 371). Nevertheless, in June of 2006 and in a rush to stay within the limited 20-day time frame required to maintain custody of the US soldiers, the four Marines were brought to trial in a Makati Regional Trial Court. This initiated a long and contentious trial that invited the attention of prominent feminist advocates including Evalyn Ursua, a high-profile legal activist and lawyer. Ursua was one of the drafters of the Philippine's 1997 rape law, and she came to represent Nicolas in the case on a *pro bono* basis (Winter 2011; Lacsamana 2011). Through the trial, three of the accused servicemen were eventually acquitted, but the charges stuck to Lance Corporal Daniel Smith, who was convicted of rape on December 4, 2006 and sentenced to life in prison.

Initially, the conviction of Smith as the first US soldier to be successfully prosecuted and sentenced for the sexual assault of a local woman was hailed as a victory for both Philippine sovereignty and for women's rights (Winter 2011). However, contrary to both Philippine law and the ruling of the courts, Smith was quietly removed from Makati prison over the Christmas break and handed over to the US embassy where he lived for two years, preparing for his appeal. As a further blow to the court ruling and to the surprise of many observers, Nicolas issued a sworn affidavit in March 2009 in which she recanted portions of her testimony. As part of her statement, Nicolas wrote that her "conscience" was bothering her,

> realizing that I may have in fact been so friendly and intimate with Daniel Smith at the Neptune Club, that he was led to believe that I was amenable to having sex or that we simply just got carried away … I would rather risk public outrage than do nothing to help the court in ensuring that justice is served.
>
> (Aurelio and Bordadora 2009)

A month later, a division of the Philippine Court of Appeals (CA) made up of Associate Justices Remedios Fernando (chair), Myrna Dimaranan-Vidal and Monina Arevalo-Zenarosa acquitted Smith of all charges. They claimed that their acquittal had nothing to do with Nicolas' affidavit and was instead the result of a "careful and judicious perusal of the evidence on record," stating

> What we see was the unfolding of a spontaneous, unplanned romantic episode with both parties carried away by their passions and stirred up by the urgency of the moment caused probably by alcoholic drinks they took

Gender, sovereignty, and insecurity 99

... Suddenly the moment of parting came and the Marines had to rush to the ship. In that situation, reality dawned on Nicole what her audacity and reckless abandon, flirting with Smith and leading him on, brought upon her.

(Philippine CA decision quoted in Pazzibugan April 24, 2012)

It was reported that Nicolas left the Philippines shortly after the CA's decision to acquit Smith, and she is believed to have immigrated to the United States with her American partner, whom she had met after the trial (Punongbayan March 19, 2009).

Not surprisingly, Nicolas' amendments to her original testimony and the decision by the Philippine Court of Appeal to acquit Smith of all charges only served to re-ignite the debate surrounding the sovereignty of the Philippines in relation to its former colonizer, the United States. Why, many asked, did the Philippine government hand Smith over to the Americans after he had been tried and convicted of a crime under Philippine law? Why did Nicolas suddenly cast doubt onto her own testimony – which as some have pointed out – occurred within days of the first official private conversation between President Obama and President Arroyo? The Subic Bay rape case became precedent-setting in the eyes of many, and "Nicole" herself unwittingly became a potent avatar of Philippine national identity and feminist solidarity, and

a symbol of the "collateral damage" brought about by the VFA ... the direct result of manipulation of both her and the judicial process by powerful US interests, supported by the corrupt Philippine state. The Subic rape case, the VFA and continued Philippine dependence on the United States have become irrevocably linked in a large section of public opinion. The more than one-century-long saga of militarization, prostitution, violence against women and US interference with Philippine sovereignty has thus been dramatically brought once again to the fore ... It is a messy and depressing story, in which poor Philippine women, as usual, have fared the worst.

(Winter 2011, 384–385)

The symbolic significance of "Nicole" has endured despite her subsequent statements and despite Smith's acquittal by the Court of Appeal.

Nicolas continued to receive the public support of her lawyer Ursua, who had been fired shortly before the recantation statement was issued. Nicolas' case also continued to receive the support of the broad-based coalition of 17 feminist organizations united under the banner TFSR (Task Force Subic Rape); the support of the Communist Party of the Philippines; and the support of nationalists within the Philippine senate who continued to lobby against the VFA. For them, Nicolas' statement was just further evidence that she had been victimized and subjected to political pressures beyond her control – and perhaps had even been the subject of a cover-up or conspiracy (Goodenough 2009). As a spokesperson from GABRIELA, a prominent feminist group in the Philippines, has stated, the widespread belief among Nicolas' supporters is that her "sudden

100 *Gender, sovereignty, and insecurity*

change of heart is unfortunate," but that they "were not angry with her" for events "that made her a victim of three aspects: rape, the government, and the VFA" (Lacsamana 2011, 211).

For many of her supporters, the details of what actually transpired between Smith and Nicolas that night in November of 2005 are less important than the fact that Philippine national identity and sovereignty had now been ascribed onto the body of "Nicole." As such, defending her honour, staking out her rights, and seeking justice for her became synonymous with the project of securing the sovereignty of the Philippines in the face of the imperial formations (Stoler 2006) of the United States after 9/11. Consequently, that the US servicemen originally charged with her rape were granted extra-judicial treatment through the VFA and ultimately escaped prosecution altogether, can be read as the inevitable "privileged exemption" that is ensured via the various gendered insecurities caused by the security architecture of the US military presence in the Philippines.

But the Subic Bay rape case was not just about sovereignty or nationalism. It also revealed the profoundly gendered effects of the US military presence. As mentioned, Nicolas' case had become a rallying point for a broadly conceived feminist-led activist coalition that had long been arguing that the presence of US bases in the Philippines led to widespread insecurity for women (Winter 2011). It is important to note that what had allegedly happened to Nicolas was not the first time – or last time – that sexual violence against women and girls at the hands of US soldiers had been reported to authorities. As Lacsamana (2011) points out, incidences of sexual assault perpetrated by U.S. servicemen against Filipino women and girls is not uncommon around US military bases. She cites several examples, including a US soldier who was allowed to leave the country despite his proven involvement in the child trafficking of 12 young girls in a prostitution ring in Olongapo; a US soldier who escaped prosecution for the alleged rape and murder of a 12-year-old girl; and "a much larger pattern of militarized violence, comprising approximately 2,000 reported cases in the post World War II period, that never reached Philippine courts" (Lacsamana 2011, 205). More recently, in Olangapo in 2014, US Marine Joseph Scott Pemberton was officially charged with the strangling and drowning murder of a young woman named Jennifer Laude, allegedly because he had discovered that she was transgendered. Although Pemberton was ultimately convicted, there was controversy surrounding the court's decision to find him guilty of the lesser charge of homicide on the basis of what the official ruling referred to as "passion and obfuscation, and intoxication" where the judges seemed to show sympathy for his "impulse and rage" on discovering that Laude was trans. Further, Pemberton's sentence was subsequently reduced to 10 years from 12.[5] Laude's family also alleged that they were offered a bribe by Pemberton's defence team to support a lesser charge and told Reuters news agency "we expected a murder conviction but instead got homicide. We are not content with the decision."

In critical feminist scholarship, it is not novel to link the exploitation and insecurity of women to the existence of foreign military bases or to the workings of international security more generally. As feminist security scholars have long asserted,[6] the connection between militarization and violence against women is not accidental, nor is it particularly exceptional. Rather, the security practices of the state are embedded within deeply entrenched gendered power structures and profoundly linked to gendered insecurities (Peterson 1992). In the case of foreign military bases in particular,

> they are engineered both through explicitly performed and reinforced cultures of masculinity within the military, which include the presumption that local women are exotic recreational commodities to be consumed, and through the actions or inactions of occupying forces and local states, who either fail to sanction sexualized violence against women or actively encourage it.
>
> (Winter 2011, 375)

Nicolas' experiences in Subic and Laude's violent death in Olangapo then, are not unique. Reports of sexual assault and abuse of women and girls by servicemen are widespread in any location where a foreign military base exists, as evidenced by the experiences of women and girls living around the Subic and Clarke, Okinawa, and South Korean US bases in East Asia (Lacsamana 2011; Enloe 1990). Nor is this problem limited to East Asia or to American bases specifically, since areas around United Nations peacekeeping bases have also shown a clear pattern of increased sexual exploitation and abuse linked to the physical presence of soldiers and military architecture (Grady 2010; Cornwell and Wells 1999). Nonetheless, these clear linkages between gendered insecurities and militarization are often ignored in conventional security analyses (Wibben 2004). The field of IR has historically struggled to engage with feminist scholarship, and prior to the 1990s, feminist IR was almost completely disregarded by the security establishment. As Wibben (2004) has noted, engagements between the mainstream and feminist scholarship have often been "troubled" and rife with misunderstandings and mischaracterizations by conventional scholars of what critical feminist scholarship actually is. This is because conventional IR scholars tend to dismiss feminist scholarship for being analytically irrelevant, or for pertaining only to the "low" politics of the domestic sphere, or because "women's issues" can be better accounted for in other fields of study (Wibben 2004). At a deeper foundational level, there continue to be misunderstandings about the actual meaning of "gender," fundamentally different ontological ideas about how the world works, and deep epistemological divides around sources of knowledge and the production of knowledge (Tickner 1992).

However, a critical feminist perspective is *required* to see how shifting security narratives that promote a heightened foreign military presence have highly gendered security implications – even if they do not fit into a conventional state-focused understanding of what "security" means. This is because gendered assumptions are deeply embedded into foundational notions of state sovereignty and security (Peterson 1992), and feminist approaches share a broad

102   *Gender, sovereignty, and insecurity*

concern with the fact that gender is a central organizing principle of the international system and that the persistence of gender hierarchies within that system is problematic. As Sjoberg (2009) argues "gender is conceptually, empirically, and normatively essential to studying international security ... accurate, rigorous and ethical scholarship cannot be produced without taking into account women's presence or the [gendered nature] of world politics" (186). It is not enough to "add women and stir" (Peterson 1992) or to simply "see like a woman," or "count the women" or "ask where the women are" if hierarchical structures of gender inequality continue to be reproduced in the security practices of states. In the same way that United Nations Security Council Resolution 1325 sought to "mainstream gender" while still reproducing the valorization of the masculine over the feminine through its discursive themes (Puechguirbal 2010), discourses of security that claim to protect "womenandchildren" are often complicit in reproducing violent patriarchy.

Consider, for example, the gendered nature of the security discourses of the War on Terror itself. It is interesting to note that the Taliban's horrendous violations of women's rights were invoked in public security narratives from the very beginning of the War on Terror in order to justify the invasion of Afghanistan (Cloud 2004; Masters 2009; Shepherd 2006; Sjoberg and Gentry 2008). First Lady Laura Bush's main talking points around the onset of the War on Terror centred around rescuing the "women over there" from their oppressors, despite the US having shown no previous care for Afghan women or for the Saudi women who continue to be oppressed by the religious laws of their main Arab ally in the Middle East (Cloud 2004; Masters 2009). Into the present, we continue to see the call to rescue women from oppressive Islamist regimes in contemporary security discourses pertaining to terrorism and the IS. Perhaps more insidiously, women's rights are often evoked by populist anti-immigration politicians in the West as a rationale for keeping out the "emergent threat" of Muslim immigrants, refugees, and asylum seekers (Eder 2006). But as Masters (2009) points out, despite these sorts of claims made on *behalf* of women, the War on Terror has nevertheless continued to reinforce the silence, erasure, and "radical exclusion of women, in varying degrees, from politics" (35). Images of helpless and faceless Afghan women (Cloud 2004) are part of the same narratives that framed US soldier Private Jessica Lynch as a "Madonna" and US soldier Private Lyndie England as a "whore" (Masters 2009), while simultaneously erasing the experiences of women who are assaulted, raped, and killed by other US soldiers stationed at bases that form part of the security architecture of the War on Terror.

Architectures of sovereignty

The situation in the Philippines outlined is notable because it demonstrates well the types of social and political complexities that have come with the War on Terror and continue to be faced by Southeast Asian states. The War on Terror itself was not solely responsible for creating the gendered insecurities that have

Gender, sovereignty, and insecurity 103

long existed around US bases in the Philippines but is notable in this respect because it provided the perfect scenario for a renewed continuation of American "imperial formations" (Stoler 2006) in Southeast Asia. The increased US military presence intersected with and brought forth complex questions relating to expressions of Philippine sovereignty and identity. Further, due to the special attention paid to the threat of Islamist terrorism in the specific context of the War on Terror, the increased US involvement in counter-terror operations also contributed to a myopic framing of security problems within the Philippines, arguably to the detriment of other issues.

During the decade after 9/11, the terrorist group *Abu Sayyaf* did launch attacks on state targets in the province of Mindanao, and there was also an increase in violence perpetrated by secessionist groups like MILF (Noor 2006). But supporters of *Abu Sayyaf* were a small minority of the Southern population, and secessionist groups like MILF themselves were not united in their use of bombing attacks and ransom kidnappings. In terms of lethality, strength, and coherence of purpose Muslims in Mindanao were not the most dangerous insurgent group in the Philippines (Swain 2010). Instead

> the most dangerous insurgent group [was] the Communist Party's New People's Army, the descendants of the Hukbalahap Rebellion of the late 1940s and early 1950 … located principally in central Luzon, they [had] been waging a guerrilla war with the central government since 1967, with the objective of overthrowing the existing system and replacing it with a communist state.
>
> (Swain 2010, 11)

Nevertheless, the combination of reduced support for the communist movement and the heightened unpopularity of Muslim separatism after 9/11 meant that despite the misgivings of nationalists and feminists, Washington was able to rely on elite and popular goodwill in the Philippines to shore up some much needed support for its War on Terror (Leheny 2005), allowing the US to re-establish a boots-on-the-ground military presence in Southeast Asia that has continued into the present.

Shifting domestic security narratives

Indonesia and Malaysia, Thailand, and Singapore all saw changes in their military and security relations with the US after 9/11. During a series of low-profile meetings between senior US officials and their counterparts from ten ASEAN nations in November of 2001, US officials stated clearly their identification of the region as an important strategic area and signalled their expectation for higher levels of military and diplomatic cooperation from member-states. This is what Cruz De Castro (2004) called the "first, cooperative security phase" of Washington's War on Terror in Southeast Asia, signalling a collaborative approach to counter-terrorism in the region. As outlined in Chapter 3, and "after

104 *Gender, sovereignty, and insecurity*

more than a decade of relative disengagement … the US dangled financial, diplomatic and military assistance to attract allies and supporters in the region in its effort to mobilize these states in the global counter-terrorism campaign" (Cruz De Castro 2004, 194). Downplaying the spectre of an American military response in the region, Washington specifically asked Southeast Asian governments for increased intelligence cooperation, and for countries to "mount an 'across the board attack' against terrorist recruits, falsification or forging of official documents for terrorists' use, and movements of terrorists from one country to another" (Cruz De Castro 2004, 199). Washington's security requests in these areas were mostly successful in re-invigorating the domestic counter-terrorism agenda in these states. As outlined below, while each country faced its own unique and complex dynamics as a result of the security pressures of the War on Terror, state elites in the region were also able to "adopt and adapt themselves to the rhetoric of the 'War on Terror' to suit their own domestic political agendas" (Noor 2006, 29).

The expectation that ASEAN states would cooperate with the US on security issues was not particularly controversial or unexpected. Countries in the region had enjoyed generally positive security relations and goodwill towards and from the US prior to 9/11. Elites in Malaysia, Indonesia, and Singapore in particular were already

> true believers in the proposition that the United States is a fundamentally benign great power. With some exceptions, members of the foreign policy community in these countries are remarkably unified and certain in their core foreign policy beliefs.
>
> (Hamilton-Hart 2012, 13)

However, this is different from saying that there was wide support for a US *military* presence, even among the elite. The specific topic of the US military setting up bases or deploying forces in the region in order to fight "Islamists" was much more sensitive than the larger question of whether or not Southeast Asian states had a generally positive security relationship with Washington. Further, the populations of Indonesia and Malaysia are principally Muslim, which meant that the domestic stakes around the role of political Islam, "radicalization," and American military responses to counter-terrorism were much higher. Indonesia is a republic with a secular constitution based on the unifying pluralist principle of "*Pancasila*," but has the largest population of Muslims in the world. Matters of religion are very much a part of the Indonesian political, social, and cultural landscape, and sectarian tensions between Muslims and Christians have long been present in some parts of the archipelago (Baswedan 2004). It is in these regions in particular that the more radical Wahhabi or Salafi influenced groups are more likely to be active (Barrett *et al*. 2016).

Malaysia is a constitutional monarchy based on the Westminster parliamentary system, with a population that is around 60% Malay Muslim. The Malaysian constitution specifically names Islam as the official state religion while also making it clear that Malaysia is not meant to be a theocracy. The Malaysian constitution also guarantees the civil rights of all Malaysians, including non-Muslim citizens who are mostly of Chinese and Indian descent, safeguarding their protection under Common Law along with their freedom of religion. But the politics of race and religion in the country can still be fraught (Chan 2018). This can be traced to the constitutional naming of the special position held by the native[7] Muslim Malays as *Bumiputera* or "Sons of the Soil," favouring them in state policies around land ownership, investment, access to education, and even marriage and adoption (Malaysian Constitution, Articles 153, 160, 181); and the *New Economic Policy*, which mandated wealth redistribution policies that favoured the Malays.[8] Not surprisingly, both have been a continued source of racial and religious tensions in the country, but other than in the aforementioned race riots of 1969, these tensions have rarely erupted into violence.

Singapore and Thailand border these two predominantly Muslim countries and have generally enjoyed close relations with them. Both the Philippines and Thailand must deal with long-standing secessionist movements from their own southern Muslim populations and all of these countries must balance their domestic and regional interests accordingly. In other words, the domestic politics within these countries are varied, but all face an assortment of competing ideas, interests, and challenges around the significance of the War on Terror and the US military presence in the region. In fact, most governments in the region have historically expressed discomfort with the existence of the Clarke and Subic US military bases in the Philippines, but 9/11 put the issue of renewed US military presence in Southeast Asia back onto the regional security agenda. The Singaporean government was the most enthusiastic about these developments, welcoming American warships to Changi Naval Base while the Malaysian government softened its general stance on American military presence as well (Capie 2004). In contrast, Thailand and the Philippines were more divided and wary about the American role in the region (Hamilton-Hart 2012), but were nevertheless motivated to support the War on Terror for a variety of reasons.

While largely welcomed by elites in Southeast Asia, the increase in American military presence and aid to the region after 9/11 was generally viewed with a mixture of ambivalence and suspicion by Southeast Asian populations more generally (Hamilton-Hart 2012; Noor 2006). As demonstrated in the previous section, along with US military interests come forms of insecurity experienced by local populations. The security politics and narratives of the War on Terror also created a historical moment that allowed for increased state repression of marginalized political groups, many of which did not necessarily espouse or condone political violence (Noor 2006). This added to the insecurities experienced by certain segments of the population and contributed to a notable rise in public anti-American sentiment (Cruz De Castro 2004; Pempel 2008a, 2008b; Hamid 2016). Such sentiment was not confined to dissidents and separatists but found expression in pro-democracy movements and the general population as well.

106 *Gender, sovereignty, and insecurity*

In the first decade of the War on Terror in Southeast Asia, the perception of American complicity in human rights abuses and harsh suppression of political dissidents by local authorities was fairly widespread among the general populations of Southeast Asian states (Hamilton-Hart 2012). This is relevant for two reasons. First, rising anti-American sentiment has contributed to successful recruitment by terrorist groups (Hamid 2016), in the process increasing the chances of terrorist attacks against regional "Western" targets or symbols of the state (Barrett *et al.* 2016). With new information available about the motivations of those who join Islamist groups like IS, we know more about the driving factors of radicalization. A series of interviews with individuals from Malaysia, Indonesia and Singapore who were arrested for joining IS show that they shared

> a romanticized notion of an Islamic caliphate … they believed that the Islamic State caliphate offered them a life of piety that would increase their chances of rewards in the afterlife … [and] some were *prepared to carry out attacks at home in support of the Islamic State* if they could not travel to Syria, and *to punish their own governments.*
>
> (Barrett *et al.* 2016, 19, my emphasis)

The willingness of IS operatives to attack civilian targets in Muslim countries comes out of the *takfiri* ideology of Wahhabism. This ideology allows jihadi-Salafists to decide that fellow Muslims have committed *shirk* (apostacy), and/or *bid'ah* (blasphemous innovation) if they reject puritanical Wahhabi teachings and show continued loyalty to the "un-Islamic" secular constitutional principles of their respective countries (Hamid 2016). The jihadi-Salafists who hold these beliefs consider Muslims or governments who support the US War on Terror to be apostates, and the Wahabbi doctrine of *al-wala' wa al-bara'* (loyalty and disavowal) promotes a Manichean world view that sanctions and encourages "militant jihad against Muslims deemed to have crossed the line of apostasy" (Hamid 2016, 8). As a result, when local states openly cooperate with American counter-terrorism policies, the risk of Islamist attacks in the region counterintuitively becomes heightened. Although the Wahhabi-Salafist views that promote the doctrine of "loyalty and disavowal" are on the extreme fringe, they nevertheless result in the terrorist attacks that do occur in the region.

Mobilizing War on Terror discourses

The War on Terror security narratives quickly became a convenient discourse under which regional governments clamped down on domestic political opposition, writ large. In this regard, Malaysia was widely thought to be a big, if not the biggest, "political winner" in US–Southeast Asian relations after 9/11 (Camroux and Okfen 2004). Diplomatic relations between the US and Malaysian governments improved considerably following 9/11 partly because "much to [then] Malaysian Prime Minister Mahathir's satisfaction, human rights issues, an old bone of contention between the Clinton administration and the Malaysian

Gender, sovereignty, and insecurity 107

government, ceased to be at the top of the US' foreign policy agenda" (Camroux and Okfen 2004, 170). It is worth noting that government officials and leaders in the region, Malaysia included, continued to express anti-American sentiment and even increased their anti-American rhetoric, especially after the US invasion of Iraq. Mindful of the implications for domestic security and stability, this anti-Americanism was largely performed for the benefit of local audiences and did not reflect the degree to which the functional relationships between regional governments and Washington were actually improving in several key respects (Capie 2004; Hamilton-Hart 2012). The disconnect between the rhetoric directed at domestic audiences and the actual level of support granted to Washington in security and intelligence indicates the importance these governments place on the "internal" stability of their regimes, which is reflected in the idea of "national resilience."

To cooperate with the counter-terrorism efforts of the Americans, the Malaysian government provided Washington with "extensive overflight rights, intelligence, and defence and law enforcement cooperation" (Capie 2004, 237). In return, US intelligence officers began assisting local Malaysian police and intelligence agencies in their own leads on Islamist individuals and organizations said to have links to *Al-Qaeda*, IS, or the various regional groups believed to be networked into transnational terrorism (Cruz De Castro 199). As a result, Washington both aided in and indicated strong support for several terror-related arrests by the Malaysian government under the country's now defunct Internal Security Act, which provided for indefinite detention of individuals without trial. This was the same act that was stridently criticized by American delegates at past APEC meetings prior to 9/11. In 2003 alone, Malaysian authorities apprehended 48 alleged Muslim extremists who were said to be members of both PAS, which is the legal opposition political party discussed in Chapter 4, and the *Kumpulan Mujahideen Malaysia* (KMM), which is an illegal militant organization with links to regional and transnational terrorism.

In response to those arrests, PAS leaders and democracy advocates – while strange bedfellows in many respects – together repeatedly denied the existence of organizational connections between PAS and the KMM, and a wide coalition of opposition voices (including non-Islamist, pro-democracy groups) demanded that the detainees be put on trial rather than be held under the ISA. However, it was clear that "the government [felt] little pressure to provide a full explanation of the security threat facing the country" (Jayasankaran 2002) and the government was able to use a security rationale rooted in the War on Terror for their exceptional use of the ISA. On more than one occasion, Malaysian politicians specifically invoked the USA PATRIOT Act as justification for the legitimacy of the ISA (Noor 2006), despite the fact that the ISA had long been used for the detention of political dissidents, had been around since 1960, and was actually enacted by the British colonial government during the *Malayan Emergency*.[9]

War on Terror discourses were also operationalized for the purposes of consolidating regime power in other ways. For example, it is interesting to note how the use of "moderate Islam" came to be mobilized in Malaysian politics. One of

108   *Gender, sovereignty, and insecurity*

the things that Washington had specifically requested from regional leadership was to appeal to "moderate Muslims in the region to counteract efforts of small but vocal groups of domestic extremists threatening violence" (Cruz De Castro 2004). But even before 9/11, the Malaysian government had already identified Islamist political groups as threats to domestic security and were particularly concerned with returning young Malays who had gone abroad to study Islam and came home espousing puritanical views as members of political parties like PAS (Noor 2006). Notably, PAS had become one of the political parties attached to the broad coalition of opposition groups that formed the *Reformasi* movement against then Prime Minister Mahathir Mohamad in 1998 – the same movement of political opposition parties led by Anwar Ibrahim at the time (Noor 2006).

Within this milieu, puritanical forms of Wahhabist or Salafist Islam were officially discredited as "*sesat*" or deviant and cast as un-Islamic in domestic political discourse. As a result, Mahathir saw the War on Terror as an opportunity to crack down hard on Islamist opposition, some of it politically legitimate but all of it cast as

> [radical terrorist] Islamist cells and networks – both real and imagined – [with] less criticism from foreign and local observers … By presenting itself as the face of "moderate" and "progressive" Islam at work, the Malaysian government had managed to out-flank the Islamist opposition and reposition itself successfully.
>
> (Noor 2006, 37)

It has long been part of Malaysian politics to define the "correct" Islam as moderate and progressive, by definition, and opposition parties like PAS have been successfully discredited on the basis of dabbling in religious ideas that the state officially deems to be "incorrect" Islam. Mahathir's successors, Prime Ministers Badawi and Najib respectively, also continued the discourse of "moderate Islam" as a way to confirm the ruling coalition's image as the keepers of "true" Islam in Malaysia, but also as a way to consolidate and legitimize strong state power and authority.

However, as Chan (2018) has pointed out, this has meant that Malaysian elites have faced a longstanding challenge of needing to control the very same discourses of "true Islam" that they themselves have created. This is because the underlying Manichean assumption that there can only be one "true Islam" – even a moderate progressive "true Islam" – makes the existence of peaceable theological pluralism among Malaysian Muslims theoretically impossible, ultimately contributing to hard-line views among both progressive and radicalized Muslims alike. This is why *Shiite, Ahmadi* and *Ismaili* forms of Islam are all outlawed in Malaysia alongside fundamentalist (but non-violent) Muslim sects that puritanically reject modern life – like the *al Arqam* movement in the 1980s and 1990s, and violent radical terrorist groups like KMM and JI. The problem with this is that in a country like Malaysia, where "nation-building and modernization is largely a statist project, perceived shortfalls and injustices from such processes

Gender, sovereignty, and insecurity 109

will invariably result in pro-orthodoxy, populist, counter-hegemonic discourses that are directed against the state" (Chan 2018, 15). This further reinforces the need for a strong-state security apparatus not only as "the lynchpin in Malaysia's counter-terror toolkit" (Chan 2018, 12), but also as a means to consolidate the power and continued legitimacy of ruling elites through the discursive linking of regime stability to state security.

In Thailand, at the height of the Asian Financial Crisis that began with the devaluation of the Thai baht in 1997, Shinawatra Thaksin's populist upstart *Thai Rak Thai*[10] party rose to power with widespread support from urbanites, the middle class, and members of the business community who all blamed the previous government for the financial crisis. Under Thaksin, Thailand saw the drafting of the new 1997 Thai constitution that was reformist in appearance but greatly expanded the power and authority of the Prime Minister (Noor 2006). Long before 9/11, Thaksin was already rallying populist support for his government through "a steady stream of state propaganda about internal threats within Thailand, ranging from drug gangs to Islamist militants in the south of the country" (Noor 2006). Not surprisingly, Thaksin went on to mobilize War on Terror discourses in service to his own domestic political aims.

Thai–US relations were never bad, but they were also not particularly good, Bangkok being historically ambivalent towards Washington's presence in the region (Cruz De Castro 2004; Hamilton-Hart 2012). And in the American view, Thailand, "with its porous borders and liberal immigration laws ... appeared to be a weak link in the region's anti-terrorism campaign" (Cruz De Castro 2004, 203). So, it was interesting to see a considerable improvement in US–Thai security relations after 9/11. From Thaksin's perspective, he now had *carte blanche* to crack down on southern Muslim secessionist violence under the pretext of counter-terrorism (Noor 2006). But for domestic audiences who were sensitive about Thai sovereignty, he was also careful not to over play the US–Thai relationship (Cruz De Castro 2004). As a result, much of the US–Thai cooperation in counter-terrorism has been relatively low profile, because unlike for neighbouring Muslim Malaysia and Indonesia, non-Muslim Thailand has no need to performatively assert its religious "moderation."

The shape taken by Thai–American security cooperation has been mostly at the level of law enforcement and covert intelligence collaboration and assistance. For example, Thai and American law enforcement intelligence agencies cooperated on a number of organized crime and terror cases after 9/11, leading to the arrest of several suspected terrorists and the breakup of a fake travel documents ring in 2002 (Cruz De Castro 2004). The Thai authorities have also allowed the US to place its own law enforcement agents in Thai airports and, notably, they have also been complicit in US rendition and black site practices by quietly allowing the CIA to "to interview suspected members of *Al-Qaeda* in secure locations" (Cruz De Castro 2004, 204). As with the secret bases-within-bases in the Philippines, these are examples of the creation of physical extra-legal spaces that operate as zones of exception where the vagaries of indeterminate jurisdiction allow for the exercise of unchecked sovereign power on abject bodies (Basaran 2008).

110   *Gender, sovereignty, and insecurity*

During this same period, Thaksin's government was implicated in several shocking human rights abuses in their crackdown on the Muslim minority secessionist movements in the south. In the early 2000s, the southern provinces experienced mass civil disturbances in response to government crackdowns following a string of small-scale bombing attacks by militant insurgent groups. In 2004, Thai police rounded up several hundred members of the southern Muslim population in what appeared, to many observers, to be an indiscriminate sweep of young men in the region. In a disturbing turn of events, at least 78 of the detainees died due to dehydration and suffocation *en route* to Bangkok for processing, because they had been placed in the back of non-air conditioned, unventilated trucks for several hours in hot and humid temperatures exceeding 30°C (*Amnesty International* October 26, 2004). This specific incident caused an uproar among regional human rights groups, including in neighbouring Malaysia. Unfortunately, the cycle of bombings and crackdowns only seemed to escalate, mutually reinforcing one another in occurrence and severity. Between 2004 and 2007 alone, the Muslim secessionist insurgency in the Southern provinces of Yala, Narathiwat, and Pattani resulted in the deaths of at least 2,000 people (Storey 2008). In early 2007, in particular, Thailand saw a sharp increase in secessionist terrorist bombings in Bangkok and in several areas in the South (Storey 2008).

Strife in the southern provinces strained Thailand's otherwise good relations with neighbouring Malaysia. The Muslim Thais in the southern regions possess an affinity for their Malay neighbours due to shared ancestry, religion, a high incidence of inter-marriage, and a relatively large number of dual citizens. Successive Malaysian governments have continued to support the cross-border networks of the counter-insurgency at the level of law enforcement and border cooperation as part of its own CVE and CT efforts. Nevertheless, Malaysian elites repeatedly found themselves in the delicate position of needing to balance regional security interests, the ongoing good will of the US, and the complicated domestic political sensitivities around such issues. While Malaysian cooperation with the Thai authorities on matters of secessionist Islamism was obviously beneficial from a state security standpoint, public opinion in Malaysia was overwhelmingly critical of the Thai authorities' crackdown on the militants, which was widely perceived as being disproportionately harsh and anti-Muslim in nature, and there was a lack of support for their government's involvement in helping the Thai authorities (Storey 2008).

In Indonesia during this same period, then President Megawati Sukarnoputri was constrained by the Islamist parties in her own coalition government and still faced the challenges of an economy hard hit by the Asian financial crisis and subsequent structural adjustment policies imposed by international financial institutions during their recovery (Hafidz 2003; Jones 2003; Murphy 2010). After 9/11, Megawati had flown to Washington on a previously planned visit, which turned into a discussion of Indonesia's potential contributions to the War on Terror. During the visit "Megawati condemned the attacks and vowed to work with the international community to combat terrorism … Bush … pledged

Gender, sovereignty, and insecurity 111

additional funding for Indonesia ... [and] the IMF resumed disbursements suspended under Abdurrahman" (Murphy 2010, 9). When the spectre of a possible security cooperation deal between Washington and Jakarta became public knowledge – and one that seemed coupled with further conditionalities around debt servicing – Islamist opposition factions and militant groups like *Laskar Jihad* took to the streets to stage mass protests against the US' military excursions into Afghanistan and Indonesia's involvement in the War on Terror (Murphy 2010). Megawati was also explicitly warned by Islamist groups and members of her own government, that "any attempts to appease the Americans would lead to a backlash at home with heavy political costs" (Noor 2006, 36). Coming in close succession with demands for economic reform and military accountability, Indonesians perceived American pressure on them to fight terrorism "as a source of unrelenting and unwarranted pressure" (Murphy 2010, 9).

As a result of these domestic political dynamics, and unlike her counterparts in Malaysia, Singapore and Thailand, Megawati was less free to use extra-judicial tools in her CT efforts, and her government demurred from engaging in anti-constitutional crackdowns on activist Muslim groups in Indonesia immediately after 9/11 (Murphy 2010). She was widely derided by Washington and the American media for this initially restrained approach to counter-terrorism, and her recalcitrance was read by some observers as evidence that "moderate" forces in Indonesia were being figuratively held hostage by the ever-strengthening force of regional Islamism (Desker 2002). Ironically however, prior to 9/11 Washington had been highly critical of the Indonesian Army's (ABRI)[11] blatant human rights abuses with regards to the East Timor situation and sectarian violence in Sumatera. So much so that in 1999 the US had instituted a congressional ban on all military contracts between the US and Jakarta and had cut off official military ties with the country after determining that the Indonesian military officers responsible for mass casualties in East Timor were not going to be prosecuted (Cruz De Castro 2004; Murphy 2010).

Washington's post 9/11 security mindset however, eventually led to a US Congressional move to resume military aid to Indonesia under the auspices of supporting counter-terrorism (The White House January 6, 2002), leading to a revitalization of military relations between Washington and Jakarta despite ABRI's "general distrust of American assistance in particular and US foreign policy in general" (Cruz De Castro 2004, 203). Nevertheless, several high-profile terrorist attacks on Western targets in Indonesia (most notably the 2002 Bali and Marriot bombings) lent increasing credence to fears of terrorism in the region and ultimately pushed Megawati to take counter-terrorism more seriously (Murphy 2010).

Adding to this complicated backdrop of the Indonesian–US military relationship was the fact that the upper echelons of ABRI had historically been dominated by Christians and secularists who had long advocated for the sidelining of Islamist interests in politics – even by legitimate organizations like NU – and generally saw all Muslim political groups as terrorist threats (Noor 2006). The post-9/11 moment then, allowed for the Indonesian ABRI generals to reassert

112 *Gender, sovereignty, and insecurity*

themselves as powerful players in Indonesian politics and Megawati ended up contentiously naming General Hendropriyono to lead Indonesia's new National Intelligence Agency (BIN) (Noor 2006). Hendropriyono was widely reviled by Indonesian Muslims and had earned the nickname the "Butcher of Lampung" because, in 1989, troops under his command brutally subdued a Sufi Islamist activist uprising in Lampung, Sumatera, leaving hundreds dead and missing (Noor 2006, 47; Della-Giacoma 2014). As with ABRI's atrocities in East Timor, the massacre at Lampung was never prosecuted.

Megawati's promotion of Hendropriyono and her open cooperation with the US in Jakarta's domestic crackdown of Islamist opposition in Indonesia "had the immediate effect of alienating her from her own Muslim-majority constituency" (Noor 2006, 38). As it turned out,

> balancing the imperatives of good relations with the US and domestic politics proved to be an extremely difficult task for the Megawati administration … The rise of political Islam during *reformasi* and the competition inherent in democracy provided incentives for Indonesian leaders to use foreign policy issues to score points domestically. Megawati's gender, status as a syncretic[12] Muslim, and the large number of Christians in her party made her particularly vulnerable to criticism on issues with an Islamic dimension.
>
> (Murphy 2010, 10)

While mainstream Muslims in Indonesia did not support the terror bombings by JI, they also did not support American military undertakings in Afghanistan and Iraq and were highly critical of what was seen by many as external foreign meddling by the "West" into Indonesia's own domestic affairs (Baswedan 2004; Sherlock 2004). This latter view was shared by the wider Indonesian public because this was not just about religion. In fact, despite a continuing steady rise in personal Islamic religious observance among Indonesians, "most voters do not seem to want an overtly political role for Islam" (Sherlock 2009).

Not unlike in the Philippines, national sovereignty is a historically sensitive topic for Indonesians due to their long and difficult history with Dutch colonialism, the Japanese occupation during World War II, the communist insurgency that followed, and harsh structural adjustment policies imposed by international financial institutions after the Asian financial crisis. Megawati's seeming willingness to bow to the demands of American pressure was seen as evidence of her unsuitability to lead a strong and resilient Indonesia. And so, after losing popular support from Indonesian voters for all the reasons mentioned and losing the confidence of her own coalition government, Megawati ultimately lost the 2004 elections to ABRI ex-General Susilo Bambang Yudhoyono (Sherlock 2004). Yudhoyono was widely seen as an underdog in the election and had previously reached out to ethnic Chinese Indonesian voters through efforts to remove several discriminatory laws affecting them (Noor 2006), garnering him a wide voter base. And despite being a syncretic secularist, Yudhoyono was also

Gender, sovereignty, and insecurity 113

able to enjoy widespread support from devout Muslim voters due partly to the credibility of his running mate, Jusuf Kalla, as a religious person with a long history of public service in government and strong ties to Muslim organizations and Islamist parties (Baswedan 2004). Yudhoyono went on to stay in power until 2014 after being re-elected in 2009. It is interesting to note that his successor, Joko Widodo, despite running on a platform of transparency and reform, has made the decision to re-instate Hendropriyono as head of BIN (Della-Giacamo August 11, 2014), furthering a strong statist approach to counter-terrorism and the possibility that legitimate Islamist organizations and parties will continue to get caught up in a very wide net of vilification.

Conclusion – "national resilience" as security

The post-9/11 period saw a marked increase in "strong state" repression of a wide range of political and religious interests under the aegis of a newly legitimized, extra-judicial, and very broad umbrella of counter-terrorism in Southeast Asia. This was because Bush's War on Terror coalition-building in the region "impacted on the distance Asian countries have been able to maintain in relation to the US" (Camroux and Okfen 2004, 163), and state elites in these countries learned quickly to leverage War on Terror discourses for their own domestic and regional political agendas (Noor 2006). As for Washington's role in actively influencing the domestic politics of Southeast Asian countries, "… where it felt appropriate the United States sought to strengthen governing regimes and thus states in dealing with internal opposition" (Camroux and Okfen 2004, 164) sometimes in opposition to the US' pre-9/11 dispositions towards those same regimes.

After 9/11 this meant that War on Terror discourses were mobilized in state projects to suppress not just Islamist groups but anti-government opposition more generally. And the processes of contestation within political Islam in the region, and between Islamist movements of all stripes and their own governments (Baswedan 2004), were further "complicated by the direct intervention of the US-led War on Terror in the region … because the War on Terror focuses almost exclusively on *increased state control* as the best means to eradicate potential terrorist threats" (Kadir 2004, 201, my emphasis). It is this increased state control that is of particular interest to a critical security analysis of War on Terror security discourses, because they have legitimized the Southeast Asian fondness for "national resilience" (Emmers 2009) as the benchmark for security. And "national resilience" includes the penchant for governments to enact a wide variety of anti-democratic and extra-judicial practices in the name of security and the integrity of the state (Burke and McDonald 2007). This is the discursive framework within which the architectures of sovereignty in post 9/11 Southeast Asia, examined in this chapter, continue to operate.

Interestingly, the concept of "national resilience" buttresses *regional* approaches to security as well, raising thought-provoking questions about the so-called "ASEAN-way" of understanding security. This leads into the issues and

114 *Gender, sovereignty, and insecurity*

questions explored in the following chapter. These questions pertain to the effects that the War on Terror has had on regional arrangements and regional dynamics. What sort of impact did the War on Terror have on regional identity and related notions of security, if any? How did 9/11 and the War on Terror affect regional institutions as well as efforts towards further regionalization? Did the War on Terror security narratives affect trade and economic relations in the region? A critical security approach to these questions prioritizes the ways that discourses and ideas play a crucial constitutive role in practices of security and the construction of identities, and the ways that the security project(s) of the state (and region) generates various forms of insecurity for non-state actors. Chapter 6 explores these questions.

Notes

1 It is worth noting that the official White Paper produced by the Singaporean government detailing the evidence against the JI 15 (and their transnational linkages) has been widely used by conventional terrorist experts as a source of information grounding subsequent analyses of terrorism in the region.

2 The ISA was repealed in 2012, when it was replaced with the Security Offences Special Measures Act (SOSMA). SOSMA requires charges in a court of law but the list of "terror offences" can include something as minor as "having a link" to "IS reading materials" on one's mobile phone (Chan 2018, 11).

3 There were some hiccups, primarily diplomatic ones, between President Obama and President Duterte in 2016. But all signs point to the continual strength of the culturally and institutionally entrenched relationship between the US and the Philippines. This will be discussed in Chapter 7.

4 Winter (2011) discusses in more detail the known and corroborated events of that evening which included the fact that "Nicole" and her cousin had been socializing with the defendants in Olangapo city and had been seen in several establishments during the course of the evening. At some later point in the night, witnesses reported seeing

> a Kia Starex van pull up at the [Alava] pier: two Caucasians emerged from the van, carrying Nicole by her hands and feet, "as if she were a pig," commented one witness ... Nicole was dressed only in her shirt and underwear. A third Caucasian picked up a pair of jeans and threw them towards Nicole ... witnesses called the Subic Bay Metropolitan Authority to report a "possible rape."

(385)

5 Nicholls April 4, 2016, CNN – http://cnnphilippines.com/news/2016/04/03/joseph-scott-pemberton-jennifer-laude-olongapo-regional-trial-court-decision-downgraded.html.

6 A rich history of feminist IR and security scholarship includes the work of Enloe (1990), who was one of the first to write specifically about the linkages between military bases and gendered violence, as well as work by Peterson 1992; Sturdevant and Stoltzfus 1993; Sjoberg 2010; Wibben 2004; Cohn 1987;Yuval-Davis 2006; Puechguirbal 2010; Golan 1997; Kumar 2004; Shepherd 2006; MacKenzie 2009; and Lobasz 2009 among others.

7 "Native" as opposed to "Indigenous." This is because the presence of Malay peoples in the Malay states and surrounding archipelagos can be traced back over several centuries, and they have been predominantly Muslim since the first documented adoption of Islam by the ruler of the Malay state Kedah, Sultan Mudzafar Shah, in the twelfth

century. Compared to the Chinese and Indian Malaysians who have mostly descended from Chinese merchants and Indian labourers who arrived in Malaya over the eighteenth, nineteenth and twentieth centuries, the Malays consider themselves to be the native people of Malaysia. They do not, however, technically fulfill the criteria of "Indigenous Peoples." Instead, hill tribe populations that live in relatively remote areas of both Peninsular Malaysia and Borneo, like the Orang Asli, the Dayaks and the Kadazan-Dusun, qualify under the United Nations definition of "Indigenous Peoples" in terms of their connection to the land, their tribal social structures, oral historical traditions, distinct languages, and their marginalized position in society as groups whose way of life is in danger of social, economic and environmental encroachment (see http://says.com/my/lifestyle/indigenous-groups-in-malaysia for a short primer on the Indigenous Peoples of Malaysia).

8 The NEP, an affirmative action plan favouring Malays, was enacted after the race riots of 1969 under the supervision of Tun Abdul Razak. The drafters of the NEP declared that its intent was to redress the inter-generational effects of economic marginalization of the Malays under British rule. But these polices are widely experienced by non-Malays as discriminatory and many Malaysians, including up to 65% of polled Malays, are now of the opinion that it should have been repealed years ago (Teoh October 9, 2008).

9 Over 10,000 people were arrested under the ISA over the course of its time.

10 "Thais Love Thais."

11 *Angkatan Bersenjata Republik Indonesia* – aka the Indonesian Armed Forces.

12 "Syncretic" Muslim refers to Clifford Geertz's term for a nominal or non-practicing Muslim, as opposed to a devout/practicing (or Santri) Indonesian Muslim, who can further be "sub-categorized" as traditionalists or modernists (Baswedan 2004).

References

Abuza, Zachary. 2005. The Moro Islamic Liberation Front at 20: State of the Revolution. *Studies in Conflict and Terrorism* 28: 453–479.

Amnesty International – Press Release. October 26, 2004. Thailand: Death of demonstrators must be fully investigated. (Index ASA 39/014/2004, news service number: 265).

Anderson, Gerald. 2006. *Subic Bay from Magellan to Pinatubo, 3rd edition*. Philippines: Anderson.

Aradau, Claudia and Rens Van Munster. 2007. Governing terrorism through risk: Taking precautions, (un)knowing the future. *European Journal of International Relations* 33(2): 251–277.

Arianti, V. and J. Singh. 2015. *ISIS' Southeast Asia unit: Raising the security threat. (RSIS Commentaries, No. 220). RSIS Commentaries.* Singapore: Nanyang Technological University.

Aurelio, Julie M. and Norman Bordadora. March 18, 2009. Nicole recants, clears Smith. *Philippine Daily Inquirer*.

Barrett, Richard, Jack Berger, Lila Ghosh, Daniel Schoenfeld, Mohamed el Shawesh, Patrick M. Skinner, Susan Sim, and Ali Soufan. 2016. *Foreign fighters: An updated assessment of the flow of foreign fighters into Syria and Iraq*. New York: The Soufan Group.

Basaran, Tugba. 2008. Security, law, borders: Spaces of exclusion. *International Political Sociology* 2(4): 339–354.

Baswedan, Anies Rasyid. 2004. Political Islam in Indonesia: Present and future trajectory. *Asian Survey* 44(5): 669–690.

Bentley, Michelle and Jack Holland (Eds). 2017. *The Obama doctrine*. London: Routledge.

116 *Gender, sovereignty, and insecurity*

Burke, Anthony and Matt McDonald (Eds). 2007. *Critical security in the Asia-Pacific.* Manchester: Manchester University Press.

Camroux, David and Nuria Okfen. 2004. Introduction: 9/11 and US–Asian relations: Towards a new "new world order"? *The Pacific Review* 17(2): 163–177.

Capie, David. 2004. Between a hegemon and a hard place: The "war on terror" and US–Southeast Asian relations. *The Pacific Review* 17(2): 223–248.

Chan, Nicholas. 2018. The Malaysian "Islamic" State versus the Islamic State (IS): Evolving definitions of "terror" in an "Islamising" nation-state. *Critical Studies on Terrorism* 1–23.

Cloud, Dana L. 2004. To veil the threat of terror: Afghan women and the "clash of civilizations" in the imagery of the US war on terrorism. *Quarterly Journal of Speech* 90(3): 285–300.

Cohn, Carol. 1987. Sex and death in the rational world of defence intellectuals. *Signs: Journal of Women in Culture and Society* 12: 4.

Cornwell, Rachel and Andrew Wells. 1999. Deploying insecurity. *Peace Review* 11(3): 409–414.

Cotton, James. 2003. Southeast Asia after 11 September. *Terrorism and Political Violence* 15(1): 148–170.

Cruz De Castro, Renato. 2004. Addressing international terrorism in Southeast Asia: A matter of strategic or functional approach? *Contemporary Southeast Asia* 193–217.

Della-Giacoma, Jim. August 11, 2014. Hope and change? Jokowi embraces the "butcher of Lampung" Crikey.Com. www.crikey.com.au/2014/08/11/hope-and-change-jokowi-embraces-the-butcher-of-lampung/.

Desker, Berry. 2002. Islam and society in Southeast Asia after September 11. Working Paper 33. Institute of Defense and Strategic Studies, Singapore: Nanyang Technological University.

Eder, K. 2006. Europe's borders: The narrative construction of the boundaries of Europe. *European Journal of Social Theory* 9(2): 255–271.

Emmers, Ralf. 2009. Comprehensive security and resilience in Southeast Asia: ASEAN's approach to terrorism. *The Pacific Review* 22(2): 159–177.

Enloe, Cynthia. 1990. *Bananas, beaches, and bases: Making feminist sense of international politics.* Berkeley, CA: University of California Press.

Felix, Victor. 2005. *Philippine-US security relations: Challenges and opportunities after the 9/11.* U.S. Army War College: Carlisle Barracks, Pennsylvania.

Golan, Gadia. 1997. Militarization and gender: The Israeli experience. *Women's Studies International Forum* 20(5): 581–586.

Goodenough, Patrick. March 19, 2009. Woman who accused US Marine of Rape Changes her story: Critics see a conspiracy. CNSnews.com.

Grady, K. 2010. Sexual exploitation and abuse by UN peacekeepers: A threat to impartiality *International Peacekeeping* 17(2): 215–228.

Gunaratna, Rohan (Ed.). 2003. *Terrorism in the Asia-Pacific: Threat and response.* Singapore: Eastern Universities Press.

Hafidz, Tatik S. 2003. The war on terror and the future of Indonesian democracy. Working Paper No. 46. Institute of Defence and Strategic Studies, Singapore: Nanyang Technological University.

Hamid, A. F. A. 2016. ISIS in Southeast Asia: Internalized wahhabism is a major factor. *ISEAS Perspective*, 16. Singapore: Yusof Ishak Institute.

Hamilton-Hart, Natasha. 2012. *Hard interests, soft illusions: Southeast Asia and American power.* Ithaca, NY: Cornell University Press.

Jackson, Richard. 2011. Culture, identity and hegemony: Continuity and (the lack of) change in US counter-terrorism policy from Bush to Obama. *International Politics* 48(2/3): 390–411.

Jayasankaran, S. March 21, 2002. Malaysia – Lost ground: The rise of the Islamic opposition may have been stunted by world events and messy politics. *Far Eastern Economic Review* 165(11): 19.

Jones, Sydney. August 29, 2003. Indonesia faces more terror. *International Herald Tribune.*

Kadir, Suzaina. 2004. Mapping Muslim politics in Southeast Asia after September 11. *The Pacific Review* 17(2): 199–222.

Kumar, D. 2004. War propaganda and the (ab)uses of women: Media constructions of the Jessica Lynch story. *Feminist Media Studies* 4(3): 297–313.

Lacsamana, Anne E. 2011. Empire on trial: The Subic rape case and the struggle for Philippine women's liberation. *Works and Days* 29(57/58): 203–215.

Leheny, David. 2005. The war on terrorism and the possibility of secret regionalism. In T. J. Pempel (Ed.) *Remapping East Asia: The construction of a region.* Ithaca, NY: Cornell University Press, pp. 236–255.

Liow, Joseph. 2015. Malaysia's ISIS conundrum. *Brookings Southeast Asia View.* www. brookings.edu/opinions/malaysias-isis-conundrum.

Lobasz, Jennifer. 2009. Beyond border security: Feminist approaches to human trafficking. *Security Studies* 18(2): 319–344.

MacKenzie, Meghan. 2009. Securitization and desecuritization: Female soldiers and the reconstruction of women in post-conflict Sierra Leone. *Security Studies* 18(2): 241–261.

Masters, Cristina. 2009. Femina sacra: The "war of/on terror," women and the feminine. *Security Dialogue* 40(1): 29–49.

Masuda, Hiroshi. 2012. *MacArthur in Asia: The general and his staff in the Philippines, Japan, and Korea.* Ithaca, NY: Cornell University Press.

Murphy, Ann Marie. 2010. US rapprochement with Indonesia: From problem state to partner. *Contemporary Southeast Asia: A Journal of International and Strategic Affairs* 32(3): 362–387.

Nicholls, A. C. April 4, 2016. Court affirms Pemberton's conviction but reduces sentence to up to 10 years. CNN Philippines.com. http://cnnphilippines.com/news/2016/04/03/ joseph-scott-pemberton-jennifer-laude-olongapo-regional-trial-court-decision-downgraded.html.

Noor, Farish. 2003. Reaping the bitter harvest after twenty years of state Islamization. In Rohan Gunaratna (Ed.) *Terrorism in the Asia Pacific, threat and response.* Singapore: Eastern Universities Press, pp. 178–201.

Noor, Farish. 2006. How Washington's "war on terror" became everyone's: Islamophobia and the impact of September 11 on the political terrain of South and Southeast Asia. *Human Architecture: Journal of the Sociology of Self-Knowledge* 5(1): 29–50.

Parameswaran, Prasanth. 2015. Exclusive: US, Malaysia and the war against the Islamic State. *The Diplomat.* November 25. https://thediplomat.com/2015/11/exclusive-us-malaysia-and-the-war-against-the-islamic-state/.

Pazzibugan, Dona. April 24, 2012. Court of Appeal: Smith not guilty of rape. *Philippine Daily Inquirer.*

Pempel, T.J. 2008a. How Bush bungled Asia: Militarism, economic indifference and unilateralism have weakened the United States across Asia. *The Pacific Review* 21(5): 547–581.

Pempel, T.J. 2008b. A response to Michael Green. *The Pacific Review* 21(5): 595–600.

118 Gender, sovereignty, and insecurity

Peterson, V. Spike (Ed.). 1992. *Gendered states: Feminist (re)visions of international relations theory*. Boulder, CO: Lynn Rienner Publishers.

Puechguirbal, N. 2010. Discourses on gender, patriarchy and Resolution 1325: A textual analysis of UN documents. *International Peacekeeping* 17(2): 172–187.

Punongbayan, Michael. March 19, 2009. Nicole leaves for US, settles for P100,000. *The Philippine Star*.

Rogers, Steven. 2004. Beyond the Abu Sayyaf: The lessons of failure in the Philippines. *Foreign Affairs* 83(1): 15–20.

Shepherd, Laura. 2006. Veiled references: Constructions of gender in the Bush administration discourse on the attacks on Afghanistan post-9/11. *International Feminist Journal of Politics* 8(1): 19–41.

Sherlock, Stephen. 2004. *Consolidation and change: The Indonesian parliament after the 2004 elections*. Canberra: Centre for Democratic Institutions.

Sherlock, Stephen. 2009. *Parties and elections in Indonesia 2009: The consolidation of democracy*. Parliamentary Report. Canberra: Australian Parliamentary Library.

Simbulan, Roland. 2010. The Pentagon's secret war and facilities in the Philippines. *Peace Review: A Journal of Social Justice* 22(2): 150–157.

Sjoberg, Laura. 2009. Introduction to *Security Studies*: Feminist contributions. *Security Studies* 18: 183–213.

Sjoberg, Laura. 2010. Gendering the empire's soldiers: Gender ideologies, the US military and the "war on terror." In Laura Sjoberg (Ed.) *Gender, war, and militarism: Feminist perspectives*. Santa Barbara: ABC-CLIO, pp. 209–218.

Sjoberg, L. and Gentry, C.E. 2008. Reduced to bad sex: Narratives of violent women from the bible to the war on terror. *International Relations* 22(1): 5–23.

Stoler, Ann Laura. 2006. On degrees of imperial sovereignty. *Public Culture* 18(1): 125–146.

Storey, Ian. 2008. Southern discomfort: Separatist conflict in the Kingdom of Thailand. *Asian Affairs: An American Review* 35(1): 31–52.

Sturdevant, S.P. and Stoltzfus, B. 1993. *Let the good times roll: Prostitution and the US military in Asia*. New York: The New Press.

Swain, Richard. 2010. Case study: Operation Enduring Freedom report by Booz Allen Hamilton, under contract to the US Army Counterinsurgency Center. www.dtic.mil/cgi-bin/GetTRDoc?AD=ADA532988.

Tan, Andrew. 2003. The Singapore experience. In Rohan Gunaratna (Ed.) *Terrorism in the Asia Pacific: Threat and response*. Singapore: Eastern Universities Press, pp. 222–248.

Teoh, Shannon. October 9, 2008. Poll shows most Malaysians want NEP to end. *Malaysia Today*. www.malaysia-today.net/2008/10/09/poll-shows-most-malaysians-want-nep-to-end/.

The White House, January 6, 2002. Press release on military aid to Indonesia.

Tickner, J. Anne. 1992. *Gender in international relations: Feminist perspectives on achieving global security*. New York: Columbia University Press.

Velasco, Mark. 2015. The Visiting Forces Agreement (VFA) in the Philippines: Insights on issues of sovereignty, security and foreign policy. *Asia Pacific Journal of Multidisciplinary Research* 3(4): 82–89.

Wibben, Annick T. R. 2004. Feminist international relations: Old debates and new directions. *Brown Journal of World Affairs* X(2): 97–114.

Winter, Bronwyn. 2011. Guns, money and justice: The 2005 Subic rape case. *International Feminist Journal of Politics* 13(3): 371–389.

Yuval-Davis, N. 2006. Intersectionality and feminist politics. *European Journal of Women's Studies* 13(3): 193–209.

6 Bicycle wheels and noodle bowls

Making sense of (South) East Asian regional relations after 9/11

Insofar as such a thing as a "Southeast Asian region" exists, its regionalization has been of interest to IR scholars for a long time. Regionalization, by definition, requires the social construction of a region through shared ideas about *what it means to be a region* and the creation of institutions that reflect and sustain them (Stubbs and Mustapha 2014). These regional designations are protean, and one could be forgiven for imagining that terms like "East Asia" and "Southeast Asia" are completely arbitrary designations. But they clearly do have purchase, as is reflected in the ongoing reality of complex regional organizations, institutions, relationships, rivalries, and affinities. As defined in Chapter 1, the term "East Asia" has been used in this book to refer generally to the larger geographically contiguous area encompassing the Western rim of the Pacific – from the Koreas, including China, and down to Indonesia. The term "Southeast Asia" has been used to refer more specifically to the sub-grouping of East Asian countries that are also members of ASEAN, which are Indonesia, Malaysia, Singapore, Thailand, the Philippines, Laos, Cambodia, Vietnam, and Myanmar/Burma. This book has been primarily interested in the impact of the War on Terror in Southeast Asia, but it is often impossible to talk about Southeast Asia as a region without necessarily bringing China, Japan, and/or the Koreas into the picture somehow. For this reason, I use the term (South)East Asia if I am referring broadly to the overlapping regional ideas and institutions that include Southeast Asia *and* East Asia.

These overlapping and unsettled iterations of what the region(s) look(s) like are part of what this chapter seeks to explore. What, if any, regional identities exist and what sort of impact did the War on Terror have on these identities and on related notions of security? How did 9/11 and the War on Terror affect regional configurations, if at all? Did the War on Terror security narratives affect trade and economic relations in the region? In exploring these questions, this chapter first looks at the evolution of regionalism and regionalization efforts in (South) East Asia, and especially those related to security. Second, this chapter is curious about how the security narratives of the War on Terror affected articulations of regional security and identity, if at all. It further examines the "securitization" of economic relations between the US and the region under the Bush Doctrine (Higgott 2004) and examines regional approaches to terrorism after

120 *Bicycle wheels and noodle bowls*

9/11. Finally, this chapter looks at how War on Terror security narratives reinforced an "ASEAN-way" of "comprehensive security" as the means by which the concepts of "regional resilience" and "national resilience" are deployed by governing elites in order to maintain *regime* security in a variety of repressive ways (Burke and McDonald 2007; Noor 2006).

Regionalism and regionalization in (South) East Asia

What does regionalism and regionalization in (South)East Asia look like? "Regionalism" can be defined as "the body of ideas promoting an identified geographical or social space as the regional project" (Hveem 2006, 72). First, regionalism may be thought of ideationally as a normative view touting the benefits of developing shared values, norms, goals and/or policies among the population and governments of a specific geographic area (Söderbaum 2003; Camroux 2006; Kim 2004). Second, regionalism may be thought of in institutional terms. That is to say, regionalism involves the formation of organizations and institutions that allow for regular formal interactions among state actors in a geographic area (Pempel 2005; Stubbs and Mustapha 2014). *Regionalism* then, is generally associated with a policy program leading to both formal and informal institution building. For example, the promotion of trade liberalization was one of the main objectives of regional agreements in the twentieth century (O'Brien and Williams 2007).

Regionalization, on the other hand, refers to the *processes* that are responsible for building concrete patterns of transactions and relationships within a regional (usually geographic) space (Hveem 2006, 72). Here we can say that regionalization refers to the process of creating connections that lead to increased cooperation, integration, or convergence across national boundaries in a particular geographic area and that serve to knit a patchwork of regional interests together (Hettne and Söderbaum 2000). Of course, the two concepts – regionalism and regionalization – are related in that for the idea of a region to be translated concretely into action it must be institutionalized through regionalization. This process, in turn, has a significant impact on the development of ideas about the most appropriate way to advance the goals of a specific region (Stubbs and Mustapha 2014). Although its post-Cold War variant had been going on for over 20 years, the regionalism seen after 9/11 was then often referred to as the "new" regionalism (Hveem 2006; Palmer 1991; Coleman and Underhill 1998; Hettne and Söderbaum 2000). "New" regionalism was named thusly in contrast to previous generations of "old" regionalism, which were strongly premised on the idiosyncrasies of the state system from a realist perspective.

Regional projects under the "old" regionalism were based on the assumption of otherwise self-interested actors whose *shared* interests were better served through limited cooperation related to security objectives or economic growth. These "old" regional arrangements tended to be at odds with multilateralism, where the cooperative grouping together of states "allowed them considerable freedom to impose barriers vis-à-vis non members" (Hveem 2006, 75). In other

Bicycle wheels and noodle bowls 121

words, the "old" regionalism was relatively inward looking (O'Brien and Williams 2007). In contrast, the "new" post-Cold War regionalism was open and outward-looking, and generally understood to be complementary to international security, trade liberalization, and neoliberal globalization (O'Brien and Williams 2007; Palmer 1991). This "new" regionalism was made distinct from the old because it did not represent a movement towards territorially based autarkies, but instead represented concentrations of competitive political and economic power competing in the global economy, with multiple inter and intra-regional flows (Mittelman 1996). Post-Cold War (South) East Asian regionalism leading up to 9/11 was "new" in this way and was "top down" rather than "bottom-up" because it was primarily state driven (Shaw and Söderbaum 2003). "New" regional arrangements showed differences in their formation (state-led or bottom-up) and the extent to which they were institutionalized and formalized. Regionalism in (South) East Asia continued to be state driven after the Cold War but was "new" in the sense of having an outward orientation. Importantly, this "new" (South) East Asian regionalism was also much less formalized than its contemporaneous counterparts in Europe and North America (Stubbs and Reed 2005).

As I have mentioned, (South) East Asia has been of particular interest to IR and security scholars for precisely this reason: a distinctively informal approach to regionalization and multilateralism that nevertheless seems to work along multiple registers. In contrast to the formality of their European and North American counterparts, East and Southeast Asian regional institutions have tended to function in a manner that is counter-intuitively both consensus-based and rule-avoidant. Yet they have continued to show "stickiness" in their ability to develop enduring institutional structures to promote regional cooperation and manage competing ideas (Stubbs and Mustapha 2014). Despite the predictions of realists and the liberal institutionalists who prefer more formalized arrangements, sometimes competing (South) East Asian regional organizations like APEC, ASEAN, ASEAN+3 (ASEAN plus China, Japan, and South Korea, also known as the APT) and the ASEAN Regional Forum (ARF) continued to play important functions in regional relations after 9/11 (Ba 2014). As such, the region has continued to perplex and challenge established notions about how regionalization is "supposed" to work.

Keeping in mind the outward-facing orientation and the relative informality of regional groupings, it is notable that (South) East Asian states are still in the process of an ever-evolving and ongoing regional project (Stubbs 2018). Prior to 9/11, the various regional groupings were still finding their footing and dealing with competing ideas around questions of regional identity and the geographic and ideational scope of the region (Pempel 2005; Ravenhill 2001; Stubbs 2000; Thomas 2012; Wesley 2001). This related to the end of the Cold War, which presented three major challenges to regional relations. First, many states in the region were still facing the "double-curse" of post-colonial independence struggles as weak states (Goh 2014); second, as discussed in Chapter 5, the region had to deal with the geopolitical shifts caused by the end of the conflicts in

122 *Bicycle wheels and noodle bowls*

Indochina and the subsequent withdrawal of the *raison d'être* for American forward operating base deployment (Goh 2014; Ba 2014); and third, states in the region came under increasingly intense pressure to become active players in a liberal international order despite the clear benefits of the "East Asian developmental approach" to state building, regime security, and economic growth (Stubbs 2018).

In response to these challenges, there emerged a dual disposition across all regional institutions that may come the closest to describing a (South) East Asian "regional identity" after the Cold War: a shared commitment to "intramural strengthening" and the "external management of great powers" (Goh 2014). In both of these commitments

> Southeast Asian states demonstrated greater strategic thinking and activism than is usually attributed to small states in international relations; they exhibited significant conceptual innovation and pragmatic adaptation, and carved a central role for ASEAN in the changing East Asian order more broadly.
>
> (Goh 2014, 466)

Holding these two commitments together meant that in most (South) East Asian societies, the post-Cold War period saw both support and contestation for a liberal regional order (Stubbs 2018). Hence, among regional elites a clear divide emerged between those advocating for a continuation of the "developmental state" model of economic growth and those who supported a more liberal market orientation. Importantly, "the views of these coalitions spilled over into the way regional economic and security relations were conducted" (Stubbs 2018, 148). As a result, during the first half of the 1990s the two dominant self-conceptions of the region were first, an expansive transpacific view embodied in the Asia Pacific Economic Cooperation (APEC) forum and; and second, a more limited Southeast Asian view institutionalized in the Association of Southeast Asian Nations (ASEAN), which would later be expanded to include the so called "plus three" of China, South Korea and Japan (Stubbs and Mustapha 2014; Goh 2014; Stubbs 2018).

Competing regional narratives

In 1990, then Malaysian Prime Minister Mahathir Mohamad called for the broadening of an explicitly "Asians-only" region. Ultimately, his efforts were sidelined by US diplomatic pressure and a lack of interest on the part of potential members (Stubbs 2002, 2009). Nevertheless, the latter half of the 1990s saw some de facto changes occur to that effect. During this period, a distinctly "Asian" regional organization in the form of the APT emerged. Then the post-9/11 period brought the gradual rolling-back of US involvement and engagement in East Asian economic multilateralism, which stemmed at least partially from post-9/11 US security policy (Higgott 2004; Ba 2014). Washington's general

Bicycle wheels and noodle bowls   123

withdrawal from multilateralism under Bush signaled a (modified) re-entrenchment of the hub-and-spokes model of bilateral relationships and ushered in further questions about the competing visions of the region.

While it was generally agreed by the original participants of the APT grouping that a wider East Asian regional association was necessary, no clear consensus emerged on what form the association should take. Indeed, its primary purpose was never properly established (Stubbs 2002; Stubbs and Mustapha 2014). As mentioned, this played into the emergence of different ideas and views of what (South) East Asian regionalism should look like. The view that gained the most strength came out of the second of the two regional visions mentioned above: that of an exclusively "Asian," relatively compact region, rooted firmly in the existing APT framework, whose purpose would fulfil both the need for increased intramural relations and the external management of the US (Goh 2014). This view became the dominant conception of the region held by most ASEAN members in the years following 9/11 (Chin and Stubbs 2011; Thomas 2012), reflecting a complex array of economic and strategic motivations woven together in a messy, but shared conception of East Asian regionalism. At its core, there was a concern with the potential for domination by "Western" actors like Australia and the US, but there was also a clear need to balance the China–ASEAN relationship as both potential threat and potential opportunity (Callahan 2005).

But what are the ideational factors that pulled together this Asian region, which as Baldwin (2004) once pointed out, resembles the messiness of a "noodle-bowl" with its seemingly ad hoc, criss-crossing, and under-formalized regional arrangements?[1] Importantly, early on in the ongoing East Asian regional project there was the emergence of a broad recognition of a shared set of values, norms, goals, and policies among the people and governments of East Asia. Two sets of global events influenced the developing conception of an "East Asian" regionalism. First, globalization and mobile capital brought regional actors together in the face of "outside" pressures. Multinational companies that were engaged in light industrial manufacturing for export had realized that parts of East Asia were particularly conducive to greater profitability. However, there was also a sense within the region of the need to manage these economic processes so as not to be sideswiped by the forces of globalization (Hveem 2006; Leu 2011; Stubbs 2012). These anxieties, of course, were validated by the events of the Asian Financial Crisis of 1997–1998 and the more recent global financial crisis of 2007–2009.

Second, the end of the Cold War brought notable changes to regional relationships in East Asia. As mentioned, this meant that the US changed its relatively relaxed economic attitude towards its regional allies by subsequently demanding that they liberalize their economies and introduce Western-style democratic reforms (Stubbs 2000; Beeson 2007a; Betts 1993). There were also calls for some of these same countries to show a greater respect for individual political and human rights. After 9/11 there was a further deconstruction of the existing Asia Pacific economic region through a new variant of the "hub and

124 *Bicycle wheels and noodle bowls*

spokes" model of US involvement in the region (Higgott 2004; Baldwin 2004), which will be explained in more detail presently. This led to new formations of securitized bilateral economic agreements between the US and (South) East Asian actors, while at the same time the US avoided meaningful or substantive participation in multilateral economic fora (Christoffersen 2002; Higgott 2004; Leheny 2005).

The ideational aspects of Southeast Asian regionalism, or the values, norms, and goals that are widely accepted by members of ASEAN, have developed over a lengthy period of time (Stubbs 2002). These values, norms, and goals revolve around ideas as to how states should relate to each other, the role of major powers in the region, and the best approach to economic development. A regional "code of conduct" was formalized in the Treaty of Amity and Cooperation (TAC), originally signed at the first ASEAN summit in Bali in 1976. The TAC is considered to be (South) East Asia's benchmark treaty as it sets out the principles by which those who accede to the treaty deal with the wider world and with each other. These principles are: *respect for the independence, sovereignty, territorial integrity and national identity of all nations; the right of states to be free from external interference; non-interference in the affairs of one another; the renunciation of the threat of force; and the peaceful settlement of disputes* (www.aseansec.org/).[2] In addition to this formal code of conduct, ASEAN members also developed an informal code governing regional interactions more generally. This is often referred to as the "ASEAN Way" and involves "a high degree of discreetness, informality, pragmatism, expediency, consensus-building, and non-confrontational bargaining styles" (Acharya 1997, 329).

It is worth noting that the values, norms, and goals of the TAC and the ASEAN Way embody a distinctive post-colonial lineage. The TAC principles and the ASEAN Way both echo the principles enunciated at the Bandung Conference of 1955, which brought together leaders from 29 Asian and African countries and led to the establishment of the Non-Aligned Movement. The ten principles set out in the 1955 Final Communiqué from the Bandung Conference are what provided the basis for the TAC later on.[3] Further, both the Bandung Conference and ASEAN were influenced by two important historical factors. First, the vast majority of leaders who met at Bandung represented countries that had experienced Western colonial subjugation, which led to a general unwillingness to serve the interests of major Western powers. Second, many of the leaders attending the Bandung Conference felt that their countries were pawns in the Cold War. There was a collective need to express opposition to the pressures that the Cold War visited on those countries that both the United States and the Soviet Union sought as allies (Mackie 2005).

The Bandung principles underscored this point by asserting a general respect for sovereignty, justice, and international obligations, and that disputes should be settled by peaceful means (Mackie 2005). Hence, there was a general sense among the Bandung participants that they had an opportunity to rethink international relations and to conduct international relations in a way that meshed

Bicycle wheels and noodle bowls 125

with their values and interests (Widyatmadja 2005). These foundational ideas about the conduct of international affairs were instantiated in ASEAN as it began to flesh out how members felt that regional and international relations should be approached. Significantly, the common experiences of the ASEAN members in terms of colonialism and the pressures of the Cold War are also reflected in the way that the ASEAN members view power (Hund 2003). Clearly, ASEAN members recognize that the major powers have an important role to play in the region, but there are differences between (and within) ASEAN countries on how this should be managed or understood. On the one hand, Singapore's Lee Kuan Yew once emphasized the value of having the United States as a partner in balancing a rising China (Hund 2003, 388). And while Emmers (2004) may be correct to note that "analysts should not underestimate the persistence of realist beliefs among political leaders" in the region (6), we still saw at the 2006 APEC meeting in Hanoi, that Asian leaders rejected the "securitization" of the APEC grouping sought by the US.

Further, a strictly neo-realist formulation of power is not very appealing to ASEAN members. As Eaton and Stubbs (2006) have pointed out, ASEAN members are states that have traditionally been the object of domination, coercion, and pressure. The question then, has been how to exercise power and shape their own world without the material capabilities that are normally associated with the exercise of "power" in the international system. One argument, of course, is that power should be seen as "the ability to resist change, to throw the costs of adaptation on others" and that, "characteristically, the ability to resist change requires fewer resources to be placed on the line than the ability to bring about change" (Brown 2001, 92). But ASEAN members are not simply in the business of resisting change. Indeed, they seek to build East Asian regionalism *not* in order to protect the status quo, but to guide change in a direction that benefits their long-term interests (Eaton and Stubbs 2006).

Costs and opportunities

On balance, 9/11 did not appear to fundamentally alter (South) East Asian regionalism in obvious ways. For the most part, a general continuation of pre-existing regional dynamics was observable. This general tendency towards continuity is partly explained by the surprisingly robust path dependency displayed by (South) East Asian institutions due to what Pierson (2000) or Stubbs (2018) might call "institutional stickiness" resulting from a combination of internal socialization and organizational culture. This was true with regards to broad patterns of economic and security cooperation between the US and the region, and among regional members as well. However, it would be a mistake to miss the subtle, but significant, shifts on several fronts, as regional actors reacted to both the costs and opportunities afforded by the War on Terror.

Where the US continued to engage in multilateral efforts after 9/11, we saw clear attempts to steer the regional agenda away from economic cooperation and towards the security anxieties of the War on Terror. So, for example,

126 *Bicycle wheels and noodle bowls*

> at the 2 APEC summits following 9/11 – Mexico in October 2001 and Shanghai in October 2003 – Bush made the War on Terror the central focus of his meetings with Asian leaders, the trade liberalization being left, much to the annoyance of some Asian leaders, on the backburner … APEC had become just another forum for coalition-building in geopolitical terms.
>
> (Camroux and Okfen 2004, 165)

This re-orientation of American participation in East Asian multilateralism, and notably Washington's marked departure from non-security regional issues, had the effect of pushing Southeast Asian regional designs even further towards an anti-hegemonist stance in the region. To be sure, this had already gained traction prior to 9/11, but Washington's post-9/11 security outlook further cemented this vision (Mustapha 2011). Individual ASEAN countries felt safer maintaining strategic and economic relations with the US at the *bilateral* level as part of their strategy to balance against Chinese hegemony (Goh 2014; Ba 2014); but *as a group* there were fears that letting great powers in to the core regional grouping would pose a potential threat to the ASEAN way of regionalism and might invite incursions into regional state sovereignty (Stubbs 2018). Because of these concerns and sensibilities, contemporary ASEAN security strategy can be summed up by the twin principles of "resilience and anti-hegemony" (Goh 2014, 474) in the face of US pressures and regional sensibilities.

As for the Americans, after 9/11 their tendency was to over-emphasize terrorism related security issues in their bilateral relations with Southeast Asian states while slowly withdrawing from multilateral relations at the same time. As a result, in the aftermath of 9/11 and within the context of the emerging security narratives of the War on Terror, Washington set about securitizing its economic and trade relations with (South) East Asia (Higgott 2004; Mustapha 2011). The concept of "securitization" suggests that to securitize something results in the suspension of "normal politics" for exceptional circumstances of threat. How and why something is placed on the security agenda depends on the authority and legitimacy of those committing the securitizing speech act, and securitizing has successfully occurred when the receiving audiences of the securitizing message accept it as such (Buzan *et al.* 1998). The degree to which regional actors actually accepted the securitizing moves is debatable, but they, nevertheless, adapted to the realities of US pressure in this area in short order.

This is partly because after 9/11, key "elements of US foreign economic policy [became] subsumed within the wider contextual discourse of the US security agenda" (Higgott 2004, 426). In this foreign policy approach, economic policy was used as both an overt and covert arm of security policy. Securitization, in this instance, was used "to justify the imposition of conditions and measures in the area of foreign economic policy that would not usually be considered the norm in the policy domain … [and] the securitization discourse [was] one of reward and threat" (Higgott 2004, 427). Hence, aspects of the War on Terror under the Bush doctrine effectively resulted in the securitization of post-9/11 economic discourse and trade policy, with great impact on the (South) East

Bicycle wheels and noodle bowls   127

Asian region (Higgott 2004; Beeson 2007a, 2007b; Ikenberry 2002, 2004; Capling 2004). In contrast, as we talked about in Chapter 3, during the late 1990s security policy was subordinate to economic policy as part of the American project "to make the world safe for the liberal economic enterprise" (Higgott 2004, 429). Bush's declaration of the War on Terror consolidated a move in the opposite direction, and the subordination of economic policy to security interests occurred "with massive accentuation following 9/11" (Higgott 2004, 429), dovetailing with Bush's existing tendencies towards unilateralist-idealist policies "under-written by US military power, and not by the collective approval of a wider (international) community" (Higgott 2004, 431). Here, as mentioned, we began to see a gradual withdrawal from, and ambivalence towards, forms of multilateralism in general.

In other words, in the years immediately after 9/11, the Bush administration rather openly brandished bilateral *economic* agreements to solidify support for the US *security* agenda under the War on Terror (Mustapha 2011). And this was happening in other places as well. For instance, then US Trade Representative Robert Zoellick testified at House Agriculture Committee Hearings that a Free Trade Agreement (FTA) with New Zealand was "very unlikely" due to sensitive agriculture issues and "some things done recently" (United States Congress 2003, 23). Savvy observers surmised that the "things done recently" referred to Prime Minister Clark's vocal opposition to the US war in Iraq and her refusal to allow US ships carrying nuclear materials to traverse through New Zealand's waters (Higgott 2004; Capling 2004; Mustapha 2007). By way of contrast, the US–Australia trade agreement was fast-tracked during this same period (Beeson 2007b; Capling 2004; Higgott 2004) and was regarded by many as a reward for Australia's staunch support for the Iraqi invasion and the War on Terror.[4]

In June 2003, in a speech to the Institute of International Economics in Washington, Zoellick further asserted that an FTA with the US was "… not something one has a right to … It's a privilege … a privilege that must be earned via the support of US policy goals … [the Bush administration] … expects cooperation – or better – on security issues" (Barry 2005). During this same period Washington was penalizing other countries that did not provide support to the military coalition for the invasion of Iraq, in a variety of ways (Mustapha 2007). This included the withdrawal of foreign aid if "… a state's behavior was seen to be inconsistent with the 'expectation' of the US government [it became] the target of punishment by the United States" (Tago 2008, 380). As such, the securitization of many aspects of American bilateralism was felt in various ways by local actors. This included the hijacking of trade and economic interests by a narrowly conceived security agenda and getting sidelined from the benefits of US trade and aid in response to levels of support provided to the War on Terror (Mustapha 2007).

Perhaps the most important aspect of the War on Terror for this analysis though, is how members of ASEAN – both individually and as members of a regional grouping – saw the War on Terror as a valuable opportunity (Gerstl 2010; Ba 2014). Despite the costs of facilitating a continued US military

128 *Bicycle wheels and noodle bowls*

dominance in the region, state elites saw Washington's pleas for help as an opportunity to prove their relevance as key regional allies and in doing so to entrench good relations with Washington (Goh 2014, 472). Further, as we saw in Chapter 5, Southeast Asian actors used the language and discourses of the War on Terror to justify illiberal security practices undertaken to protect the stability of their own regimes. But they had to be careful about balancing the delicate machinations of improving their global reputation, while continuing to function well as a resilient region according to the ASEAN Way through the maintenance of strong state apparatuses and dispositions to retain power domestically.

ASEAN after 9/11

Before the 1990s. "Asia proved infertile ground for regional security institutions" (Ba 2014, 667). As outlined in the previous sections, after the end of the Cold War the regional security landscape changed considerably and saw the formation of several regional security institutions and arrangements including the ASEAN Regional Forum (or ARF), the East Asia Summit, and the ASEAN Defence Ministers Meeting Plus (ADMM-Plus) as additions to the Asian security architecture (Ba 2014; Tow and Taylor 2010). The role of ASEAN in this shift cannot be understated, as regional security trends after the Cold War and into the post 9/11 period have highlighted ASEAN's role as a well established institution – despite its "messiness" – with a key role in "expanded cooperative activity" extending beyond its immediate members and including key powers in the larger Asian region as well as Western powers like the US (Ba 2014, 669). Notably, ASEAN and its related security arrangements are relatively decentralized, consensus-driven, and conceive of security broadly (Ba 2014), all of which helps to explain the unique way that Southeast Asia, as a region, was able to leverage the security politics of the War on Terror for the purposes of both regional "comprehensive security" and strong-state "national resilience."

As the relationship between securitization and politics is usually understood, positioning something as a security problem often results in the exceptional suspension of "normal" politics and its replacement with security politics. In a related but slightly different manoeuvre, *as a region* the War on Terror compelled ASEAN to *semi*-securitize terrorism with the intention of *de*politicizing regional counter-terrorism activities in order to overcome unique regional political challenges (Gerstl 2010). Hence, after 9/11 ASEAN reacted to the complex political obstacles standing in the way of closer counter-terrorism cooperation between members in a double move of balancing regional sensibilities with regime interests. First, ASEAN members securitized the terrorist threat specifically as a trans-national issue that required a collaborative *technocratic* response; and second, ASEAN members did this as a measured attempt to depoliticize regional counter-terrorism so as to not threaten the ASEAN way principles of non-interference and mutual respect for state sovereignty (Gerstl 2010).[5]

This deliberate move to depoliticize counter-terrorism cooperation served the specific needs of the ASEAN governing regimes at the state level. Although it was the case that in the US, the UK, and Australia leaders felt the political need to "discursively portray terrorism as an existential threat in order to justify new legislative measures to limit certain individual rights in the War on Terror" (Wolfendale 2007 quoted in Gerstl 2010, 60), this was not a necessity for the Southeast Asian governments that already practiced more (soft) authoritarian forms of government. Rather, much more important for ASEAN countries were the priorities of maintaining regime stability and, in some cases, reducing domestic perceptions of an unfair anti-Muslim bias in counter-terrorism practices. At the same time, ASEAN state elites needed to also convince Washington of a serious and concerted effort by them to combat regional terrorism (Mustapha 2011). As such, the case of ASEAN's responses to 9/11 demonstrated that securitization does not always mean a straightforward moving away from "normal" politics to security politics (Gerstl 2010). Rather, under certain circumstances securitization can lead to *de*politicization altogether, which allows for a formerly politicized issue to be regarded instead as a technocratic security issue "that is best dealt with through non-political, technical measures" (Gerstl 2010, 62) and the knowledge of experts.

In the case of ASEAN, this had several effects. First, it allowed for a greater resolution of the difficult-to-reconcile tensions that exist between state, regime, and human security in the region. Second, it allowed for greater accord among ASEAN state leaders who would otherwise be hesitant to share sensitive security information with one another, and who grapple with their own intra-regional security tensions. Third, the technocratic and seemingly apolitical nature of the cooperation helped to maintain an anti-hegemonist "Southeast Asians only" vision of ASEAN (Goh 2014; Stubbs 2018) and to assuage local fears of slavish capitulation to American interests (Noor 2006). And fourth, it served as a "deliberate move to limit the scope and sensitivity of human security as a matter of discourse and policy" (Gerstl 2010, 54) because of the presumption that the continued subversion of human security discourses was required for the continued maintenance of regime legitimacy.

From a critical security perspective, this is significant on several levels. First, when a security issue is taken *out* of the realm of the political (as opposed to when its politics are re-framed), there can be "no genuine political debate about the counter-terrorism approach" (Gerstl 2010, 62) at all and in the case of ASEAN, this "depoliticization strategy [was] evident with regards to ASEAN's treatment of political Islam" (Gerstl 2010, 62), which as outlined in Chapters 4 and 5 resulted in increased repressive state measures against political resistance more generally – whether or not a legitimate threat of terrorism exists. And it is here where we can see that the dangers of a comprehensive security approach that buttresses the further consolidation of the ASEAN "strong state" to the detriment of individuals and groups residing within these states. This last point is particularly noteworthy because ASEAN's vision of security has always been based on national stability and regime security rather than on human security. This ASEAN vision of security is known as "Comprehensive Security," and refers to a state-centric, top-down understanding of security that subverts the

130   *Bicycle wheels and noodle bowls*

security of individuals as an adjunct to regime security. And as Acharya (2005) and others (see Caballero-Anthony 2005; Noor 2003) have pointed out, "Comprehensive Security" has been used as an instrument of regime legitimization in Southeast Asia.

This allows us to understand better the seeming lack of cohesion in the messaging of state elites regarding threats of terrorism, their respective relationships with the US, and the role of political Islam in domestic politics: on the one hand, framing regional terrorism as an existential threat to the state would be politically risky for the ASEAN grouping as it would necessarily then introduce difficult questions pertaining to the limits of sovereignty and the possibilities for state intervention; while on the other hand, framing regional terrorism as a threat to the safety of individuals or as a violent expression of otherwise legitimate political grievances would necessarily then introduce questions around human security and human rights. Framed either way, none of the potential outcomes are particularly compatible with the political and security goals of ASEAN member-states – both as a group and as individual governing regimes. The solution then, was to frame terrorism *regionally* as a practical problem that required only a politically "neutral" technocratic response; to frame terrorism *domestically* as a way to discredit and delegitimize various forms of political opposition; and to frame terrorism *globally* as counter to the progressive forces of "moderate Islam," of which elites in Southeast Asia became self appointed champions after 9/11.

Conclusion – "regional resilience" as security

In Southeast Asia, notions of regional security relate very much to the long-standing centrality of the idea of "national resilience" as an organizing principle of security politics. Among the ASEAN members, a high importance continues to be placed on the military dimension as the most important aspect of security, but political, economic and socio-cultural dimensions are folded into a broader conceptualization of security factors that characterizes the so-called ASEAN Way (Burke and McDonald 2007). This is the afore-mentioned "comprehensive" understanding of security, which has origins in the TAC and is a core principle of the ASEAN charter and of regional security cooperation in general. This concept is what ultimately enabled the formation of ASEAN as a regional "security community" whose members agreed to respect each other's internal sovereignty via the doctrine of non-interference; agreed to collaboratively minimize the intrusion of great powers despite ASEAN's "omni-enmeshment" (Goh 2014) with them; and agreed to remain committed to "the maintenance of 'internal security,' in which sovereignty … is paramount, and regime security a dominant objective" (Burke and McDonald 2007, 12).

In this "comprehensive" conceptualization of security then, "security" is closely related to the concept of "national resilience," or the idea that domestic economic, political and socio-cultural stability in combination with a norm of non-interference between states is necessary for maintaining the stability of the region and the strength of individual regimes. In other words, to flip the comprehensive regional security model around, a stable and happy region (i.e. free of military inter-state conflict and unwanted "outside" intervention) makes for stable and happy governing regimes (i.e. free of internal conflict and "outside" influences). In his analysis of the formation of the ASEAN Regional Forum, Katsumata (2006) points out that the interests and policies that initiated the ASEAN Regional Forum were "defined by what can be regarded as a norm of security cooperation in Asia … [that contained] two sets of ideational elements: common security … (and) the ASEAN Way of diplomacy" (181). Neither of these norms pose a threat to the governing regimes of ASEAN members, and, in fact, both reinforce their authority. As such, we can observe a style and understanding of Southeast Asian security regionalism that remains "tellingly essentialist, particularly [with] concessions to state-centrism and ideational/normative determinism" (Tan 2006, 239).

But what is the significance of this? Why does the state-centrism and distinctive ASEAN*ness* of regional security merit attention? Because, as outlined in Chapter 3, this reading of Southeast Asian security, which emphasizes the significance of multilateralism and ideational norms as they relate to inter-state conflict, "tends to soft-soap the darker side of the ASEAN-way, and the essentially statist *(and internally coercive)* character of its norms" (Burke and McDonald 2007, 13). Importantly, a critical reading of this Southeast Asian concept of comprehensive security reveals that along with the norms of national resilience and non-interference that are incorporated into its structures, ASEAN security regionalism – reinforced and consolidated by the War on Terror – has been a source of, and a site of, insecurity. The very principles that drive Southeast Asian enthusiasm for expanding the scope of security cooperation leave important issues at the

> subnational and transregional levels outside the regional conceptual and policy frameworks … [and] threats to the security of individuals or communities posed by state-perpetrated or sanctioned political violence also tend to be "black-boxed" in continuation of the ASEAN association of regional interference.
>
> (Goh 2014, 473)

This is because "comprehensive security as 'resilience,' links internal security paradigms preoccupied with the (often violent and repressive) defense of regime security … with regional frameworks that … place a primacy upon sovereign freedom, non-interference and 'political stability'" (Burke and McDonald 2007, 13). As part of the ongoing relevance of ASEAN as a mechanism for intramural strengthening and the external management of powers (Goh 2014, 466), member-states saw the opportunities presented by 9/11 and took them. And as such, ASEAN regionalism

> tends to *strengthen* statist norms and insulate regional governments from scrutiny over their approach to human rights and internal claims to justice, separatism and difference … if this is a security community, it is a community

132 *Bicycle wheels and noodle bowls*

of economic, political and military elites, and the security that it provides is morally (and conceptually) incoherent, being too often premised on the insecurity of others.

(Burke and McDonald 2007, 13, emphasis in original)

9/11, and the War on Terror that followed, has only served to strengthen these statist and regime-centric norms, allowing for an ever-growing emphasis on the primacy placed on the internal "stability" of states through the tacit approval of anti-democratic practices under the guise of anti-terrorism.

Notes

1 Baldwin was referring to Free Trade Agreements, but the "noodle bowl" metaphor also works when one considers the degree to which East Asian regional and bilateral relations more generally display overlapping relationships, divergent interests, and different levels of cohesion and/or formalization.
2 It is notable that the US had refused to sign on to the TAC until then Secretary of State, Hillary Rodham Clinton, signed the TAC on behalf of President Obama on July 22, 2009.
3 These included an emphasis on non-intervention in the affairs of other countries; respect for the sovereignty and territorial integrity of all nations; the equality of all races and nations, large and small; the right of all states to collective self-defence but not in order to further the interests of great powers; and the promotion of mutual interests and cooperation. Moreover, the Bandung Conference deliberations were conducted in a manner that later came to characterize ASEAN meetings. For example, contentious issues were avoided; informality was encouraged; and the importance of wide consultation, compromise, and consensus-building was stressed (Acharya 2005; Mackie 2005).
4 It is worth pointing out that the politics of the American War on Terror, while clearly responsible for fast-tracking an FTA agreement that many were doubtful would actually occur (see Beeson 2007b, 222–224), also compelled the Australian government to agree to rather unfavourable terms. This was driven by "Howard's desire to strengthen Australia's political and strategic links with the US, and objective that had assumed an even greater importance with the War on Terror" (Capling 2004 quoted in Beeson 2007b, 223).
5 Interestingly, the Americans were doing the exact opposite. Before 9/11, East Asian terrorism was generally framed as trans-national crime in American security policy, but after 9/11 and as part of the War on Terror it was a necessary maneuver to frame Southeast Asian political Islam and secessionist terrorism as relating to *Al-Qaeda* and IS. I explored some of this discursive switching in Chapters 4 and 5.

References

Acharya, Amitav. 1997. Ideas, identity, and institution-building: From the "ASEAN way" to the "Asia-Pacific way"? *The Pacific Review* 10(3): 319–346.
Acharya, Amitav. 2005. Do norms and identity matter? Community and power in Southeast Asia's regional order. *The Pacific Review* 18(1): 95–118.
Ba, Alice D. 2014. Asia's regional security institutions. In Evelyn Goh, Saadia Pekkanen, John Ravenhill, and Rosemary Foot (Eds) *The Oxford handbook of the international relations of Asia*. Oxford: Oxford University Press. pp. 667–689.

Bicycle wheels and noodle bowls 133

Baldwin, R. E. 2004. *The spoke trap: Hub-and-spoke bilateralism in East Asia.* CNAEC Research Series 04-02. Seoul: Korean Institute for International Economic Policy.

Barry, Tom. June 15, 2005. Zoellick plies new trade. *Asia Times* (*Asia Times Online*: www.atimes.com/atimes/Global_Economy/GA14Dj01.html).

Beeson, Mark. 2007a. The United States and Southeast Asia: Change and continuity in American hegemony. In K. Jayasuria (Ed.) *Crisis and change in regional governance.* London: Routledge. pp. 215–231.

Beeson, Mark. 2007b. *Bush and Asia: America's evolving relations with East Asia.* London: Routledge.

Betts, Richard. 1993. Wealth, power and instability: East Asia and the United States after the Cold War. *International Security* 8(3): 34–77.

Brown, Drusilla K. 2001. Labor standards: where do they belong on the international trade agenda?. *Journal of Economic Perspectives* 15(3): 89–112.

Burke, Anthony and Matt McDonald (Eds). 2007. *Critical security in the Asia-Pacific.* Manchester: Manchester University Press.

Buzan, Barry, Ole Waever, and Jaap de Wilde. 1998. *Security: A new framework for analysis.* Boulder: Lynne Rienner.

Caballero-Anthony, Mely. 2005. *Regional security in Southeast Asia: Beyond the ASEAN way.* Singapore: Institute of Southeast Asian Studies.

Callahan, William A. 2005. The rise of China: How to understand China: The dangers and opportunities of being a rising power. *Review of International Studies* 31(4): 701–714.

Camroux, David. 2006. "Regionalism," "regionalisation" and "three level games": Towards an Asian response to Eurocentrism in the analysis of regional integration, paper prepared for the ECPR Joint Sessions of Workshops, April 25–30 in Nicosia, Greece.

Camroux, David and Nuria Okfen. 2004. Introduction: 9/11 and US–Asian relations: Towards a new "New World Order"? *The Pacific Review* 17(2): 163–177.

Capling, Ann. 2004. *All the way with the USA: Australia, the US and Free Trade.* Sydney: University of New South Wales.

Chin, G. and Stubbs, R. 2011. China, region-building and the China-ASEAN free trade area. *Review of International Political Economy* 18(3): 277–298.

Christoffersen, Gaye. 2002. The role of East-Asia in Sino-American relations. *Asian Survey* 42(3): 369–396.

Coleman, Will and Geoffrey R. D. Underhill (Eds). 1998. *Regionalism and global economic integration: Europe, Asia and the Americas.* Routledge: London.

Eaton, Sarah and Richard Stubbs. 2006. Is ASEAN powerful? Neo-realist versus constructivist approaches to power in Southeast Asia. *The Pacific Review* 19(2): 135–155.

Emmers, Ralf. 2004. *Cooperative security and the balance of power in ASEAN and the ARF.* London: Routledge.

Gerstl, Alfred. 2010. The depoliticization and "ASEANization" of human security in Southeast Asia: ASEANs counter-terrorism and climate change policies. *ASEAS* 3(1): 48–75.

Goh, Evelyn. 2014. Southeast Asia's evolving security relations and strategies. In Evelyn Goh, Saadia Pekkanen, John Ravenhill, and Rosemary Foot (Eds) *The Oxford handbook of the international relations of Asia.* Oxford: Oxford University Press, pp. 462–480.

Hettne, Björn and Fredrik Söderbaum. 2000. Theorising the rise of regionness. *New Political Economy* 5(3): 457–473.

134 *Bicycle wheels and noodle bowls*

Higgott, Richard. 2004. After neoliberal globalization: The "securitization" of US foreign economic policy in East Asia. *Critical Asian Studies* 36(3): 425–444.

Hund, Markus. 2003. ASEAN Plus Three: Towards a new age of pan-East Asian regionalism? A skeptic's appraisal. *The Pacific Review* 16(3): 383–418.

Hveem, H. 2006. Explaining the regional phenomenon in an era of globalization. In Richard Stubbs and G. R. D. Underhill (Eds) *Political economy and the changing global order*. Oxford: Oxford University Press, pp. 294–305.

Ikenberry, G John. 2002. America's imperial ambition. *Foreign Affairs* 81(5): 44–60.

Ikenberry, G. John. 2004. Liberalism and empire: Logics of order in the American unipolar age. *Review of International Studies* 30(4): 609–630.

Katsumata, Hiro. 2006. Establishment of the ASEAN regional forum: Constructing a "talking shop" or a "norm brewery." *The Pacific Review* 19(2): 181–198.

Kim, Samuel. 2004. Regionalization and regionalism in East Asia. *Journal of East Asian Studies* 4(1): 39–67.

Leheny, David. 2005. The war on terrorism and the possibility of secret regionalism. In T. J. Pempel (Ed.) *Remapping East Asia: The construction of a region*. Ithaca, NY: Cornell University Press, pp. 236–255.

Leu, G. 2011. ASEAN Preferential trade agreements (PTA) strategy. *Journal of Current Southeast Asian Affairs* 30(2): 31–64.

Mackie, Jamie. 2005. *Bandung 1955: Non-alignment and Afro-Asian solidarity*. Kuala Lumpur: Editions Didier Millet.

Mittelman, James. 1996. Rethinking the new regionalism in the context of globalization. *Global Governance* 2(2): 189–208.

Mustapha, Jennifer. 2007. Re-assessing East Asian security regionalization after 9/11. In Anita Singh and David McDonough (Eds) *Defence to development: Resolving threats to global security*. Halifax: Centre for Foreign Policy Studies, Dalhousie University, pp. 257–281.

Mustapha, Jennifer. 2011. Threat construction in the Bush administration's post-9/11 foreign policy: (Critical) security implications for Southeast Asia. *The Pacific Review* 4(24): 487–504.

Noor, Farish. 2003. Reaping the bitter harvest after twenty years of state Islamization. In Rohan Gunaratna (Ed.) *Terrorism in the Asia Pacific, threat and response*. Singapore: Eastern Universities Press, pp. 178–201.

Noor, Farish. 2006. How Washington's "war on terror" became everyone's: Islamophobia and the impact of September 11 on the political terrain of South and Southeast Asia. *Human Architecture: Journal of the Sociology of Self-Knowledge* 5(1): 29–50.

O'Brien, Robert and Marc Williams. 2007. *Global political economy: Evolution and dynamics*. New York: Palgrave.

Palmer, Norman. 1991. *The new regionalism and the Asia Pacific*. Lexington, KY: Lexington Books.

Pempel, T. J. 2005 *Remapping East Asia: The construction of a region*. Ithaca, NY: Cornell University Press.

Pierson, P. 2000. Increasing returns, path dependence and the study of politics. *American Political Science Review* 94(2): 251–267.

Ravenhill, J. 2001. *APEC and the construction of Pacific Rim regionalism*. Cambridge: Cambridge University Press.

Shaw, Timothy M. and Fredrik Söderbaum (Eds). 2003. *Theories of new regionalism: A Palgrave reader*. London: Palgrave Macmillan.

Söderbaum, Fredrik. 2003. Introduction: Theories of new regionalism. In Fredrik Söderbaum and Timothy M. Shaw (Eds) *Theories of new regionalism: A Palgrave reader.* London: Palgrave Macmillan, pp. 1–21.

Stubbs, Richard. 2000. Signing on to liberalization: AFTA and the politics of regional economic integration. *Pacific Review* 13(2): 297–318.

Stubbs, Richard. 2002. ASEAN Plus Three – Emerging East Asian regionalism. *Asian Survey* 42(3): 440–455.

Stubbs, Richard. 2009. Meeting the challenges of region-building in ASEAN. In Mark Beeson (Ed.) *Contemporary Southeast Asia, 2nd edition.* Basingstoke: Palgrave Macmillan, pp. 237–247.

Stubbs, Richard. 2012. The developmental state and Asian regionalism. In M. Beeson and R. Stubbs (Eds) *Routledge handbook of Asian regionalism.* London: Routledge. pp. 90–99.

Stubbs, Richard. 2018. Order and contestation in the Asia-Pacific Region: Liberal vs developmental/non-interventionist approaches. *The International Spectator* 53(1): 138–151.

Stubbs, Richard and Jennifer Mustapha. 2014. Regional economic institutions in Asia: Ideas and institutionalization. In Evelyn Goh, Saadia Pekkanen, John Ravenhill, and Rosemary Foot (Eds) *The Oxford handbook of the international relations of Asia.* Oxford: Oxford University Press, pp. 690–702.

Stubbs, Richard and Austina Reed. 2005. Regionalism and globalization. In Richard Stubbs and Geoffrey R. D. Underhill (Eds) *Political economy and the changing global order, 3rd edition.* Toronto: McClelland and Stewart, pp. 289–293.

Tago, Atsushi. 2008. Is there an aid-for-participation deal?: US economic and military aid policy to coalition forces (non)participants. *International Relations of the Asia-Pacific* 8(3): 379–398.

Tan, See Seng. 2006. Rescuing constructivism from the constructivists: A critical reading of constructivist interventions in Southeast Asian security. *The Pacific Review* 19(2): 239–260.

Thomas, N. 2012. China–ASEAN relations: The core of Asian regionalism. In M. Beeson and R. Stubbs (Eds) *Routledge handbook of Asian regionalism.* New York: Routledge, pp. 138–151.

Tow, William T. and Brendan Taylor. 2010. What is Asian security architecture? *Review of International Studies* 36(1): 95–116.

United States Congress. 2003. Hearing transcript, House Agriculture Committee http:// agriculture.house.gov/hearings/108/1085.pdf.

Wesley, M. 2001. APEC's mid-life crisis? The rise and fall of early voluntary sectoral liberalization. *Pacific Affairs* 74(2): 185–204.

Widyatmadja, Josef Purnama. April 6, 2005. The spirit of Bandung. *The Jakarta Post.*

7 Beyond the Bush Doctrine

New narratives and new questions

The questions asked in this book have focused primarily on War on Terror narratives in (South) East Asia in the decade immediately after 9/11. But they also gesture towards broader questions about critical security concerns in general, and to emerging questions relating to the ongoing effects of US foreign policy in East and Southeast Asia in the years beyond the Bush administration. As we now know, Barack Obama became the 44th president of the United States and took office in 2009, serving two terms until the election of the 45th and current president of the United States, Donald Trump, who took office in 2017. At the time of this book's publication, we are only into the second year of the Trump administration and it can be politely stated that his foreign policy continues to be a bit of a moving target. We will briefly discuss aspects of what we do know about the "Trump Doctrine" – as far as it does exist – at the end of this chapter. But I will focus primarily on Obama's approach to foreign policy following the Bush years and what it can tell us about both continuities and changes in security discourses and practices relating to the threat of terrorism, and its impacts on (South) East Asia (Jackson and Tsui 2017; Bentley and Holland 2017; Bentley 2013). We can ask the following questions using the same critical security approach that I have outlined in this book, by re-orienting our questions to the particular case and particular security logics of the Obama administration: What did the Obama administration's security policies and discourses bring to this region? Did we witness a change in the understanding and practices of security in East and Southeast Asia in a post-Bush era? Or did we see a continuation of familiar security discourses that marked the region? More importantly, what can a critical security analysis of these questions tell us about how American security policy continues to influence actors in the region?

Hope? Change? Or more of the same?

Immediately upon taking office, the Obama administration appeared to consciously shift the White House's public narratives relating to the War on Terror. At first glance, this shift destabilized the central themes in the security narratives of Bush's War on Terror. But, as will be discussed, the degree to which Obama's security practices actually did differ from that of his predecessor is debatable. As

Beyond the Bush Doctrine   137

I have outlined in this book, security under the Bush Doctrine was based upon America's ongoing "responsibility" as a purveyor of liberalism abroad. But it was also rooted in a clear narrative of fear that emerged after 9/11 – the fear of terrorist threats, and the fear *of fear* itself. As such, the security narratives of Bush's War on Terror expressed a necessity for the aggressive maintenance of both US hegemony and homeland security. The corollary to this was a strategy of pre-emptive military action; a rejection of multilateralism in favour of unilateralism; and on the domestic front, the systematic erosion and subversion of constitutional rights in the name of security.

As mentioned in Chapter 3, herein lay the greatest *problematique* of the War on Terror. Items in the War on Terror toolbox that were employed in the pursuit of security – such as pre-emptive strikes, extraordinary rendition, the use of waterboarding, and other forms of prisoner abuse and humiliation, and unlawful detentions of "enemy combatants" at Guantanamo Bay – actually contributed to *in*security. Insecurity that occurred both in the sense that these policies provided fodder for those very groups that would seek to do America harm, leading to more recruitment and attacks by terrorist groups; but also, insecurity felt within the communities and populations "subject" to War on Terror security practices rooted in the management of risk and emergent threat (Mustapha 2011).

On the surface at least, the narratives of Obama's policies initially set out to confront this *problematique* head on (Jackson and Tsui 2017; Bentley 2017). In his inaugural presidential speech, Obama pointedly rejected key elements of the Bush Doctrine. In contrast to Bush's emphasis on threat and fear, Obama spoke of "hope over fear, unity of purpose over conflict and discord" (The White House January 20, 2009). In rejecting unilateralism and Bush's doctrine of pre-emption, Obama recalled "that earlier generations faced down fascism and communism not just with missiles and tanks, but with sturdy alliances ... and [understands] that our power alone cannot protect us, nor does it entitle us to do as we please" (The White House January 20, 2009). In contrast to Bush's exhortation of American hegemony as the nation's birthright, Obama declared his understanding "that greatness is never a given ... it must be earned" (The White House January 20, 2009). On suspending civil rights in the name of security, Obama declared

> as false the choice between our safety and our ideals ... our Founding Fathers drafted a charter to assure the rule of law and the rights of man ... those ideals still light the world and we will not give them up for expedience's sake.
>
> (The White House January 20, 2009)

In pursuit of the "safety of the American people," Obama's administration refuted "the false division between our values and our security" (White House 2009, *Guiding principles of President Barack Obama's foreign policy*).

As part of these assurances, the first foreign policy item on the Obama administration's agenda was the announcement of two executive orders issued on

138 *Beyond the Bush Doctrine*

January 22, 2009. The first ordered the closure of the Guantanamo Bay Detention Center (The White House January 22, 2009, *Executive order – Review and disposition of individuals detained at the Guantanamo Bay naval base and closure of detention facilities*). The second explicitly prohibited the use of torture on anyone under United States custody detained in armed conflicts (The White House January 22, 2009, *Executive order ensuring lawful interrogations*). The expediency of these orders was clearly part of a larger communications strategy to distance the Obama administration from that of his predecessor. In hindsight, we now know that this was part of a concerted communications strategy above all else (Jackson and Tsui 2017), especially because Guantanamo ultimately remained open for the duration of his presidency and continues to operate today under President Trump.

Nevertheless, the call to close Guantanamo and the explicit prohibition of torture were talking points that hinted at the changing narratives of Obama's (then) declared approach to combat terrorism. In a move away from Bush's hard and fast policy of non-negotiation with "evil-doers," Obama seemed to be moving towards an approach to "win hearts and minds." His administration also largely did away with the term "War or Terror," in clear efforts to re-brand his administration's counter-terrorism policies. The phrase continued to be used only sparingly in official White House documentation and in Obama's briefings and remarks throughout his two terms. In replacing some of the central themes in War on Terror discourses, Obama avoided specifically targeting the religion of Islam, "Islamists" or "Islamic fundamentalism." Instead, he issued general statements against "those who seek to advance their aims by inducing terror and slaughtering innocents" (The White House January 20, 2009). In these general terms, he spoke also of "relentlessly confront[ing] violent extremists who pose a grave threat to our security – because we reject the same thing that people of all faiths reject: the killing of innocent men, women and children" (The White House, June 4, 2009).

At the beginning of his now famous Cairo Address, Obama also broke from Bush's positioning of terrorism by acknowledging that existing tensions between the United States and Muslims are

> tensions rooted in historical forces that go beyond any current policy debate … tension fed by colonialism that denied rights and opportunities to many Muslims, and a Cold War in which Muslim-majority countries were too often treated as proxies … violent extremists have exploited these tensions in a small but potent minority of Muslims.
>
> (The White House June 4, 2009)

Here, Obama acknowledged the historical contexts of contemporary grievances and rejected as false the idea that there is some sort of innate rupture between America and Islam. Instead, he emphasized that they "overlap, and share common principles – principles of justice and progress; tolerance and the dignity of all human beings … and that Islam has always been a part of America's story"

Beyond the Bush Doctrine 139

(The White House June 4, 2009).[1] It was a fairly significant discursive move to consciously and carefully shift characterizations of Islam in the counter-terrorism discourse coming out of the White House.

Instead of perpetuating the "common sense" assumption that all Muslims, by definition, hold the potential for extremism and violence, he repeatedly asserted that the "violent extremists" are an extremely small minority. Among other statements to support this, Obama said that "the partnership between America and Islam must be based upon what Islam is, not what it is not" (The White House June 4, 2009). This shift in rhetoric was imperceptible to many observers, but its importance to Muslims in the campaign to win back goodwill should not be underestimated. According to Ipsos-Reid and Pew research polling, Obama's approval ratings among Muslims, both at home and abroad, rose considerably in his first term (Ohlheiser 2014). Interestingly, his approval ratings among Muslims abroad, however, plummeted in his second term and were actually lower than Bush's in his final year of office (Wan and Clement 2016).

This speaks to the fact that in looking at the entire course of his two terms in office, Obama's presidential legacy continues to be fiercely debated. Bentley and Holland (2017) point out that those who speak of Obama's successes tend to focus on his domestic record, while those more skeptical of his deliverance of "Hope and Change" tend to focus on perceived failures in his foreign policy decisions and legacy. Indeed, the notable drop in his approval ratings among global Muslims implies a measure of disappointment in his administration's perceived failures to live up to promises of change in US foreign policy. Despite the skepticism, we did see measurable successes in Obama's foreign policy promises – especially in his second term – as he brokered a nuclear deal with Iran; normalized relations with Cuba; improved economic relations with China; was part of achieving a climate change agreement in Paris; and was Commander in Chief presiding over the covert operation to finally find and kill Osama bin Laden (Bentley and Holland 2017; Jackson and Tsui 2017; Bentley 2017; Christensen 2015).

Though contested, the Obama Doctrine – with its emphasis on more careful strategic assessment and issue management in foreign policy (Kitchen 2017), and a Jeffersonian hesitation about slaying monsters abroad (Bentley and Holland 2017) – was, in some senses, "highly significant and, arguably, a necessary if imperfectly realized, remedy for the excesses of the Bush Doctrine" (Bentley and Holland 2017, 2). On the other hand, a wider perspective of Obama's two terms indicates that his attempts to re-focus American foreign policy faced considerable constraints from the sedimented material realities and discursive structures of not only the Bush Doctrine (Bentley and Holland 2017) but also a longer historical legacy of American ideas about its place in the world as an upholder of "civilization" (Fermor 2017).

It is reasonable then, to assert that although they were not without their successes, the departures in the central themes of the Obama Doctrine as compared to the Bush Doctrine resulted in only incremental changes (Jackson and Tsui 2017). All told, Obama's security strategy was marked mostly by continuities.

140 *Beyond the Bush Doctrine*

These continuities included the persistent centrality of terrorism in security discourses; that terrorism continued to be seen as the biggest threat to America and the world; and that "forceful military-based strategies [continued] to dominate the Obama administration's counter-terrorism response" (Jackson and Tsui 2017, 73) comprising materially of military interventions, targeted killings, drone strikes, and rendition programs (Jackson and Tsui 2017, 72; Bentley 2017). In short, changes in the Obama Doctrine, while significant in their own way, were mostly stylistic, whereas in substance we saw the momentum of the powerful connections that exist between hegemonic security discourses, epistemic communities (Leander 2005; Stampnitzky 2013), and material practices (Jackson 2005).

In assessing the Obama Doctrine, it is possible to see how Bush's well-established War on Terror was already firmly "embedded as a powerful and ubiquitous narrative … into the political-cultural economy of American society … it [had] become a hegemonic discourse and a counterterrorism 'regime of truth'" (Jackson and Tsui 2017, 78). A war on terror, whatever it is called, continues to exist precisely because we continue to observe it as a set of ideational and material structures and practices *that continue to exist*, and which

> now involves plethora of government and private agencies, bureaucracies, corporations, companies, think tanks, research centres and the like, along with lobbyists and industry financiers … and represent a powerful set of material interests for maintaining and even expanding … the scope of activities of the war on terror.
>
> (Jackson and Tsui 2017, 80)

The stickiest aspects of this discourse continue to manifest in the enduring centrality of risk management approaches to security in the form of pre-emptive security practices like mass surveillance of populations; the widespread use of targeted shelling by unmanned aerial vehicles; and the anticipatory apprehension of suspected terrorists. This is because, despite the slightly shifted rhetoric under Obama, the larger structural conditions of the War on Terror have largely remained unchanged (Bentley and Holland 2017).

The Obama Doctrine in Asia

In terms of the Obama administration's relations with Asia, there was a clear departure from Bush's more bilateral approach towards more of a diplomatic-multilateral approach to the region. Under its *Pivot Asia* policies, Washington returned to the table of regional multilateral fora pertaining to security, trade, and the environment indicating more of an activist disposition towards what was, nevertheless, a fairly close adherence to "pragmatic and constructive US approaches to key Asia issues in recent years" (Sutter 2009, 212). Although still relatively low on the foreign policy agenda, Southeast Asia – in particular – enjoyed revitalized diplomatic relations with the US under Obama. This was

Beyond the Bush Doctrine 141

evidenced by the fact that, in July of 2009, (Hillary) Clinton's first official foreign visit as Secretary of State was to Asia where she signed the ASEAN Treaty of Amity and Cooperation (TAC) on behalf of the United States.

Another indicator of Obama's pivot to Asia was his high-profile ten-day trip to the region in November of 2009, which included stops in Japan, China, South Korea, and Singapore. During that trip, Obama attended the Asia-Pacific Economic Cooperation (APEC) summit in Singapore and afterwards attended the very first US-ASEAN (Association of Southeast Asian Nations) summit. He also met with individual ASEAN leaders, and, in a great departure from his predecessors, engaged Burma/Myanmar in discussions about the detention of opposition leader Aung San Suu Kyi and the upcoming elections, which as we now know, was a prescient diplomatic move. Again, this was a show of renewed interest in the Asia-Pacific region and in multilateralism in particular. In contrast, the Bush administration was notorious for its avoidance of multilateral engagement, showing a clear preference for bilateral security and economic relationships in East Asia. Under Bush, Secretary Rice had snubbed several ASEAN and ASEAN Regional Forum meetings that the US had been invited to attend (Stubbs 2018). Overall, this was the beginning of a larger attempt by the Obama administration to "re-engage with the Asia-Pacific and re-energize hopes for a liberal regional order" (Stubbs 2018, 146), which culminated in the successful negotiations for a Trans-Pacific Partnership (TPP), which included historically significant commitments by regional members like Malaysia, Singapore and Vietnam to tighten up their environmental and labour laws and regulations.

The Obama administration also expressed a continued commitment to pre-existing bilateral military and security relationships in the region throughout his terms in office. In March 2009, President Obama and President Arroyo of the Philippines reaffirmed their commitment to the "long-standing US-Philippines alliance, including the Visiting Forces Agreement, which remains critical to the bilateral relationship and our strategic interests" (The White House March 13, 2009). In January 2010, Secretary Clinton gave a speech on American principles and priorities in the "regional architecture" of Asia, where she reaffirmed the importance of bilateral ties to the region. According to Clinton, US "engagement and leadership in the region," still hinged upon the US' bilateral strategic partnerships, including those with Japan, South Korea, Australia, Thailand, and the Philippines (US Department of State January 12, 2010). The US also continued, and in some cases expanded, their cooperative arrangements with regional members in "Track II" areas like law enforcement and intelligence sharing as mentioned in Chapter 5.

The one notable – and perhaps telling – exception was the very fast deterioration of the US–Philippines relationship after President Duterte came to power. In 2016, in response to Obama's criticism of Duterte's anti-crime policies that included mass extra-judicial street-side killings of drug users, Duterte famously called Obama a "son of a bitch" and told him to "go to hell" in a speech to reporters regarding the issue. Specifically, he expressed disdain for Obama's presumption of authority over him and went on to blame the US for their problems in Mindanao saying,

142　*Beyond the Bush Doctrine*

as a matter of fact, we inherited this problem from the United States ... Because they invaded this country and made us their subjugated people. Everybody has a terrible record of extrajudicial killing. Why make an issue about fighting crime?

(McKenzie and Liptak 2016)

He then went on to invoke the 1906 Battle of Bud Dajo in southern Moro in which hundreds of people, including women and children, were massacred by the US army who were trying to suppress a separatist uprising against the Americans (McKenzie and Liptak 2016).

On the whole, however, and despite rhetorical flourishes to the contrary, Washington's core security relations with (South)east Asia remained very similar to those of the preceding administration (Sutter 2009; Stubbs 2018). Washington's willingness to engage with Burma was probably the most revolutionary aspect of Obama's strategic policies in the region and getting ASEAN states to include human rights and environmental commitments in the TPP agreement was notable. But there was nothing particularly novel about the "new regional architecture" as outlined by Secretary Clinton save for a heightened *diplomatic* emphasis on the region. That is to say, while Obama demurred from discussing China's rise as a strategic power in the region – emphasizing instead economic relations with the regional powerhouse – it was evident that tensions continued to exist and that the region was still subject to many of the same "balance of power" issues between the US and China (Christensen 2015). Multilaterally, the status-quo of official US–Southeast Asia relations also remained fairly static even though the President was now personally attending or sending high level representatives like the Secretary of State to regional summits instead of lower-level officials, or snubbing meetings altogether. Furthermore, the bilateral alliances with Southeast Asian nations maintained their status as top billing on Washington's agenda, and always took priority over multilateral relations.

The Obama administration's principles and priorities for the "regional architecture" still revolved around "security" and the contention that the region continued to face an uncertain future because:

Asia's progress is not guaranteed. Asia is home not only to rising powers, but also to isolated regimes; not only to longstanding challenges, *but also unprecedented threats*. The dangers of nuclear proliferation, military competition, natural disasters, violent extremism, financial crises, climate change, and disease transcend national borders and pose a common risk.

(US Department of State January 12, 2010, emphasis added)

This was a continuation of Bush's fear and uncertainty discourse, in contrast to the rhetoric being relayed by Obama himself. The solution, according to Clinton, was that the US would continue to play the stabilizing role of benevolent hegemon, where "the United States not only continues to have dynamic and durable bilateral ties, but plays a central role in helping to deal with the

Beyond the Bush Doctrine   143

difficulties that individual states and this region confront" (US Department of State January 12, 2010).

As such, the following points outline the approach of the Obama administration to East and Southeast Asia: first, that existing bilateral strategic partnerships continued to be the "cornerstone of [American] regional involvement," and that the US commitment to bilateral relationships is "entirely consistent with – and will enhance – Asia's multilateral groupings"; second, that regional institutions, both strategic and economic, were key to advancing US objectives; third – and this was a pointed challenge to the loose and informal characteristics of the "ASEAN way" and may have been realized in the TPP – that institutions must be effective, with clear goals, and that "concrete and pragmatic considerations" should drive the formation and operation of regional institutions; fourth, that there still needed to be "flexibility in pursuing the results we seek," which meant that "where it makes sense," informal and ad-hoc arrangements were still to be used in specific situations (such as the Six-Party Talks on North Korea) for which a special Ambassadorship to ASEAN was created to respond to these needs; and fifth, that regional institutions were to be prioritized and the more "important" ones be identified, which was another way of saying that although the US officially committed to multilateralism in the region, it was not willing to waste its time with make-work groupings that served no immediate purpose (US Department of State January 12, 2010). In short, the real change in the substance of the Obama administration's Asia policy was that they showed up more often. While Obama's larger security narrative and rhetoric underwent a marked change, what the regional architecture action plan actually revealed was that it was going to be mostly business as usual.

Obama's ~~War on Terror~~ war on terror

Obama's foreign policy rhetoric, we can easily concede, was markedly different from that of Bush's. But it was mostly in the area of rhetoric that we observed any great shifts in Washington's approach to the world. In many ways, the *substantive* aspects of Obama's foreign policy and counter-terrorism agenda were not remarkably different from Bush's War on Terror. That is to say, there was an observable continuity in American policies on the ground (Mustapha 2011). However, these threads of continuity *were* tempered by the loftier values of a regional liberal order that was consistently evangelized by President Obama (Stubbs 2018). As a discursive analysis would suggest, even the "talk" can mean more than Obama's detractors would grant him. Obama promised engagement and dialogue, where Bush promised pre-emptive strikes and non-negotiation with "evil-doers." In his Cairo address, Obama extended an olive branch to the Muslim world in a speech where he extensively and knowledgably quoted the Qur'an and emphasized the shared traditions of the Abrahamic faiths. In relations with Asia, he personally attended ASEAN meetings and spoke directly to Southeast Asian leaders, discounted the realist preoccupation with relative gains in relation to the rise of China, and endeared himself to Indonesian audiences

144   *Beyond the Bush Doctrine*

with his personal knowledge of their country. He used terms like "militant" and "extremist" rather than "Islamist" to describe terrorists. Perhaps most significantly, he rarely used the term "War on Terror" in a seemingly conscious disavowal of the previous administration's security narratives.

What Obama's security narratives reminded us – at least rhetorically – was that it was the "open society and liberties and values that we cherish as Americans" that *should* be the referent of security. These were the values that were among the casualties of Bush's War on Terror. In *naming* those values as objects to be "secured" and in constructing the idea that the loss of those values is something to fear, Obama suggested a plausible counter-scenario for how "security" could now be understood in the context of combating terrorism. In so far as his policies have actually reflected this, there is little evidence that an enduring "counter-scenario" was successfully constructed. Osama bin Laden is now dead, killed extra-judicially in a covert Navy Seal operation in Abbottabad on May 2, 2011, in Pakistani sovereign space. Guantanamo is still open for business and "enhanced" interrogation tactics continue to be defended by members of the American defence and intelligence establishment, with impunity. Drone warfare has killed thousands of innocent people in Pakistan and Afghanistan and continued to be deployed by the Obama administration despite its illegality from an international law perspective. Obama not only demurred from rolling back the assault on civil liberties brought by Bush's USA PATRIOT Act, he further increased executive privilege in this regard as well. And in East and Southeast Asia, Washington continued to support and legitimize repressive regimes.

Donald Trump is now the 45th president of the United States. And we know that the demise of the term "War on Terror" and a shift in Presidential rhetoric did not bring the promised sea-changes in US foreign policy. The security narratives of the Obama administration did not successfully destabilize the hegemonic security narrative of Bush's War on Terror nor did Obama successfully construct a "counter-scenario" (Lipschutz 1995) to undermine the centrality of fear in American political and security discourses. If anything, we might wonder what role Obama's rhetorical counter-narratives played in deflecting attention away from the continued insecurities brought forth by the de facto continuation of the War on Terror.

The attempted terrorist attack against a US passenger plane by Nigerian national, Umar Farouk Abdulmutallab, on December 25, 2009 was a clue about Obama's ability to construct a plausible "counter-scenario" to Bush's War on Terror. Faced with the reality of a system-wide intelligence and security failure and the fact that the so-called "underwear bomber" could have succeeded in his goal to detonate explosives onboard an aircraft in American airspace, Obama's rhetoric noticeably shifted gears back to one of fiery statism. In this instance, Abdulmutallab was not a "violent extremist," he was most definitely a "terrorist" (The White House January 7, 2010). In his remarks in response to the attempted attack, Obama's use of language revealed a much more hard-line sentiment than in any of his previous statements regarding the threat of terrorism:

Beyond the Bush Doctrine 145

We are at war. We are at war against Al-Qaeda, a far-reaching network of violence and hatred that attacked us on 9/11, that killed nearly 3,000 innocent people, and that is plotting to strike us again. And we will do whatever it takes to defeat them.

(The White House, January 7, 2010)

His response to that first major Homeland Security threat under his presidency was foretelling, and subsequent terrorist attacks were met with discursive and material responses that signaled the de facto continuation of Bush's War on Terror.

There is no doubt that President Obama succeeded in a lot of ways. His outreach was meaningful in many areas, and for a brief period the United States enjoyed renewed goodwill and approval ratings from around the world. But Obama's rhetorical platitudes never stood a chance against the already materially entrenched machinations of a national security discourse rooted in fear – a discourse that continued to be fuelled by the rise of the Islamic State and a series of high-profile incidences of IS-linked terrorism in the Western world. Or a divisive electoral landscape that has become increasingly polarized, where these same War on Terror narratives – still alive and well – have found their way into the domestic political discourses of countries in the liberal Western world who now must reckon with rising ethno-nationalist populism and increasing rates of hate-fuelled crimes against marginalized communities. When we consider that both national identity and the practice of security *require* the definition of threats along with the identification of the referent objects that must be "secured," it becomes easier to understand how this all could have happened.

Conclusion: the Trump Doctrine – from chess to checkers

President Donald Trump's emerging foreign policy stance has been described as a neo-mercantilist "American First" strategy (Stubbs 2018; Liow 2017; Townshend 2017); "Tweet diplomacy" (Tow, 2017); "bellicose ... unconventional and confrontational" (Hamilton-Hart 2017); "No Friends, No Enemies" (Goldberg 2018); "Permanent Destabilization creates American Advantage" (Goldberg 2018); and perhaps most vividly, a senior White House official reportedly described the Trump Doctrine as "We're America, Bitch" (Goldberg 2018). Trump's electoral campaign rhetoric clearly indicated that with him as president of the United States, business would most certainly *not* be happening as usual. On the campaign trail, Trump promised to "Make America Great Again," capitalizing on his base's nostalgia for a mythical time when (presumably white) middle class Americans were upwardly mobile and freed from the "economic anxieties" of an increasingly globalized economy and the social anxieties of an increasingly diverse America.

Trump has shown sympathy towards "ethno-nationalist" hate groups protesting the removal of statues commemorating confederate soldiers (Shear and Haberman 2017) and has lashed out at the Black Lives Matter movement through

146 *Beyond the Bush Doctrine*

vitriolic statements denouncing NFL players who kneel during the anthem to protest ongoing racial injustices in America (Graham 2017). He promised to build a wall between the US and Mexico and declared that he would order "a total and complete shutdown" of travel by Muslims to the United States "until our country's representatives can figure out what the hell is going on" (Johnson 2015). During his campaign, he also tipped his hat to his future administration's grand strategy by declaring that the US would not "surrender to the false song of globalism and [w]ouldn't spread 'universal values' that not everyone shares" (Tow 2017, 7).

From the start of his presidency, the Trump administration has, in fact, "shown him to be what he appeared to be during the campaign and in his earlier career: narcissistic, capricious, and willing to play to the anxieties and prejudices of the crowd" (Hamilton-Hart 2017, 42). His choices for cabinet and senior White House positions have included people with clear derision for a liberal international order, "who have expressed extreme anti-Muslim and socially conservative attitudes and who deny that humans are responsible for climate change" (Hamilton-Hart 2017, 42). Economically, Trump is *en route* to eviscerating NAFTA and one of the first things he did as president was formally withdraw the US from the TPP (Stubbs 2018). He has decried the terms of Free Trade under the WTO as heavily weighted against US interests and has started a trade war with Canada, imposing tariffs on Canadian steel and aluminum, and provoking a targeted response by Ottawa against key industries and consumer goods from some of Trump's key voting districts (Dale 2018). As I write this, Trump is in the process of starting a trade war with China (Pesek 2018).

In short, Trump's approach to the world is so far quite unlike Obama's "cerebral to a fault" (Goldberg 2018) foreign policy approach – or even Bush's, who for all his personal shortcomings was at least surrounded by those who were well-informed. Instead, Trump is proving to be "the most glandular president in American history" (Goldberg 2018) both at home and abroad. Trump's specific Asia policies indicate a clear withdrawal of the US' presence from regional multilateralism (Stubbs 2018) and appear to be a reflection of

> a more deep-seated crisis in the United States, where there has been a breakdown in the social foundations that underpinned US leadership of a liberalizing and (more or less) rules-based world order.
>
> (Hamilton-Hart 2017, 43)

Trump has shown no interest in developing economic or security multilateralism in the region, nor has he sought to promote or protect human, environmental or democratic rights in the Asia-Pacific (Stubbs 2018). (Then) Malaysian Prime Minister, Najib Abdul Razak, proudly repeated Trump's assessment of him as his "favourite Prime Minister" (Hamilton-Hart 2017, 43) and Philippine President Duterte and Trump have revived amiable diplomatic relations between the two countries after Trump visited the Philippines and expressed open admiration for some of the very policies that brought forth Obama's criticism of the leader

(Stubbs 2018). Trump has also welcomed to the White House Thai Prime Minister Prayuth Chan-ocha – who took power in Thailand by leading a coup in May 2014 – and has repeatedly failed to express concern about the political situation in Cambodia, where the Hun Sen government has just won a rigged national election after dismantling political opposition and cracking down on the press (Stubbs 2018).

For regional elites, Trump's open rejection of a rules-based world order represents a "double-edged sword" (Hamilton-Hart 2017) that presents both costs *and* opportunities. In terms of potential costs, Trump's foreign policies are a clear threat to the idea of a (South) East Asian liberal regional order that the Obama administration was supportive of, and that provided substantial gains in terms of regional cooperation on certain key issues. Accordingly, both new and existing structural stresses in Southeast Asia may well be tested over the course of Trump's administration. For one, ASEAN is at a cross-roads regarding disagreements over the handling of South China Sea disputes and regarding ongoing contention around regional economic issues and trade (Chong 2017). Southeast Asia is economically very vulnerable to a trade war between China and the US or to rising US interest rates (Hamilton-Hart 2017). The regional grouping is further challenged by the continued state-sanctioned persecution and genocide of the Rohingya people in Myanmar, with all of its attendant diplomatic complexities and the transborder regional complexities produced by forced migration.

Regional observers have predicted that the main regional policy challenges caused by the Trump administration in East Asia will be the ongoing threat of a nuclearizing North Korea and "the transition of US alliance politics and multilateralism in Southeast Asia … potentially leading to a substantial power vacuum subject to Chinese exploitation" (Tow 2017, 3). So far, we have seen the surprising development of a Trump–Kim Nuclear Summit in Singapore, and a historically remarkable thaw in North–South Korean relations. Many have directly credited Trump for these developments and there is little doubt that his recent actions have *contributed* to the current diplomatic thaw between the two Koreas, but

> this is very different from saying that Mr. Trump actually deserves to take credit for it. In fact, his contributions to the current diplomatic détente are largely accidental. As much as the Trump administration's security disposition has acted as a catalyst in the lessening tensions between Seoul and Pyongyang, it could have just as easily escalated the tensions between them. In the worst-case scenario, Trump's bombast and disregard for the prevailing regional security architecture could have caused the outbreak of a nuclear war.
>
> (Mustapha 2018)

This last point is key. Trump's bellicose midnight tweeting, erratic behaviour, and reactive diplomacy put millions of East Asian lives in the crosshairs of a

148 *Beyond the Bush Doctrine*

potential nuclear exchange, highlighting the biggest problem with our prevailing understanding of a regional security architecture that continues to place the US and its interests in the centre: it downplays the degree to which regional state actors have their own agendas, both regionally and domestically, and it ignores the actually occurring insecurities of the region's *populations*.

A critical security analysis requires us to look at the ways that US security policy acts both as a set of practices and as a powerful discursive framework that influences actors in the region. It is noteworthy then that, so far, Trump's East Asia policies seem focused mainly on North Korea and on economic relations with China. Unlike both Obama and Bush before him, the Trump administration does not appear overly concerned with combating the threat of Islamism in the region. In fact, it seems possible that Trump is simply unaware of the degree to which an ongoing threat of terrorism in Southeast Asia exists. In the meantime, regional intelligence, law enforcement, and military actors will likely continue to cooperate within existing counter-terrorism and CVE security arrangements, but perhaps more so on their own terms and with less of a need to balance US interests. In many ways then, we are seeing a continuation of familiar security relationships and discourses within the region, despite Trump's apparent withdrawal from multilateralism. This is because Obama's liberal regional order was more of a challenge to the authoritarian-leaning developmental regional order that still dominates elite perspectives in Southeast Asia, and also because Southeast Asian states are themselves committed to maintaining positive regional relations (Stubbs 2018).

Which brings us to the *opportunities* provided by Trump's apparent disregard for a liberal regional order. It is precisely this indifference that will allow East and Southeast Asian actors to go about pursuing their domestic interests in maintaining strong-state "national resilience," unfettered by outside scrutiny (Hamilton-Hart 2017). While it is still too early to tell what larger impact Trump's presidency may have on the region over the long run, for now it appears that most of his foreign policy decisions are easily explained as theatrics for his own domestic audiences (Mustapha 2018), without any apparent long-term regional goals or strategy. Commentators and analysts are still grappling with Trump's Asia policies, wanting so badly to make sense of them. But, if we are honest about

> the revolving door of leadership in the US State Department over the past year, and the confusion and mixed messages from the highest levels of US diplomacy [on the region], there is very little evidence that Trump has been playing some sort of complex strategic game of multilevel chess with the long-term goal of peace … In fact, the suspension of disbelief that is required for that particular take is considerable.
>
> (Mustapha 2018)

In the meantime, regional elites know that for as long as Donald Trump is president of the United States, he is unlikely to object to the clear preference by

Beyond the Bush Doctrine   149

Southeast Asian governments for informal regional arrangements, non-interference in domestic affairs, and sacrosanct respect for state sovereignty. Insofar as Southeast Asian "comprehensive security" continues to be defined in terms of national resilience, nothing about Trump's foreign policy disposition appears to challenge the continued power of ruling elites in the region.

Note

1 In the same Cairo speech, Obama also outlined his vision for the issues that must be dealt with in America's relations with Islam and Muslims. They include combating terrorism by "confronting violent extremism in all of its forms"; dealing with the Israel–Palestine problem by acknowledging the challenges faced by Palestinians under Israeli occupation and pursuing a two-state solution; pursuing the eventual elimination of nuclear weapons while recognizing the right of nations – including Iran – to pursue peaceful nuclear power "if they comply with their responsibilities under the NPT"; that democracy should be promoted but that "no system of government can or should be imposed on one nation by any other"; that religious freedom should be protected including the religious freedom of Muslims in America, because "we can't disguise hostility towards any religion behind the pretense of liberalism"; the protection of women's rights and education; and the promotion of economic development and opportunity (The White House June 4, 2009).

References

Bentley, Michelle. 2013. Continuity we can believe in: Escaping the war on terror. In Michelle Bentley and Jack Holland (Eds) *Obama's foreign policy: Ending the War on Terror*. London: Routledge, pp. 101–117.

Bentley, Michelle. 2017. Ending the unendable. The rhetorical legacy of the war on terror. In Michelle Bentley and Jack Holland (Eds) *The Obama Doctrine*. London: Routledge. pp. 57–69.

Bentley, Michelle and Jack Holland (Eds). 2017. *The Obama Doctrine*. London: Routledge.

Chong, Ja Ian. 2017. Deconstructing order in Southeast Asia in the age of Trump. *Contemporary Southeast Asia: A Journal of International and Strategic Affairs* 39(1): 29–35.

Christensen, Thomas J. 2015. Obama and Asia: Confronting the China challenge. *Foreign Affairs* 94(5): 28–36.

Dale, Daniel, Bruce Campion-Smith, and Tonda MacCharles. May 31, 2018. Canada to hit US with retaliatory tariffs. *The Toronto Star*. www.thestar.com/news/canada/2018/05/31/us-will-hit-canada-with-steel-and-aluminum-tariffs-as-of-midnight-tonight.html.

Fermor, Ben. 2017. Shifting binaries: The colonial legacy of Obama's war on terror. In Michelle Bentley and Jack Holland (Eds) *The Obama Doctrine*. London: Routledge. pp. 84–98.

Goldberg, Jeffrey. June 11, 2018. A senior White House official defines the Trump Doctrine: "We're America, bitch." *The Atlantic*. www.theatlantic.com/politics/archive/2018/06/a-senior-white-house-official-defines-the-trump-doctrine-were-america-bitch/562511/.

Graham, Bryan. September 22, 2017. Donald Trump blasts NFL anthem protesters: "Get that son of a bitch off the field." *Guardian*.

150 *Beyond the Bush Doctrine*

Hamilton-Hart, Natasha. 2017. Deal-makers and spoilers: Trump and regime security in Southeast Asia. *Contemporary Southeast Asia: A Journal of International and Strategic Affairs* 39(1): 42–49.

Jackson, Richard. 2005. *Writing the War on Terrorism: Language politics and counterterrorism*. New York: Manchester University Press.

Jackson, Richard and Chin-Kuei Tsui. 2017. War on terror II: Obama and the adaptive evolution of US counterterrorism. In Michelle Bentley and Jack Holland (Eds) *The Obama Doctrine*. London: Routledge, pp. 70–83.

Johnson, Jenna. December 7, 2015. Trump calls for "total and complete shutdown of Muslims entering the United States." *Washington Post.* www.washingtonpost.com/news/post-politics/wp/2015/12/07/donald-trump-calls-for-total-and-complete-shutdown-of-muslims-entering-the-united-states/?noredirect=on&utm_term=.d24df4f4d623.

Kitchen, Nicholas. 2017. Ending "permanent war": Security and economy under Obama. In Michelle Bentley and Jack Holland (Eds) *The Obama Doctrine*. London: Routledge, pp. 9–25.

Leander, A. 2005. The power to construct international security: On the significance of private military companies. *Millennium – Journal of International Studies* 33(3): 803–826.

Liow, Joseph. 2017. *The rise in Trump and its global implications: Trump's Asia policy, two months on*. RSIS Commentaries No. 049. Singapore: Nanyang Technological University.

Lipschutz, Ronnie D. 1995. *On security*. New York City: Columbia University Press.

McKenzie, Sheena and Kevin Liptak. September 6, 2016. After cursing Obama, Duterte expresses regret. *CNN.* www.cnn.com/2016/09/05/politics/philippines-president-rodrigo-duterte-barack-obama/.

Mustapha, Jennifer. 2011. Threat construction in the Bush administration's post-9/11 foreign policy: (Critical) security implications for Southeast Asia. *The Pacific Review* 4(24): 487–504.

Mustapha, Jennifer. May 5, 2018. To give Trump full credit on North Korea is to deny regional realities. *The Globe and Mail.* www.theglobeandmail.com/opinion/article-to-give-trump-full-credit-on-north-korea-is-to-deny-regional-realities/.

Ohlheiser, Abby. July 11, 2014. Here's how Obama's approval ratings break down by religion. *The Atlantic.* www.theatlantic.com/politics/archive/2014/07/heres-how-obamas-approval-ratings-break-down-by-religion/374276/.

Pesek, William. July 20, 2018. China's four trump cards in the trade war. *Nikkei Asian Review* https://asia.nikkei.com/Opinion/China-s-four-trump-cards-in-the-trade-war.

Shear, Michael and Maggie Haberman. 2017. Trump defends initial remarks on Charlottesville; Again blames "both sides." *New York Times*, 15.

Stampnitzky, L. 2013. *Disciplining terror: How experts invented "terrorism."* Cambridge: Cambridge University Press.

Stubbs, Richard. 2018. Order and contestation in the Asia-Pacific region: Liberal vs developmental/non-interventionist approaches. *The International Spectator* 53(1): 138–151.

Sutter, Robert. 2009. The Obama administration and US policy in Asia. *Contemporary Southeast Asia: A Journal of International and Strategic Affairs* 31(2): 189–216.

The White House. 2009. Guiding principles of President Barack Obama's foreign policy. www.whitehouse.gov/issues/foreign-policy.

The White House. January 20, 2009. President Barack Obama's inauguration address.

The White House. January 22, 2009. Executive order ensuring lawful interrogations.

The White House. January 22, 2009. Executive order – Review and disposition of individuals detained at the Guantanamo Bay naval base and closure of detention facilities.

The White House, March 13, 2009. President Obama's telephone call to President Arroyo of the Philippines.

The White House. June 4, 2009. Remarks by President Obama on a new beginning, Cairo University, Cairo, Egypt.

The White House. January 7, 2010. Remarks by President Obama on strengthening intelligence and aviation security.

Tow, William T. 2017. President Trump and the implications for the Australia–US alliance and Australia's role in Southeast Asia. *Contemporary Southeast Asia: A Journal of International and Strategic Affairs* 39(1): 50–57.

Townshend, Ashley. March 2017. *America first: US Asia policy under President Trump.* Sydney: United States Studies Centre.

US Department of State. January 12, 2010. Remarks by Secretary of State Clinton on regional architecture in Asia: Principles and priorities at the East–West center, Honolulu.

Wan, William and Scot Clement. November 18, 2016. Obama's legacy. Interactive graphic from the *Washington Post*. w.washingtonpost.com/graphics/national/obama-legacy/global-approval-rating.html.

Conclusion

Future questions in writing Southeast Asian security

As I have been at pains to emphasize throughout this book, my point is not to discount the threat of terrorism as far as it does exist. Nor do I think that the security of or between states is irrelevant to assessments of regional security – rather, a state-centric understanding of security only tells us so much and precludes a host of other considerations that relate to insecurity. The point of the type of critical security analysis deployed in this book is to ask *different* questions than ones commonly asked, so as to uncover some of the less obvious ways that the threat of terrorism, along with reactions to it, can manifest. Hence, the central research question guiding this project has been: *What can a critical security analysis tell us about the War on Terror and about security in Southeast Asia?* This book, then, set out to explore the tensions inherent in seeking "security" within the hegemonic security narratives of the War on Terror, with the larger purpose of demonstrating that the pursuit of security by states often contributes to forms of *in*security, critically defined. Utilizing a "weak ontology" critical security approach, which demands historically and geographically contingent methods of critique, I was able to examine and explore some of the lesser-known "contrapuntal" effects that terrorism and counter-terrorism have had on the production of insecurity in the region.

In doing so, this book has demonstrated that forms of insecurity were constructed and abetted by the security narratives and material practices of the War on Terror itself, and that these forms of insecurity occurred in concert with the practices of traditional forms of state-centric security. In other words, *operating as an empirically grounded critical post-structuralist critique* in the historical and geographic context of East and Southeast Asia, this project has demonstrated and affirmed the critical security supposition that the pursuit of "security" by states both necessitates and exacerbates various forms of insecurity. Further, I saw this project as an opportunity to demonstrate that an epistemologically deconstructive critical analysis of security based in post-structuralist commitments *need not be anathema to engagements with pragmatic problems and issues, nor should it have to preclude the possibility of enacting the politics and ethics that are required to address and remedy actually-occurring insecurity* (Mustapha 2013).

The book demonstrated this by conceptually and theoretically contextualizing the empirical cases explored by situating and explaining a "weak ontology"-based

Conclusion 153

critical approach to theorizing security. Utilizing Stephen K. White's (2000, 2003, 2005, 2009) idea of "weak ontology" in *re*constructing foundations, I argued for the benefits of employing (modified) post-structuralist methods of analysis that stress the interwoven relationships between knowledge, power, and subjectivity. This is done to move beyond *de*construction and to make space for engagements with the (contingent) empirical realities of actually-occurring security logics (Mustapha 2013). By focusing on the role of knowledge-production; the importance of ontological theorizations of critical security; and by deploying a context-specific, reflexive, and empirically grounded method similar to what Wyn-Jones (1999) might call "immanent critique," this book showed how it is possible to engage critically with the politics and ethics of security practices in Southeast Asia in the specific context of the War on Terror.

The book also examined existing IR scholarship on the region, surveying the dominant literature on Southeast Asian security and highlighting first, the debates between realist and conventional constructivist scholarship; second, the conceptual gaps in the existing literature; and third, the various critical ideas that have emerged. Approaching academic bodies of literature discursively like this reminds us that these are not homogenous or monolithic areas of inquiry, because each contain unique and sometimes competing representations of the subjects that they pertain to. Understanding this, it is important to critically engage with various literatures in ways that recognize which points of view are privileged and which are marginalized. The book specifically looked at realist and (mainstream) constructivist images of security in East and Southeast Asia, and their corresponding "hub and spokes" and "comprehensive security" models.

The "hub and spokes" model of security corresponds with the realist image of security in East and Southeast Asia. This model sees the maintenance of an American hegemonic balance of power via bilateral alliances as the lynchpin of East Asian security, which is defined as stability through an absence of inter-state warfare in the region. For the social constructivist view however, security goes beyond the military dimension, albeit without excluding it. Constructivist approaches still consider the military dimension to be the most important aspect of security, but include the political, economic and socio-cultural dimensions into a broader conceptualization of security. Importantly, this "comprehensive" understanding of security is central to conceptualizations of Southeast Asian regional security, enabling the formation of ASEAN and closely related to the concept of "national resilience." This is the idea that domestic economic, political, and socio-cultural stability in combination with a norm of non-interference between states is necessary for maintaining the stability of the region. In other words, stable and happy states make for a stable and happy region.

This constructivist image of security brings with it many of the same problems that a realist one does. The rationalist tendency to couple subjectivity with sovereignty means that the realist shortcoming of treating agency as ultimately pre-given remains a central feature of constructivism (Tan 2006). As such, the constructivist image of East Asian security remains "tellingly essentialist, particularly [with] concessions to state-centrism and ideational/normative determinism,

154 *Conclusion*

both due partly to an uncritical emulation of rationalist constructivist perspectives in IR theory" (Tan 2006, 239). As mentioned, this has allowed for the continued "soft-soaping" of the "darker side of the ASEAN way" (Burke and McDonald 2007, 13), in ways that serve to strengthen the state and shield Southeast Asian governments from criticisms of how "internal claims to justice, separatism and difference" (Burke and McDonald 2007, 13) are dealt with. Hence, if ASEAN is a security community according to this view, it is a community of "economic, polit-ical and military elites, and the security that it provides is ... too often premised on the insecurity of others" (Burke and McDonald 2007, 13).

Following this, the book delved into the constitutive effects of US foreign policy in East and Southeast Asia after 9/11 and argued that the Bush Doctrine set the stage for how the War on Terror continues to operate as a dominant security narrative. First, the different ways to define and approach "foreign policy" were explored, and I ultimately argued for the utility of a *critical* con-structivist analysis of foreign policy as informed by David Campbell's (1998) persuasive call to reorient our understanding of it. Campbell (1998) sees "foreign policy" as performative and constitutive, and as a boundary-producing practice "central to the production and reproduction of the identity in whose name it operates" (68). As such, it is an integral aspect of the narratives of *Self* and *Other* that both construct and define threats and the security practices of states in response to those threats. This informed a critical reading of the Bush Doctrine and the *2002 National Security Strategy* as the foundational (con)text of the security narratives of the ongoing War on Terror. Along these lines, the argu-ment was made that the US-led War on Terror, as a security narrative, operated through discursively constructed "regimes of truth." Finally, I sketched out significant aspects of US foreign policy towards East Asia, revealing both the continuities and discontinuities in US policy from "before 9/11" and into the "post-9/11" era. This was the context in which the empirical cases of the follow-ing chapters were examined.

Chapters 4 through 6 were conceptually linked through the use of a critical security lens to explore regional examples of specific security issues. This crit-ical security lens allowed us to see a persistent theme emerge: that the "common sense" of the War on Terror has introduced the idea of risk-mitigation and the management of emergent threat as central organizing logics of security. Chapter 4 scrutinized common assumptions present in the "expert" understandings of terrorism in the region within the context of War on Terror discourses and challenged three commonly made claims that emerged out of the post-9/11 security narrative and related "expert" discourses. These claims are inter-related and flow into one another: first, *that all forms of political Islam necessarily represent an imminent threat of terrorism*; second, *that there exists a regionally cohesive radical Islamist identity with robust organiza-tional and ideological links to Al-Qaeda and the Islamic State (IS)*; and third, *that terrorism in Southeast Asia is best understood as pathology* which results in narrowly conceived state-responses to behaviours understood to be irrational and evil, rather than political.

Contesting each of these claims from a critical security perspective allowed us to see that conventional expertise around counter-terrorism (CT) and countering violence and extremism (CVE) in Southeast Asia contributed twofold to increasing insecurity. On the one hand, much of the existing expertise on terrorism in Southeast Asia renders a vast territory and its people as a contingent, emergent threat, homogenously transformed into epistemic objects by the knowledges that seek to govern their potential for becoming dangerous. As a result, large populations of people who pose no specific threat are themselves rendered insecure through the risk management policies and pre-emptive security practices of the state (Lacher 2008). Second, and related to the previous point, counter-terrorism discourses and CVE rationalities are mobilized by the state in service to a variety of manoeuvres and practices designed to consolidate the political power of ruling elites rather than address the problem of terrorism. Finally, I explained how CT measures and CVE policies have actually contributed to radicalization and the formation of anti-establishment Islamist identities. Hence, these "epistemic objects," and the potential threat they pose may *come out of* problematizations of security and not just the other way around.

Picking up on that theme, Chapter 5 utilized critical feminist and post-structuralist methods of analysis to ask after the gendered implications of regional security politics in Southeast Asia in the context of the ongoing War on Terror. After 9/11 there was a concerted re-establishment of a regional US military presence as well a discursive re-framing of US relations in Asia more generally. This contributed to an escalation of gendered insecurities around regional military architecture; re-configurations of post-colonial constructions of national identity; and a discernible rise in state repression due to the coupling of counter-terror security policies with statist notions of "national resilience." Chapter 5 explained how the War on Terror itself is not unique in creating these insecurities but provided a felicitous scenario for the renewed continuation of American imperial formations in Southeast Asia. Further, these heightened gendered and post-colonial insecurities intersect with and bring forth complex questions relating to expressions of sovereignty and identity in the region.

Chapter 6, in turn, looked at the overlapping and unsettled iterations of what the "region" of (South) East Asia looks like. It asked: what sort of impact did the War on Terror have on regional identities and on related notions of regional security after 9/11? How did 9/11 and the War on Terror affect regional configurations, if at all? Have War on Terror security narratives affected trade and economic relations in the region? In exploring these questions, Chapter 6 examined the evolution of regionalism and regionalization efforts in (South) East Asia, and especially those related to security. It demonstrated the "securitization" of economic relations between the US and the region under the Bush Doctrine (Higgott 2004) and examined regional approaches to terrorism after 9/11. Finally, it demonstrated how War on Terror security narratives have reinforced an "ASEAN-way" of "comprehensive security" as the means by which the concepts of "regional resilience" and "national resilience" are deployed by governing elites in order to maintain *regime* security in a variety of repressive ways (Burke and McDonald 2007; Noor 2006).

156 *Conclusion*

Finally, Chapter 7 pointed us towards emerging questions relating to the ongoing effects of US foreign policy in the region in the years beyond the Bush administration. Barack Obama became the 44th president of the United States and took office in 2009, serving two terms until the election of 45th and current president of the United States, Donald Trump, who took office in 2017. Chapter 7 assessed Obama's approach to foreign policy following the Bush years, as well as the early days of the Trump administration and asked what both can tell us about the continuities and changes in security discourses and practices relating to the threat of terrorism in (South) East Asia (Bentley and Holland 2017). Ultimately, Chapter 7 argued that we can observe a continuing retrenchment, and in many cases escalation, of the same types of security practices observable under the Bush administration, indicating the power of discursive sedimentation, the limited possibilities for discursive transformation, and the different ways that security discourses continue to make certain material practices possible.

Weak ontology and (immanent) critique

Significantly, it would have been difficult to draw the conclusions that I have drawn without deploying the critical security approach articulated in this book. This is a critical security approach with post-structuralist underpinnings, but that demurs from strawman postmodern tendencies to eschew any and all foundational assumptions. Instead, I have articulated and deployed a method of critique informed by Stephen K. White's notion of "weak ontology," which calls for a thoughtful engagement with complex security questions using a case-based examination of empirical actualities. This exercise is about contingently situating one's theorizations of security in response to *particular cases* and in *particular contexts*. This creates opportunities to still engage in the types of empirically grounded foundational ontologizing that is required to cope with the political and ethical problematics of security. But it also reminds us to do so in ways that avoid reproducing the violent aspects of problematic security structures. This does not mean that we have to avoid engagement with statist structures, either analytically or practically. But it does require us to shift our focus in the questions we ask and in *which* security problems we seek to address.

As such, my analysis of the many-layered critical security effects of the War on Terror in (South) East Asia is predicated on the presupposition that it is not only desirable, but necessary, to situate critical security perspectives within particular empirical contexts – historical, geographical, and discursive. This is the key to bridging the divide between a postmodern "post-ponism" (Connolly 1989) that is disengaged from the empirical realities of actually-occurring insecurity and that allows us to move from deconstruction towards a practical engagement with the world. As mentioned, this exercise is not about trying to operate without ever making foundational claims, but rather calls on us to be very careful not to naturalize particular security logics as being timeless and inevitable. It is about being able to see and understand the various insecurities engendered by the security narratives of the War on Terror in a specific time and place.

I used this book to demonstrate that a critical security analysis can "see" the causes and the implications of identifying entire populations as emergent threats; the gendered insecurities that were heightened with the return of US military interests to the region; the complex issues around post-colonial sovereignties and identities that regional actors must continue to navigate; the mobilization of War on Terror discourses and security practices by governing regimes in the region in pursuit of "national resilience"; and the different ways that regional multilateral fora have been influenced by the War on Terror agenda. And once again, the whole point of this project was never to discount the threat of terrorism in Southeast Asia or the existence of more "traditional" security problems as far as they do exist. Rather, the point has been to ask different questions than the ones traditionally asked by the "experts" – in order to reveal some of the less obvious ways that terrorism, along with reactions to terrorism, can influence the security of groups and individuals.

But now what? How do we actually *use* a critical security disposition rooted in empirically grounded immanent critique to avoid the post-ponism of deferring indefinitely our engagement with the world? Goh (2014) points to a promising area of research that this type of critical security approach would be well equipped to tackle. In her critique of the state-centric focus of research relating to ASEAN, Goh suggests IR scholars "undertake research that would specify nationally and comparatively across the subregion *other pressing security issues at the subnational and transboundary levels – as well as state-sanctioned political violence*, which are specifically excluded from the regional agenda" (Goh 2014, 476, my emphasis). This is different from saying that regional institutions are irrelevant, or that we cannot engage with the state – conceptually or practically – because of some theoretical fear of "essentializing" existing structures. The state exists. Its institutions exist. Its security politics exist. And the state can, and does, cause actually-occurring forms of insecurity. And we need to be able to appeal to these claims in efforts to address that insecurity.

Unfortunately, the "common sense" that a dichotomy exists between "problem-solving theory" and "critical theory" has contributed to *the misguided idea that critical theories can never solve problems*. But I argue that trying to "solve security problems" is still possible from a weak ontological perspective. Which leads me into some of my own areas of current and future research. My previous work on regionalization, in combination with the research that I have been engaged in on borders, citizenship, security politics, forced migration, and sovereign violence has led me to a project regarding the plight of the Rohingya people in Myanmar in the context of ASEAN. I am interested in how notions of ASEAN-ness have been affecting regional responses to the increasingly horrifying humanitarian tragedy unfolding in Myanmar's Rakhine province. We know that ASEAN's core working principles – *respect for member state sovereignty, non-interference in the affairs of member-states, and consultation and consensus among member-states* – continue to inform ASEAN's policies and organizational practices. This "ASEAN-way" also contributes to the persistent dominance of (conventional) constructivist scholarship and expertise on the region

158 *Conclusion*

that, due to a tendency to focus on state-level understandings of regional norms and institutions, often sees ASEAN as inherently ineffectual.

Some of my current research is focused on an examination of how the Rohingya crisis in Myanmar – along with regional responses to it – challenges both the core working principles of ASEAN as well as the conventional constructivist understanding of them. This is because, first, the plight of the Rohingya people raises fundamental questions around the very concepts of citizenship, identity, and sovereignty itself, all of which challenge the core ASEAN principle of "respecting member state sovereignty." Second, the Rohingya crisis, by definition, requires the suspension of "non-interference" between members. This is a crisis that crosses borders; that moves along different scales of jurisdiction and governance; and that necessarily disrupts tidy ideas about what – or who – is inside and outside the state. And third, regional discourses around the Rohingya crisis highlight both the negatives and positives of the ASEAN commitment to consultation and consensus, and challenge simplistic state-centric notions about what constitutes an "effective response" to regional problems such as this one.

It is arguable that the prevalence of "Track II diplomacy" in ASEAN, which is often seen as a weakness in conventional IR approaches, is precisely what is required to functionally address the humanitarian crises of mass killings, forced migration, and gender-based violence that the Rohingya people are currently facing. ASEAN is part of the problem, but an immanent critique helps us to envision ways that ASEAN can also be part of the solution. What is crucial to point out here, is that my primary concern – the concern that informs *the politics and ethics of this project* – is *not* the well-being of ASEAN as a regional organization; or of the "resilience" of the region's comprehensive security; or the consolidation of the ruling elites of its member-states. Rather, *the concern that informs the politics and ethics of this project is the well-being of the Rohingya people themselves.* These are real people whose corporeal security – whose lives – are in jeopardy. And in order to address their insecurity, we have to talk about – and yes, *engage* with – the actually occurring security logics that they find themselves in.

References

Bentley, Michelle and Jack Holland (Eds). 2017. *The Obama Doctrine*. London: Routledge.

Burke, Anthony and Matt McDonald (Eds). 2007. *Critical security in the Asia-Pacific*. Manchester: Manchester University Press.

Campbell, David. 1998. *Writing security: US foreign policy and the politics of identity*. Manchester: Manchester University Press.

Connolly, William. 1989. Identity and difference in global politics. In J. Der Derian and M. Shapiro (Eds) *International/intertextual relations: Postmodern readings of world politics*. Toronto: Lexington Books. pp. 323–342.

Goh, Evelyn. 2014. Southeast Asia's evolving security relations and strategies. In Evelyn Goh, Saadia Pekkanen, John Ravenhill, and Rosemary Foot (Eds) *The Oxford handbook of the international relations of Asia*. Oxford: Oxford University Press, pp. 462–480.

Higgott, Richard. 2004. After neoliberal globalization: The "securitization" of US foreign economic policy in East Asia. *Critical Asian Studies* 36(3): 425–444.

Lacher, Wolfram. 2008. Actually existing security: The political economy of the Saharan threat. *Security Dialogue* 39(4): 383–405.

Mustapha, Jennifer. 2013. Ontological theorizations in critical security studies: Making the case for a (modified) post-structuralist approach. *Critical Studies on Security* 1(1): 64–82.

Noor, Farish. 2006. How Washington's "war on terror" became everyone's: Islamophobia and the impact of September 11 on the political terrain of South and Southeast Asia. *Human Architecture: Journal of the Sociology of Self-Knowledge* 5(1): 25–29.

Tan, See Seng. 2006. Rescuing constructivism from the constructivists: A critical reading of constructivist interventions in Southeast Asian security. *The Pacific Review* 19(2): 239–260.

White, Stephen K. 2000. *Sustaining affirmation: The strengths of weak ontology*. Princeton, NJ: Princeton University Press.

White, Stephen K. 2003. After critique: Affirming subjectivity in contemporary social theory. *European Journal of Political Theory* 2(2): 209–226.

White, Stephen K. 2005. Weak ontology: Geneology and critical issues. *The Hedgehog Review* 7(2): 11–25.

White, Stephen K. 2009. Violence, weak ontology and late modernity. *Political Theory* 37(6): 808–816.

Wyn-Jones, Richard. 1999. *Security, strategy, and critical theory*. London: Lynne Rienner.

Index

Abu Sayyaf (terrorist group) 74, 93, 103, 118
Abuza, Zachary 70–71, 92
Acharya, Amitav 31, 34, 36, 53, 59, 84, 124, 130, 132
Alagappa, Muthiah 28
alliances, bilateral security 27, 29, 31, 142, 153
America *see* USA
anti-American sentiment 80, 90, 106–107
"anti-foundationalism" 16–17, 19, 35
"anti-terrorist assistance" 93
APEC *see* Asia Pacific Economic Cooperation
Aradau, Claudia 47
ARF *see* ASEAN Regional Forum
ASEAN 9–11, 24–26, 28–29, 31–34, 36–38, 103–104, 113, 116, 119–135, 141–143, 147, 153–155, 157–158; members 10, 24–25, 119, 123–125, 127–128, 130–131; security regionalism 126, 131; state leaders 129; visions of security 129
ASEAN Regional Forum 26, 28–29, 32, 121, 128, 131, 133, 141
"ASEAN Way" 124, 128, 130, 132, 143
Ashley, Richard 21, 48
Asia 5, 8, 10–11, 36–39, 49, 52–53, 60–61, 63, 89, 117–118, 128, 131–133, 135, 140–143, 149–151; and the financial crisis 29, 37, 53, 59, 109–110, 112, 123; leaders of 125–126; policies 146; and security 29, 128, 135
Asia-Pacific Economic Cooperation 121–122, 126, 134, 141
Asia-Pacific Region 28, 38, 54, 85–86, 116, 123, 127–128, 133, 135, 141, 146, 158
Association of Southeast Asian Nations

10–11, 24, 26, 31–34, 36–38, 119, 121–122, 124–131, 133–135, 141, 143, 147, 153–154, 157–158

Baldwin, R.E. 123–124, 132–133
ballistic missile defence 50, 55
Bandung Conference 124
Bangkok 109–110
Barrett, Richard 72, 83–84, 104, 106
Baswedan, Anies Rasyid 104, 112–113, 115
Beeson, Mark 10–11, 29, 36, 52, 59, 83–85, 123, 127, 132–133, 135
Bentley, Michelle 9, 28, 91, 136–137, 139–140, 156
Betts, Richard 24–25, 29, 36, 123, 133
bilateral security alliances 27, 29, 31, 142, 153
BMD *see* ballistic missile defence
bombings 2, 54, 83–84, 110
Booth, Ken 14, 17, 35n3
Bordadora, Norman 98
border security 2, 47, 117
Browning, Christopher S. 14–15, 19–20
Burke, Anthony 10, 14, 158
Bush, George W. 49–51, 53–55, 57, 60–61, 85–86, 90, 93, 95, 117, 126–127, 136, 138–141, 143–144, 146, 148; administration of 3, 9, 49, 53–56, 70, 80, 89, 91–93, 118, 127, 136, 141, 156; declaration of war against global terrorism 3, 127; Doctrine of 2, 7, 9, 41, 44, 49–52, 56, 58, 61, 87, 119, 126, 136–151, 154–155; National Security Strategy 50; and the response to 9/11, 3; security narratives of 136–137; War on Terror 3–5, 7, 50, 90, 107, 113, 136–138, 143–145, 154, 157
Buzan, Barry 14, 18, 28, 126

Index 161

CA *see* Court of Appeals
campaigns 104, 109, 139, 145–146; global counter-terrorism 104; region's anti-terrorism 109
Campbell, David 2–3, 7, 17, 22, 35, 41, 45–47, 51–52, 64, 80, 154
Camroux, Cameron 90–91, 93, 106–107, 113, 126
Capie, David 10, 90, 93, 105, 107
Chan, Nicholas 10–11, 67, 74, 76, 84–85, 91, 105, 108–109, 114, 116
China 10, 24–25, 28–29, 54–55, 60, 62, 95, 119, 121–123, 125, 133, 135, 139, 141–143, 146–150; development of nuclear weapons 55–56; and the EP-3 spy-plane incident 55; and North Korea 94; plans to develop offensive nuclear forces 55; relationship with USA 54; as a rising economic and military power 26
Christoffersen, Gaye 53–54, 124
Clark Base (military) 93–95
Clement, Scot 139
Clinton, Pres. William 53–54, 141–142
Clinton administration 49, 53–54, 59, 90, 106
Cold War 2, 17, 23–24, 26–30, 36, 49, 52–53, 80, 121–125, 128, 133, 138; bipolar system 25; discipline 25; and regionalism 121
Collier, Kit 76–77, 80
commitments 26, 122, 141; collective 32; environmental 142; epistemological 23; ontological 15–16; political 90; post-structuralist 21, 152; strategic 25
constructivism 23, 29–34, 39, 153; conventional 33; critical 36; social 36
cooperation 33, 56, 93, 127, 129, 132; border 110; diplomatic 26, 103; economic 29, 125; increased intelligence 104; regional 121, 147
"Copenhagen School" of security studies 14, 35
counter-terrorism 2–5, 8, 47–48, 51–52, 58, 61, 66–70, 82–83, 103–104, 109, 111, 113, 150, 152, 155; approach to 129; conventional 70, 89; and cooperation between members 128; and depoliticizing cooperation 128; discourses 8, 67–68, 139, 155; existing 148; measures 8, 67; operations 58, 103; practices 4, 129; regional 128
countering violence and extremism 8, 67, 155; and CT in Southeast Asia 66, 82; and expertise in Southeast Asia 89; and

rationalities 8, 67, 155; and security arrangements 81, 148; strategies 70
Court of Appeals 11–12, 36–37, 86, 98, 116
Cox, Michael 56
critical security 6, 9–11, 15, 19, 22, 35–37, 60, 85, 116, 133, 136, 153, 158; analyses 4–6, 9–10, 34, 36, 41, 56–57, 96, 113, 136, 148, 152, 157; approach 4, 9, 13, 18, 21–22, 57, 114, 136, 152, 156–157; disposition 157; exploration 4; ideas 35; methods 13, 89; perspectives 8, 10, 21, 66, 82, 129, 155–156; projects 6, 20; studies 6, 12, 14–15, 17–23, 39, 61, 66, 159; theories 20–21
Croft, Stuart 46, 48
Cruz De Castro, Renato 90–93, 95, 103–105, 107–109, 111, 116
CT *see* counter-terrorism
cultures 11–12, 37, 47, 60, 85–86, 116–117; organizational 125; popular 3; prevailing security 59; reinforced 101

Daalder, Ivo H. 49–51, 54
deaths 37, 68, 85, 110, 115–116
Dillon, Michael 64, 78–82
disputes 24, 31–32, 124

East and Southeast Asia 6, 9–10, 13, 23–24, 28–31, 35–36, 41, 44, 48, 52, 56–57, 136, 143–144, 152–154; governments of 5, 26, 29, 121, 148; post-Cold War 25; relations 29; security and economic regional institutions 26; security in 13, 23, 27, 34; studies in 30, 33
Eaton, Sarah 27–28, 31, 125
economic multilateralism 58, 122
economic policies 52, 80, 126–127
economic relations 8, 114, 119, 126, 142, 148, 155
elections 5, 9, 90–91, 112, 118, 136, 141, 156; federal 74; in Indonesia 118; presidential 12; rigged national 147
engagements 6, 9, 18, 21–22, 79–81, 101, 122, 141, 152–153, 156–157; deferring 14; multilateral 141; promised 143; regional 53
Enloe, Cynthia 35, 101
Europe 5, 14, 26, 35, 37, 116, 133; and East and Southeast Asian regional institutions 121; and East Asian regionalism 121; and reconstruction in Asia 49

162   *Index*

evidence 83, 111, 114, 144, 148; linkages to Al-Qaeda and IS 78; of the peripheral influence of Islam 72, 76; required to prosecute the US servicemen under domestic rape laws 97–99; of the unsuitability of Megawati 112
executive orders 137–138
expertise 2, 37, 45, 47, 50–51, 62, 64–65, 67–69, 71, 76, 78–79, 81–83, 111, 137, 144–145; conventional 8, 66, 70, 76, 82, 155; existing 8, 66, 82, 155; and terrorism 67–69, 79–80

fear 47, 50, 129, 137, 142; based rationalizations 50; of biological death 47, 50; "evangelism of" 51; path of 50; of terrorism 5, 51, 137; theoretical 157
feminist advocates 35, 39, 98, 101, 103, 114, 118
Fierke, Karin M. 17–18, 20, 35
forces 24, 27, 31–32, 73, 123–124; armed 92–93; coalition 135; counter-civilizational 1; "gradual repositioning of" 90; historical 138; linear 73; nuclear 55–56; occupying 101; rapid reaction 90; social 75, 77, 85; threats and uses of 15
foreign fighters 83, 85, 115
foreign policy 7, 41, 43–44, 154; agendas 56, 107, 140; analysis 43, 46, 60–61; discourses 2, 12, 17, 45, 48, 51–52; ongoing effects of US 9, 136, 156; powerful constitutive effects of US 7, 56; practices 41, 45; social/cultural/political practices of 48, 59
Free Trade Agreement 127, 132
freedom 2, 51–52, 105, 120; political 71; religious 55, 149; sovereign 33, 131
Friedberg, A. 24–25, 38
FTA *see* Free Trade Agreement

gendered insecurities 8, 89–90, 97, 100–102, 155, 157
Gershman, John 57, 71, 74, 81
Gerstl, Alfred 127–129
global politics 4, 37, 50, 60, 158
globalization 1, 11, 36, 39, 73, 85, 123, 134–135; economic 53; era of 11, 85, 134; neoliberal 12, 60, 86, 121, 134, 159
Goh, Evelyn 25, 121–123, 126, 128–131, 157
Goldberg, Jeffrey 145–146
governance 62, 82, 158; global 38, 134; regional 59, 133; security 48, 50–51; Shariah 76

Gunaratna, Rohan 10, 76–77, 92, 116
Gusterson, Hugh 3, 17, 65

Hamid, A.F.A. 52, 58, 67, 72–74, 83, 105–106
Hamilton-Hart, Natasha 12, 24–26, 34–35, 57–58, 69–70, 75–76, 78–80, 104–107, 109, 145–148
hegemonic security narratives 3–4, 6, 56–57, 144, 152
Higgott, Richard 5, 9, 53, 119, 122, 124, 126–127, 155
Hill, Cameron J. 28, 38, 42–44, 60
Holland, Jack 4–5, 9, 18, 28, 91, 136, 139–140, 156
Holsti, Ole R. 42–43, 60–61
hostages 93, 111
human rights 33, 37, 55, 58, 92, 123, 130–131, 142; abuses 54, 58, 95, 106, 110–111; and Indonesia 58; violations 58
human security 10, 66, 129–130, 133
Huysmans, Jef 47, 50, 58–59, 61

Ikenberry, John 28, 38, 61, 87, 127, 134
individuals 4, 41, 64–65, 69–71, 77–78, 91–92, 106–107, 129–130, 138, 157; affiliated 78; Islamist 107; security of 10, 66, 129–131, 133
Indochina 122
Indonesia 10, 30, 63, 74–75, 77, 83–84, 87–88, 90–91, 103–104, 106, 109–112, 115, 117–119; counter-terrorism 84; independent Islamist organization in 74
Indonesians 74, 104, 111–112
insecurity 4–6, 8–9, 12, 18–20, 33–34, 38, 52, 56–57, 67, 86, 89–118, 131–132, 137, 152, 154–158; constructions of 89; corporeal 21; increasing 8, 66, 82, 155; local 90; remedying 22
instability 24, 32, 36, 57, 133; arising from imbalances in strategic power 33; associated with insecurity 34; and military uncertainty 24
intelligence 107, 141, 151; agencies 69, 107, 109; and American defence 144; communities 71; regional 148
inter-state conflicts 24, 30, 33–34, 57, 131
Internal Security Act (Malaysia) 92, 107, 114–115
international politics 35, 37, 39, 44, 61, 86, 116–117
international relations 1, 10–11, 13, 30–31, 37–40, 42, 44–46, 49, 59–62, 83, 115, 118, 122, 124–125, 135; Cold War

Index 163

period of 49; and foreign policy 43; theory 28, 43, 46
interrogations 138, 151; enhanced tactics for 144; lawful 138, 151
Iraq 2, 12, 51, 81, 83, 85, 107, 112, 115
Iraqi invasion 127
ISA *see Internal Security Act*
ISIS 29, 72, 123; and Malaysia 117; networks in Southeast Asia 72
Islam 66, 69–74, 76–78, 80, 82, 108, 112, 114, 116, 138–139, 149; moderate 74, 107–108, 130; and political organizations in Southeast Asia 75; regional 71; religion of 70, 138; "true" 108
Islamic State 7, 11, 52, 66, 69–70, 84–85, 106, 116–117, 145, 154
Islamism 56–57, 72, 76, 148; global 77–78, 82; regional 76, 79, 111
Islamists 72, 75, 77–78, 92, 104, 108, 138, 144; groups in Southeast Asia 73–75, 77, 82, 106, 113; opposition 108; and terrorism 91, 103; terrorism in Southeast Asia 52, 57, 62, 71, 87, 92; violence of 72, 75
Islamiyah, Jemaah 74–75, 77, 83–84, 91, 108, 112, 114
"Islamization" 72–73

Jackson, Richard 2–4, 44, 46, 48, 51–52, 57, 61, 65, 67–68, 70, 79–80, 91, 136–140
Japan 10, 24–25, 28–29, 53, 117, 119, 121–122, 141; occupation during Wold War II 112; and the Red Army 91; security relationship with the US 54; and South Korea 122
Jarvis, Lee 4, 18, 48
Jemaah Islamiyah (terrorist group) 74
Jervis, Robert 48, 50

Kadir, Suzaina 58, 71, 73–74, 76, 113, 117
Kang, David C. 24–26
KMM *see* Kumpulan Mujahidin Malaysia
Korea *see* South Korea
Korean Peninsula 10, 24, 54, 119, 147
Kumpulan Mujahidin Malaysia (terrorist group) 74, 91–92, 107–108

Lacsamana, Anne E. 95–98, 100–101
lawful interrogations 138, 151
liberalism 49–50, 137, 149
Lindsay, James M. 49–51, 54

Malaysia 10, 58, 72, 74–75, 77–78, 85–88, 90–93, 103–108, 110–111, 115–119, 141; and the dismantling of the Communist Party in 29; governments of 105–108, 110; and the Muslim population in 72; politics of 107–108
Malaysian Constitution 104–105
MBA *see* Military Bases Agreement
McDonald, Matt 9, 14–15, 18–20, 27, 31–34, 57, 83, 113, 120, 130–132, 154–155
member-states 26, 103, 131, 157–158
MILF *see* Moro Islamic Liberation Front
militarization 91–92, 99, 101, 116
"militarization as a preponderant policy tool" 91–92, 99, 101
military 28–29, 34, 50, 80, 83, 92–94, 101, 103, 118; American 8, 31, 53, 89–91, 94–96, 100, 104–105, 118, 127, 155; inter-state conflicts 32, 131; power 24, 26, 28, 31, 35; security 24; stability 25; threats 29, 33
Military Bases Agreement 94–95
Moro Islamic Liberation Front (separatist group) 75, 84, 103, 115
multilateral regional security framework 30
multilateralism 33, 49–50, 53, 120–121, 123, 127, 131, 137, 141, 143, 146–148
Muslim countries 105–106
Muslims 67, 69–78, 80, 104, 106, 111–112, 114–115, 138–139, 146, 149–150; global 139; Indonesian 72, 112, 115; mainstream 112; Malaysian 72, 108; politicized 75; and politics in Southeast Asia 71, 73, 82; radicalized 108
Mustapha, Jennifer 6, 13–23, 26, 29, 31–32, 43, 50, 70, 119–123, 126–127, 129, 137, 143, 147–148, 152–153

national identity 2, 8, 11, 44–45, 89, 92, 94, 99–100, 124, 145, 155; American 51; re-configurations of post-colonial constructions of 8, 89, 155
"national resilience" (notion of) 8–9, 32–33, 89–90, 107, 113, 120, 128, 130–131, 148–149, 153, 155, 157
National Security Strategy 7, 50, 56, 62, 80–81, 88, 154
Neack, Laura Jeanne 42–43, 58
Nicolas, Suzette 97–101
Noor, Farish 5, 9, 58, 67, 70, 74, 76, 79, 83, 92, 103–105, 107–109, 111–113, 120, 129–130

164 *Index*

North Korea 51, 54–55, 94, 143, 147–148, 150

NSS *see* National Security Strategy

Obama, Pres. Barack 36, 86, 99, 114, 117, 132, 137–146, 148–151

Obama administration 92, 136, 138–141, 143–144, 147

O'Brien, Robert 120–121

Okfen, Nuria 90–91, 93, 106–107, 113, 126

Operation Enduring Freedom 92–94

operations 58, 70, 84, 93–94, 96, 103; counterinsurgency 84; covert 139; hostage-taking 93; joint task force exercises 93; Navy Seal 144

"pathologizing terrorism" 79

Pempel, T.J. 91, 105, 117, 120–121, 134

Peterson, V. Spike 17, 35, 39, 101–102, 114, 118

Philippine Constitution 93, 96

Philippine Senate 93, 95–96, 99

Philippines 10, 30, 58, 71, 75, 83–84, 90–100, 102–103, 105, 109, 112, 114–115, 117–119, 141, 151; government 98–99; law and ruling of the courts 98–99; military in counter-terror operations 58; and Southeast Asia 96; sovereignty and identity 103; sovereignty of the 93, 98–99; and the US military and security relationship 92, 94–95, 141

policies 2–3, 5, 7, 32, 34, 44, 47, 49, 54, 57, 83, 129, 131, 144, 146; administration's counter-terrorism 138; American counter-terrorism 3, 86, 106, 117; American security 9, 52, 132, 136; of Barrack Obama 137; Duterte's anti-crime 141

political Islam 64, 72, 74–76, 81–83, 112–113, 129, 132, 154; ASEAN's treatment of 129; and counter-terror policies 3; represents an imminent threat of terrorism 7, 66–67, 69–72; role of 104, 130

political violence 4, 30, 60, 72, 75, 80–81, 85, 105, 116

politics 11, 14, 36, 39, 42, 45, 62, 64, 73, 80–82, 101–102, 118, 128–129, 132, 134–135; balance-of-power 25; contemporary 48; electoral 5; and ethics of security practices in South East Asia

6, 14–15, 19, 152–153, 158; global 4, 37, 50, 60, 158; international 35, 37, 39, 44, 61, 86, 116–117; level of 13, 80; Malaysian 107–108; Muslim 73; of representation 12, 39

"post-ponism" approach 19, 21, 56, 156–157

post-structuralist approach to critical security 19–21

post-structuralist methods of analysis 6, 8, 22, 89, 153, 155

post-structuralist theorizing 19–21, 35–36

"privileged exemption" (US soldiers) 96–97, 99–100, 114

prostitution 99–100, 118

Al-Qaeda 2, 66, 69–71, 76–80, 84–86, 91, 107, 109, 132, 145, 154; affiliated operation 77; arrests of suspects linked to 91; and Islamist identity with organizational and ideological links to 7; recruitment afforts by 52; rise and reach of 1

radicalization 3, 8, 67, 70–71, 87, 104, 106, 155

rape 98, 100, 117; and the law 97–98; and the Subic Bay rape case 97–99, 117–118

Ravenhill, John 11, 39, 121

regime security 9, 32–33, 120, 122, 129–131, 150, 155

regional 7–11, 24–34, 36–39, 57–59, 70–72, 76–79, 82–83, 85–87, 89–92, 105–108, 113–114, 119–135, 140–143, 146–155, 157–158; agreements 120; architecture of Asia 141–143, 151; elites 122, 147–148; governments 33, 92, 106–107, 131; groupings 121, 126–127, 147; identities 8, 26, 114, 119, 121–122, 155; institutions 26–29, 31, 114, 121–122, 143, 157; members 125, 141; network 76–78; observers 92, 147; order 36, 122, 132, 141, 147–148; projects 120, 123; relations 119, 121, 148; security 5, 8, 26–31, 33–34, 38, 41, 57, 86, 90–91, 119, 128, 130, 148, 152–153, 155

regionalism 36, 39, 120–121, 126, 131, 133–135, 155; evolution of 8, 119; participatory 36; secret 117, 134

regionalization 114, 119–121, 134, 157; evolution of 8, 119, 155; and regionalism 120

Index   165

relationships 24, 28, 41, 55, 81–82, 92, 119–120, 128; bilateral 123, 141, 143; regional 123; strategic inter-state 27

religion 39, 70, 72–74, 76, 87, 104–105, 110, 112, 149–150; of Islam 70, 138; official state 104; terrain of 73, 82

Republic of Korea *see* South Korea

research 6, 70, 83, 157; counter-terrorism evaluation 87; terrorism-related 74

rogue states 50–51

Rohingya crisis (Myanmar) 147, 157–158

Rosenau, J.N. 42–43

Second Indo-China War 24

security 2–3, 5–15, 17–20, 22–41, 45–47, 56–61, 64–67, 101–102, 113–115, 128–130, 132–133, 136–138, 142–144, 152–155, 157–159; bilateral 92, 141; of borders 2, 47, 117; community 32–33, 36, 68, 130–131, 154; "comprehensive" 9, 31, 33, 120, 128–131, 149, 153, 155, 158; cooperation 29, 32, 125, 131; critical approaches to 14–29, 31–40; discourses 9, 20, 22, 35, 67, 80, 102, 136, 140, 144, 156; domestic 3, 107–108; dominant 7, 41, 56, 154; in East and Southeast Asia 13, 23, 28–29, 153; governance 48, 50–51; homeland 2, 137, 145; human 10, 66, 129–130, 133; internal 32, 130; international 11–12, 24, 36–38, 61, 68, 73, 86–87, 101–102, 121, 133, 150; logics 6, 8, 15, 19, 22, 51, 89, 154, 158; narratives 4–5, 7–8, 34, 41, 51–52, 57, 64, 70, 80–81, 89, 92, 96, 152, 154, 156; national 2, 49, 51; notions of 4, 17, 66, 114, 119; policies 47, 50, 126–127; the political and ethical problematics of 9, 22, 156; politics 2, 4, 8, 20, 22, 37, 58, 67, 89, 105, 128–130, 155, 157; practices 6–7, 9, 15, 47–48, 52, 57, 68, 78–79, 81, 101, 114, 153, 156–157; problems 14, 20, 52, 65, 103, 128, 156; pursuit of 6, 52, 137, 152; referents of 4, 144; regime 9, 32–33, 120, 122, 129–131, 150, 155; and regional cooperation 31, 130; regional relations 26, 34, 47, 54, 92, 103, 122, 133, 158; state-centric understanding of 5, 24, 152; study of 4, 14, 23, 26, 65; theorizations of 9, 15, 20, 156; threats 52, 95, 107, 115; understanding of 17, 31, 113, 130, 153

security agenda 126–127; national 54–56; regional 105; US 126–127

security policies 47, 50, 126–127; counterterror 8, 89, 155; of the Obama administration 136, 153; of the United States 52, 80, 122

security studies 4, 13–17, 19, 23–24, 33, 35, 39, 43, 117–118; conventional 17; critical 6, 12, 14–15, 17–23, 39, 61, 66, 159; mainstream 34; traditional 4–5, 18; understanding of 18

sexual violence 96

Shariah governance 76

Sidel, John 58, 70–72, 77–78, 80

Singapore 10–11, 37, 60, 77, 85–86, 90–91, 103–104, 106, 111, 115–119, 133–134, 141, 147, 150; civilians 91; government of 105, 114; and Lee Kuan Yew 125; and the Thailand border 105

Sjoberg, Laura 102, 118

Smith, Daniel 97–100

social forces 75, 77, 85

Söderbaum, Fredrik 120–121

South China Sea 54, 147

South Korea 121, 141; and Japan 122; and relations with North Korea 147; and US bases in East Asia 101

Southeast Asia 5–13, 22–24, 26–31, 34–39, 56–57, 59–62, 64–67, 69–78, 81–82, 84–92, 103–106, 113, 115–117, 128–136, 147–155; continuation of American imperial formations in 8, 89, 155; and East Asia 10–11, 119; gendered implications of regional security politics in 8, 89, 155; and Muslim support for Al-Qaeda 71; Muslims in 71, 82, 85; security 160–166; states 26, 102, 104, 106, 122, 126, 148; threat of terrorism in 64, 71, 148, 157

sovereignty 8, 17, 26, 32, 62, 89–118, 124, 130, 132, 153, 155, 158; imperial 118; internal 32, 130; national 90, 93–95, 112

Spanish-American War 94

stability 27–29, 32, 34, 53–54, 57, 66, 107, 128, 130, 132, 153; political 33, 131; regional 26–28, 31, 90; socio-cultural 32, 130, 153

Stampnitzky, L. 52, 67–68, 72, 79–80, 82, 140

state-centrism, concessions to 32, 131, 153

166 *Index*

state identity 17, 45–47
state security 8, 17, 41, 67, 92, 109–110
state sovereignty 48, 101, 126, 128, 149, 157–158
Stubbs, Richard 26–33, 119–126, 129, 141–143, 145–148
Subic Bay (military base) 95, 97, 99–101, 115
Subic Bay rape case 97–99, 117–118
Swain, Richard 93–95, 103

TAC *see* Treaty of Amity and Cooperation
tensions 29, 80, 105, 138, 142, 147, 152; between Muslims and the United States 138; difficult-to-reconcile 129; existing 138; intra-regional security 129; religious 105; sectarian 104
terror 1–13, 21, 36–38, 41, 44, 47–52, 55–94, 102–111, 113–120, 125–134, 136–140, 143–145, 148–150, 152–157, 159; attacks 77, 81; bombings 112; an crime cases 109; governing of 81–82, 85; and security narratives in Southeast Asia 67, 79; and security practices 78, 137; transnational Islamist 78
terrorism 2–5, 8–12, 51–52, 56–59, 61–62, 64–70, 72, 74, 76, 78–93, 114–119, 129–130, 140, 148–150, 157; attacks of September 2, 69; combatting 56, 68, 91, 110, 138; experts 65, 67–68, 72, 83; imminent threat of 7, 66, 76, 82, 154; regional 70, 72, 83, 91, 129–130; semi-securitizing of 128; solutions to 70, 80; in Southeast Asia 7, 12, 38, 60, 65–66, 70–71, 84, 86, 91–92, 154–155; threats of 4–5, 9, 58, 70–71, 76, 78, 91, 130, 136, 144, 152, 156; transnational 87, 107; understandings of 7, 154
terrorism expertise 67–70, 72, 76–80, 83, 92; contemporary 70; conventional 76, 92; regional 72, 77–78, 83
terrorist attacks 1, 3, 49–50, 55, 57, 71, 106, 144–145; coordinated 78; high-profile 111; large-scale 55, 77; of September 11, 2001 2
terrorist groups 2, 50–52, 73–75, 80, 106, 137; active 77; fringe 69; localized 79; radical 108; single 84
terrorists 4, 51, 58, 62, 70, 75, 78–81, 88, 104, 144; activities 74, 77, 92–93; allies 50; cells 83; incidents 82; individual 74; irrational 82; Muslim 72; networks 50; organizations 75–76; radical 108;

sleeper cells 91; suspected 91, 109, 140; tactics 91
threats 2, 7–8, 10–12, 41, 45–47, 50–51, 57, 64–65, 72–73, 75–78, 80, 116–118, 126, 130–131, 154–155; existential 4, 66, 129–130; national security 87; ongoing 147–148; potential 8, 48, 55, 67, 79–80, 123, 126, 155; terrorists 51, 70, 81, 111, 113, 128, 137
Tow, William 28, 128, 145–147
TPP *see* Trans-Pacific Partnership
trade wars 146–147, 150
Trans-Pacific Partnership 141, 143, 146
Treaty of Amity and Cooperation 124, 130, 132, 141
Trump, Pres. Donald 9, 136, 138, 144–151, 156; East Asia policies of 148, 150; electoral campaign rhetoric 145

United States *see* USA
USA 1–2, 7–9, 11–12, 27–29, 48–50, 52–57, 59–62, 80–81, 90–100, 102–104, 109–114, 116–119, 122–130, 132–149, 154–156; and counter-terrorism policies 3, 86, 106, 117; economic policy 126, 146; foreign policy in East Asia 7, 41, 53, 55, 58; Marines 96–97, 116; military personnel 95–96, 104; Philippine security relationship 94

Velasco, Mark 90–91, 93–95
VFA *see* Visiting Forces Agreement
violence 11–12, 30, 40, 47, 75–77, 81, 84, 87, 99, 101, 103, 105, 108, 139, 145; countering 8, 66, 82–83, 155; Islamist 72, 75; sovereign 37, 157; terrorist 66, 81–82, 90
Visiting Forces Agreement 95–100, 118, 141

Waever, Ole 14
War on Terror 1, 104, 140, 144; discourses 3–5, 7, 50, 90, 107, 113, 136–138, 143–145, 154, 157; and migration and border control 70; and President Obama 143; and questions about the pursuit of security by the state 52; and security narratives in Southeast Asia 67, 79; and security practices of states 78; in Southeast Asia 6, 10, 89, 103, 106, 119
warfare 50, 91, 144; inter-state 31, 153; sub-state 90
"weak ontology" 6, 14, 16–17, 19, 22, 35–36, 46, 152–153, 156

Weldes, Jutta 11, 38, 43–44, 46
"Welsh School" of security studies 14
White, Stephen K. 6, 14, 23, 153, 156
White House 50–51, 53–55, 62, 81, 88, 111, 118, 136–139, 141, 144–145, 149–151; and Donald Trump's "Make America Great Again" 145–146, 149; and Prayuth Chan-ocha (Thai Prime Minister) 147
Wibben, Annick T.R. 101, 114, 118

Williams, Marc 15, 121
women 37, 85, 99–102, 116–117, 138, 142; Afghan 102, 116; Filipino 100; Muslim 76; Philippine 95, 99, 117; rights of 98, 102, 149; Saudi 102
World War II 27, 29, 49, 94, 112
Wright-Neville, David 58, 62, 69, 71, 74–77, 83–84, 88
Wyn-Jones, Richard 6, 14, 19, 153